Professor Helen McGrath has worked for many years as a counselling psychologist in both a hospital setting and in private practice. She has also lectured for many years on a range of topics in psychology and educational psychology at Deakin University, and run hundreds of workshops for educational and health professionals on key aspects of psychology. She is currently an adjunct professor at both Deakin University and RMIT University. Helen has also been involved in the development of a number of Australian national and state frameworks related to the promotion of mental health and the safety and wellbeing of children and young people. She is the author/co-author of 22 books for psychologists, other professionals and the general community, including *Difficult Personalities* and *Bounce Back! A Positive Education Approach to Wellbeing, Resilience and Social–Emotional Learning.*

Cheryl Critchley is a respected Melbourne investigative and freelance journalist with more than 30 years experience on a range of publications, including the Melbourne *Herald Sun* newspaper and the *Weekly Review* magazine. She has written about state and federal politics, psychology, education, general news and features. Cheryl's books cover topics as diverse as AFL football and parenting. She now writes and edits for a range of publications, volunteers with the AFL Fans Association, and works as a communications professional. Cheryl has a strong interest in psychology, and has produced parenting columns, feature articles and opinion pieces with a psychological focus.

Also by Dr Helen McGrath and Cheryl Critchley

Why Did They Do It?

Dr Helen McGrath and Cheryl Critchley

MIND BEHIND THE CRIME

Pan Macmillan Australia

First published 2018 in Macmillan by Pan Macmillan Australia Pty Ltd
1 Market Street, Sydney, New South Wales, Australia, 2000

Cataloguing-in-Publication entry is available
from the National Library of Australia
http://catalogue.nla.gov.au

Typeset in 12.5/15.5 pt Granjon LT by Midland Typesetters, Australia
Printed by IVE

The paper in this book is FSC® certified.
FSC® promotes environmentally responsible,
socially beneficial and economically viable
management of the world's forests.

This book is dedicated to those who lost their lives, and the family members and friends who loved and supported them, as well as the dedicated police and other legal professionals who worked tirelessly in seeking justice for all of those affected by the crimes covered in this book.

CONTENTS

HOW TO USE THIS BOOK

In our first book, *Why Did They Do It?*, we attempted to explain the motives behind some of Australia's most puzzling murders, to help people to understand *why* they happened. As well as outlining the circumstances of each crime, we explained how, in each case, a specific type of personality disorder, combined with other factors, led to the murder. In this second volume, we have dissected and analysed new cases and explored several additional personality disorders that had an impact on the perpetrators' behaviour and decision-making in the lead-up to their murder or manslaughter. Where appropriate, an outline of the relevant personality disorder is provided as an introduction to many of the specific crimes that are discussed and analysed. Some of the cases, such as those that involve filicide or familicide (the killing of one's family members), don't necessarily involve personality disorders, and the relevant motivational factors are explained by reference to other key psychological research studies. At the back of the book you will find a glossary of technical terms, some useful contact details for those seeking assistance, references and further/recommended reading.

INTRODUCTION

Why Did They Do It? attempted to explain the inexplicable – crimes that shocked Australia and were perpetrated in some cases by the most unlikely killers. Among others they included Robert Farquharson, the seemingly unassuming Winchelsea father who intentionally drove his three young sons into a dam and left them to drown; Melbourne retiree Peter Caruso, who bludgeoned to death Rosa, his wife of almost 50 years, and tried to blame burglars when police arrived; and Gerard Baden-Clay, a cocky Queensland real estate agent who murdered his wife Allison, left her on the banks of a creek and maintained his innocence as friends and family tried desperately to find her.

We explained how each of these killers was largely driven by their specific personality disorders. In Farquharson's case it was avoidant personality disorder (AvPD), while Caruso and Baden-Clay both had a narcissistic personality disorder (NPD). Farquharson's crime was an act of revenge against his estranged wife, Cindy Gambino. Caruso and Baden-Clay both wanted to silence their wives, who had, finally, after years of torment, called them out on selfish and hurtful behaviour. The positive response to our analysis of these and other cases we covered, which are recapped in this book, was overwhelming. People told us that our explanations helped them understand why some people kill, and alerted them to people they knew who might be dangerous. Several chapters from that book have been used as a reference in court cases.

In this book, we look at another collection of equally shocking and distressing cases. By trying to understand the motives of the perpetrators, we hope to alert people to some of the personality and behavioural traits shared by potentially dangerous people. In some cases, it is almost impossible to predict whether someone is capable of murder. But in others, there may be enough information to alert those at risk of being the victims of a violent attack. In this second volume, we have analysed a range of crimes that involve murder or manslaughter to explain how the perpetrator's personality disorder, and/or other relevant psychological factors, influenced their lethal actions. The cases include:

- **Geoff Hunt**, who killed his wife Kim and their three children, Fletcher, ten, Mia, eight, and Phoebe, six, before killing himself.
- **Arthur Freeman**, who threw his daughter Darcey, four, off Melbourne's West Gate Bridge to take revenge on his wife during a custody dispute.
- **Akon Guode**, who intentionally drove into a lake, allowing three of her four children in the car to drown, including four-year-old twins Hanger and Madit, and seventeen-month-old Bol.
- **Damien Little**, who shot his sons Koda, four, and Hunter, nine months, and then himself, before driving them all off a pier in Port Lincoln to their certain deaths in the ocean.

- **Darren Milne**, who drove his car into a tree in rural New South Wales, killing himself, his wife Susana Estevez Castillo, and their son Liam, eleven. Their other son, Ben, seven, survived.
- **Michael Cardamone**, who tortured and then murdered his neighbour, Karen Chetcuti, in rural Victoria.
- **Vincent Stanford**, who killed young NSW teacher Stephanie Scott just before she was due to be married.
- **Man Haron Monis**, who perpetrated the Lindt Chocolate Café siege in Sydney.
- **Megan Haines**, a nurse who murdered two elderly residents in a NSW nursing home because they complained about her rude and unprofessional behaviour.
- **Robert Xie**, who murdered his brother-in-law and sister-in-law, their children, Henry, twelve, and Terry, nine, and his sister-in-law's sister, who was staying with them in Sydney.
- **Michael O'Neill**, who bludgeoned to death with a cooking pan his long-term partner, well-known Melbourne interior designer Stuart Rattle.
- **Dr Chamari Liyanage**, a physician who killed her husband, also a doctor, in the Western Australian town of Geraldton after years of being verbally, physically and sexually abused by him in horrific ways.
- **Anthony Sherna**, who strangled his partner of eighteen years, Susie Wild, in their outer suburban Melbourne home after he said he could no longer take her emotional abuse.
- **Cia Xia Liao**, who exacted violent revenge on her ex-partner by taking him hostage in his Melbourne home and then brutally killing his wife and young grandson.
- **Ian Jamieson**, who shot three of his neighbours in rural Victoria over a minor dispute.

Among the most dangerous perpetrators are those with malignant narcissism, an extreme form of NPD. Those who have this disorder believe that they are justified in using and abusing other people for their own ends, and that anyone who stands in their way is expendable. Man Haron Monis, who perpetrated Sydney's Lindt café siege, is a classic malignant narcissist. Monis spent his adult life shamelessly manipulating and using others. He changed his name at will and targeted vulnerable people whom he exploited financially and emotionally. Monis sexually abused women through a shonky 'spiritual healing' business, and his actions became increasingly erratic and dangerous, to the point where he was prepared to order a partner to murder his former wife, who was also the mother of two of his children.

When these and other criminal actions began to catch up with him, Monis took hostages in the Lindt Café and opportunistically linked himself to terror organisations. His actions were designed to draw attention to himself, deflect attention from his wrongdoing and provoke police into a violent confrontation. He had no qualms about shooting café manager Tori Johnson in a final and horrific act of selfishness as police closed in on him. Lawyer Katrina Dawson was tragically killed in the crossfire as Monis literally went out guns blazing.

Nurse Megan Haines, who murdered two elderly NSW nursing home residents, also has malignant narcissism. Fearing that her history of poor behaviour in other nursing jobs would be exposed by a resulting investigation of the patients' claims against her, she injected them with insulin, knowing it would kill them. Haines was arrogant enough to think her crime would go undetected, but astute authorities soon uncovered her plan.

Another malignant narcissist is Robert Xie, who killed five members of his wife's family because he was jealous of the attention his brother-in-law received from his wife's parents.

Xie bludgeoned three adults and two children to death in their bedrooms simply to get rid of them. In his mind, this would improve his status in the family. Xie also sexually abused a young relative both in the months before and also after committing his crime. This took a special kind of evil and a warped belief that his actions were justified.

Some killers are driven by extreme paranoia. Ian Jamieson, who shot and killed three of his neighbours he believed were abusing a shared track beside his house in rural Victoria, was deluded in thinking they were deliberately trying to make his life miserable. At worst, his neighbours, Peter and Mary Lockhart and Mary's son Greg Holmes, occasionally stirred up a small amount of dust when driving along the shared track they were completely entitled to use. But Jamieson, who has a paranoid personality disorder (PPD), amplified this into a serious 'feud' that, in his mind, the victims had started. Even after he was arrested over the murders, he continued to blame his victims and claimed that they drove him to do it.

This book also investigates several cases in which men and one woman killed their children (filicide) or their whole family (familicide). Apart from possible mild depression, which is not associated with an increased likelihood of perpetrating a violent crime, these killers were not suffering from a mental illness nor experiencing a psychotic episode that made them unable to identify what was real and what wasn't. These cases don't necessarily involve personality disorders, but all demonstrated irrational, non-resilient and self-focused thinking of some kind, which led to their choosing to commit horrendous murders.

Popular and highly regarded NSW farmer Geoff Hunt shot his wife Kim and their children Fletcher, ten, Mia, eight, and Phoebe, six, before turning the gun on himself. Friends and family were shocked, telling the media that Hunt was a respected farmer and a great bloke who must have been in a terrible place to even think about doing this. Like many other men who have perpetrated familicide, he was eulogised in the media and in his community as a loving father who must have 'cracked'. In other cases, South Australian father Damien Little shot himself and his young sons before driving them all off a pier to their deaths. In New South Wales, Darren Milne drove his car into a tree, killing himself, his wife and one of their two sons. Hunt, Little and Milne were all remembered as respected members of their local communities, but they should be seen for what they were – fathers who murdered their own children or whole family. This book argues that there is no excuse or justification for what they and others like them have done.

Some familicide cases are so shocking, however, that the perpetrator is instantly and universally condemned. This is what happened when Arthur Freeman threw his daughter Darcey, four, off Melbourne's West Gate Bridge on the way to her first day of school. It was a clear case of revenge against his estranged wife, Peta Barnes, whom Freeman even rang while he was driving to tell her she'd never see her children again. He then drove to the top of the bridge and threw his terrified little daughter over the edge as her two brothers watched in horror. Freeman tried to argue in court that he was mentally impaired, but this argument was rejected.

The situation of Sudanese refugee Akon Guode was somewhat more complex. After escaping to Australia from her war-torn homeland, where her first husband was killed, she started an affair with a married Sudanese man with whom she then had four children. The local Sudanese community did not approve, and Guode found herself in a difficult situation. After deciding she couldn't cope any more, she intentionally drove her car – with her four children – into an outer suburban lake and fled the vehicle, leaving her children inside. One child escaped as she watched three of the four children drown. Regardless of what led her to make this choice, her actions were also inexcusable.

In another complex case, Vincent Stanford, who killed young NSW teacher Stephanie Scott just before she was due to marry, was influenced by several factors. Stanford has an autism spectrum disorder, but there is no evidence that those who have autism are any more violent or crime-prone than the general population. Stanford had a specific subtype of autism called 'criminal autistic psychopathy', and was also obsessed with violent and sadistic sexual fantasies. Michael Cardamone had an antisocial personality disorder that led to him brutally torturing and killing his neighbour, Karen Chetcuti, when she refused to reciprocate his sexual interest. Rather than move on, Cardamone decided to harm and kill Karen in a way that showed extreme sadism and lack of empathy towards his victim.

We also look at several killers with a dependent personality disorder (DPD) that influenced them to become dependent and over-reliant on a more dominant partner. When the relationship became overly strained, they irrationally felt that the only way to deal with what was happening was to kill their partner rather than leave and try to cope on their own. Michael O'Neill bludgeoned to death his long-term partner, well-known interior designer Stuart Rattle, with a cooking pan, after Stuart allegedly continually belittled him. Cia Xia Liao's actions were even more extreme. As well as having a DPD, she also displayed many features of a histrionic personality disorder. After becoming dependent on her Victoria-based lover Brian Mach, who eventually returned to his wife, Liao exacted violent and dramatic revenge by taking Brian hostage and brutally killing his wife and grandson.

Western Australia–based Dr Chamari Liyanage became desperate when she found herself overly dependent on her partner,

Dinendra 'Din' Athukorala. Din treated Liyanage appallingly, and after years of regular sadistic sexual and emotional abuse, she could no longer cope. By all accounts the abuse was shocking, but rather than leave, Liyanage violently killed Din in their home with a mallet. After being convicted of manslaughter, she said she had felt trapped, did not see a way out and could not actually remember killing her husband. The Melbourne case of Anthony Sherna, who strangled his partner Susie Wild, had some similarities, as he felt trapped and emotionally abused with no way out. Sherna claimed that Susie, whom he described to police as overly controlling and cruel, drove him to do it.

None of these killings was justified, but understanding the perpetrators' personality disorders and/or irrational non-resilient thinking can help explain why they committed some of Australia's worst crimes. Like the killers we analysed in our first book, those described in this second book also knew what they were doing. None was mentally ill (a personality disorder is not a mental illness, as we will see shortly) and most felt that their actions were justified. We have used psychological analysis, combined with scientific evidence from research studies, to identify their flawed reasoning and behaviours and their probable motives for actions that may seem inexplicable.

Callous killers are rare. But the analysis of these cases can help alert us to warning signs in partners, friends, family members and social acquaintances who may, despite appearances to the contrary, be capable of serious, harmful and criminal acts. While unusual, these people exist, and they can be dangerous. They are often such good actors that their criminal behaviour comes as a complete surprise to those who know them. But when you dig a little deeper, the signs may have been there: a pattern of selfishness, lack of empathy, controlling behaviour or callous indifference to suffering may indicate a seriously flawed personality. In the case of those with a DPD, they may show the opposite traits, such as being overly dependent on a more dominant partner.

Our analysis of these cases has enabled us to gain an insight into the killers' behaviour and motives, and the context in which their killings occurred. Professor Helen McGrath has spent many years researching the available scientific information about personality disorders and irrational and non-resilient thinking and behaviour patterns. She has also counselled many patients, some of whom have relatives, colleagues or partners whose lives have been affected by people with these patterns of behaviour. This book aims to provide an understanding of these crimes, but it in no way excuses them. Nor do we wish to imply that all people with personality disorders are dangerous. Most are neither dangerous nor violent. What we hope to convey is an understanding of why some people with certain personality disorders or other psychological factors can cross the line and seriously hurt someone. Being alert to the potential signs can help us all feel a bit safer. We hope to provide an understanding of why some people with certain personality disorders or irrational, non-resilient and self-focused types of thinking can murder.

Mental illness or personality disorder?

A mental disorder can be described as a pervasive and repeated pattern of behaviour characterised by disturbances in an individual's thinking, management of emotions and behaviour (DSM-5, APA, 2013). A personality disorder is an example of a mental disorder, as defined above, but it is *not* a 'mental illness'. It is important to distinguish personality disorders from mental illness, as they differ in several ways. An individual's *personality* is their relatively consistent, pervasive and permanent pattern of thinking, feeling and behaving. If this pattern becomes inflexible and maladaptive (dysfunctional and non-productive), is demonstrated in many areas of their life, and causes distress to themselves and/or others, then it can become a 'personality disorder'. One study found that almost 5 per cent of the UK population is living with a personality disorder (Coid et al., 2006). A review of research by Quirk et al. (2016) concluded that the prevalence rate was more likely to be somewhere between 4.4 and 21.5 per cent.

Essentially, personality disorders are pervasive patterns of thoughts and behaviours that tend to persist through life and cause problems at work and with relationships. Someone with a personality disorder usually has difficulty dealing with problems and everyday stressors, partly due to the lack of empathy they feel for others, their lack of resilience, and their flawed thinking and decision-making. In some cases, they neither realise nor care that their actions have caused distress to another person. They also tend not to learn readily from their mistakes, and they often continue to repeat them.

Such disorders are different from mental illnesses, which are enduring and deeply ingrained and maladaptive patterns of behaviours that are very difficult to treat. Mental illnesses are at least partly influenced by a 'disease' that adversely affects one or more organs, including the brain, in a way that significantly impairs normal thinking and functioning. Many mental illnesses can be treated with medication. Most are usually recognisable, and in most cases they severely impair a person's thinking and perceptions of reality. They can also cause distressing behaviour towards self and others.

The term 'mental illness' is more often used in a legal context than in a medical one. Most legal definitions describe it as a clinically significant medical condition that significantly impairs (temporarily or permanently) the person's mental functioning and judgement, and strongly indicates that they need care, treatment and/or control. It is characterised by serious disturbance in many of the following: thought processes, emotions, orientation, mood, perceptions, memory and/or decision-making. It usually results in one or more of the following symptoms: delusions, hallucinations, serious disorder of thought, self-harm, a severe disorder of mood and/or sustained or repeated irrational behaviour that indicates the presence of one of these symptoms.

These indicators are mostly associated with the more severe mental disorders, which often include a temporary or longer-term psychosis, such as schizophrenia, bipolar disorder, and some severe mood disorders, such as post-partum depression or major depressive disorder. When somebody is in a psychotic state, their thoughts and emotions are seriously impaired to the point where they are unable to distinguish what is real and what is not. Typical symptoms displayed by someone who is in a psychotic state include delusions, hallucinations (hearing voices, receiving 'commands' from people who aren't there, or 'seeing' things that aren't there), seriously impaired memory, very confused thinking, and a severe inability to reason effectively, solve everyday problems or make plans.

Someone who has been charged with a crime can claim 'mental impairment' and, if successful, may be declared unfit for trial. To do this, they must be assessed as unable to assist in their own defence and unable to understand the court process. 'Mental impairment', which usually means mental illness, intellectual disability, brain damage and/or senility, can also be used as a defence during a trial. Some Australian states have laws that specifically exclude substance abuse from the definition of mental illness. It is possible for some people with a personality disorder to have a separate mental illness too, such as schizophrenia, but this isn't the situation in the cases explored in this book.

Is depression a mental illness? Not always. Mild to moderate depression is often a normal part of life and is not therefore a mental illness in the sense of significantly impairing thought processes and perceptions. Most people have times when they feel unhappy, lack energy or have a low mood. This may follow a sad, stressful, worrying or traumatic life event such as a family death, separation or job loss. In some cases, this depression is more severe, prolonged and considered a mental illness. An example outlined in the DSM-5 (APA, 2013) is 'major depressive disorder'. Those who have it are likely to have a depressed mood most of the day, nearly every day. They feel chronically sad, empty, hopeless and teary, may lose weight or overeat, have problems with insomnia or oversleeping nearly every day, feel de-energised, lack the desire to engage in formerly pleasurable activities, have a diminished capacity to think clearly, concentrate and solve problems, and may consider suicide. These symptoms are severe enough to cause clinically significant distress or impairment in their social life, work life and other parts of their lives. In these cases, antidepressant medication can help.

Rather than behaviours that are controlled by an illness or disease, personality disorders are essentially extremes of the normal personality spectrum. They reflect an individual's characteristic lifestyle, pervasive style of relating to and communicating with others, and, ultimately, their identity. The key features of any personality disorder are: distorted and inflexible patterns of thinking and behaviour, low levels of resilience, problematic emotional reactions and responses, problems with impulse control (sometimes too much, sometimes too little), and difficulties with interpersonal communication, empathy and relationships. A personality disorder can range from mild to severe, and two people with the same disorder may behave differently in some ways, depending on which combination of that personality disorder's criteria they meet. Some people with an NPD, for example, are simply annoying because they brag all the time and exaggerate various achievements, while others are prepared to kill to protect or enhance their image.

Two aspects of all personality disorders are especially maladaptive, self-defeating and sometimes dangerous to others (Millon et al., 2004; 2011). The first is a lack of resilience under stress. Someone with a personality disorder lacks the capacity to respond to problems and difficulties in their life with flexible, appropriate and varied strategies. Unlike most other people, if their first strategy doesn't work, they often won't try a different approach. Instead, they usually keep using the same strategy, often turning a problem into a crisis, with even higher levels of stress and anger that adversely affect those around them. In Man Monis's case, he continually used the legal system to push his various causes. When it finally became clear that the law was catching up with him, he orchestrated what was almost certainly destined to be a fatal siege rather than face serious criminal charges in court.

The second aspect is stubbornness and rigidity, and an inability to adapt to changing circumstances. In situations that make new demands of them, such as a partner wanting to change something in their relationship, someone with a personality disorder will often continue to try to control the outcome to suit themselves rather than rethink things in terms of their partner's needs. Again, this often leads to an interpersonal crisis, such as Ian Jamieson's refusal to accept the rights of his neighbours to use the track between their properties. In Jamieson's mind this was a major problem, when to anyone else it clearly wasn't. These maladaptive ways of dealing with life's challenges and hurdles often lead to a series of repeated, ineffective and self-defeating behaviours that blight the lives of both the people who have them and the people with whom they live, work or interact. In extreme cases, they can result in violence and even murder, which is what happened when Jamieson's paranoia became extreme and he decided the only way to stop his neighbours 'infringing on his rights' was to kill them.

Personality disorders are also associated with relatively low levels of empathy and concern for others. Most people with serious personality disorders have a diminished capacity to empathise, which is why some, such as Michael Cardamone, can commit serious crimes without feeling guilt or remorse, cover them up and then calmly lie when they are caught. Cardamone even blamed someone else for his crime, and involved his mother, who also ended up spending time in jail, by asking her to pay a hit man to kill the man he had falsely accused of his own crime. Some aspects of empathy appear to be developmental. As children develop, their experiences with other people help their brain to create efficient neural pathways, and they become more and more capable of empathy.

What is empathy?

Empathy is one of the most important building blocks of respect, compassion, conscience development and moral behaviour. It has four components, each drawing on different skills:

1. **emotional recognition**: knowing intellectually how someone else is feeling (and perhaps thinking) as a result of seeing their expressions or actions and/or listening to their voice and words
2. **emotional resonance**: when you actually 'feel' some of the same emotion that you recognise another person is feeling. For example, when you are listening to someone who is upset

as they tell you about something sad they have recently experienced, you might also feel sad and a bit teary
3. **empathic concern**: when, having recognised and understood that another person is distressed, you react by saying or doing something that might help them feel better
4. **empathic prediction**: when you take the time to think about and anticipate how another person *might* respond and react to something you are thinking of doing or are planning to do.

The skills that underpin empathic behaviour are learned mostly from childhood experiences of seeing and experiencing empathy, kindness, support and nurture at home and at school. We also learn it from opportunities to practise showing empathy, kindness, support and nurture to family members, friends, classmates, neighbours and pets. Children start to develop empathy from about the age of two, and may cry when an adult or another child cries.

The degree to which those with personality disorders lack empathy will vary according to the type and severity of the disorder, but most will display a pattern of putting their wants and needs ahead of those of others. Megan Haines is an example of someone with a serious case of malignant narcissism whose selfish actions continued to become more serious. She had been able to perpetrate unprofessional nursing behaviour over many years, so felt emboldened to act in a criminal way, thinking she was smart enough to always get away with what she did. She went too far, however, and was quickly caught after murdering two nursing home residents in the same way at the same time. Haines's lack of empathy meant she did not realise other people would investigate the deaths and suspect her as a result of both the recent complaints that had been made about her and her previous poor track record.

Nature or nurture?

Personality disorders are usually the result of a complex interplay of genetic and environmental factors. Genetics don't directly cause a personality disorder, but they often play a role in predisposing a person to developing one or more components of a disorder. Genes can predispose someone to behave in a certain way, or make them more susceptible to the negative effects of certain situations. In a health-related example, someone with the gene predisposing them to type 2 diabetes and who is also overweight is more susceptible to developing type 2 diabetes than someone who has the same gene but isn't overweight. Other genes can minimise the effects of one specific gene, as can environmental factors. Similarly, other genes or negative environmental factors can exaggerate the effects of a specific gene.

As we pointed out in our first book, the level of 'heritability' is the degree to which genetic differences explain the differences between large groups of people in terms of specific behaviours and characteristics such as shyness or impulsivity. The influence of genetics is larger in some personality disorders than in others, but biology isn't destiny, and many environmental factors also play a significant role. Parenting significantly impacts on the development of a person's temperament and overall personality. Warm, caring parents who are calm and resilient under stress can help a child to self-calm and feel safe. Such parents also model resilience, and show their children how to manage uncomfortable feelings and cope with difficult situations. Parents who teach their children strong moral values and directly teach their children to consider the rights, needs and feelings of others make it more likely those children will behave that way. Parents can also minimise a child's predisposition to shyness by teaching them specific social skills and encouraging them to connect with other people.

A child's attachment style, or how they establish emotional bonds, is developed through their early childhood experiences and becomes their working model for adult relationships. A child is more likely to develop a positive and trusting working model of how relationships should be when they are raised in a loving, secure, responsive and predictable family situation where their physical and emotional needs are reliably met, boundaries about acceptable behaviour are clearly communicated, and adults can be trusted to care for them and keep them safe. This helps the child develop a 'secure attachment' style that leads to confident and independent adult behaviour, the ability to trust others in relationships, positive social interactions, and an ability to meet both their own and another person's needs.

However, when a child is raised in a family situation that is non-responsive to their needs, unpredictable, chaotic or unsafe, they are likely to develop a negative and non-trusting working model of relationships and an 'insecure attachment' style. As adults, they are less able to trust those close to them, more likely to fear isolation, may have difficulties in managing feelings such as anger, and can become over-controlling and/or over-dependent in relationships.

These children are more likely to develop a personality disorder, especially if they already have a genetic predisposition to some of its components, such as high levels of emotionality and irritability, impulsivity, anxiety, shyness and/or low levels of empathy.

Often 'shared genes' also result in a 'shared environment'. This can increase the likelihood that the child will develop a personality disorder. A parent who has passed on a specific gene to their child may be more likely to parent in a way that reflects that same genetic predisposition in themselves. For example, a parent with a genetic predisposition for anxiety may pass it on to their child while also modelling anxious behaviour by overly focusing on potential danger in their own and their child's world. A child's early temperament can also influence the way their parents respond to them. Parents of babies with an 'easygoing' and sociable temperament often find it relatively easy to be calm, warm and nurturing towards them. Parents of irritable, socially withdrawn or overly emotional babies may respond to them in a more impatient or avoidant way. Parents of fearful and inhibited babies may respond to them in a more protective way that calms them down but also may reduce their confidence and independence.

Some environmental factors that influence how a child's personality develops are the result of random good fortune or misfortune. An example of good fortune is having regular contact with another caring and supportive adult who displays care and affection, such as a family friend, teacher, sports coach or grandparent. Conversely, the death of a parent when a child is young is an example of misfortune. Other factors that can affect a child's personality development include the quantity and quality of their friendships, whether they are bullied or included at school, the quality of their educational experiences, and their involvement in positive or negative activities outside school, such as music, art, drama and sport.

Adjustment disorder

Some of the killers in this book, including Anthony Sherna and Cia Xia Liao, were also diagnosed with an adjustment disorder, which means they had difficulty coping with and managing one or more stressful life event. This short-term and thus temporary condition involves distressing emotional or behavioural symptoms, and usually develops within three months of experiencing one or more stressful life events such as major relationship problems, the end of a significant relationship, developing a serious illness, the failure of a business or job loss. It rarely lasts longer than six months after the stressful situation has passed. Normal bereavement, such as the loss of an elderly relative, is not considered to be a stressor in this context.

An adjustment disorder is different from post-traumatic stress disorder (PTSD), which is most often a reaction to experiencing or witnessing a life-threatening event and tends to last longer. With an adjustment disorder, the degree of emotional distress is generally out of proportion to the severity of the stressor. It has significant negative effects on most aspects of the individual's day-to-day life such as their social life, work life or academic functioning. Typical emotions, reactions and behaviours that might be experienced by someone with an adjustment disorder include:

- strong feelings of anxiety
- feelings of hopelessness
- physical reactions such as palpitations
- a chronic lack of energy
- changes in appetite or sleeping pattern
- frequent crying and tearfulness
- social withdrawal
- absenteeism from work or school/university
- dangerous or destructive behaviour
- increased use of alcohol and drugs.

Both Sherna and Liao reacted in the worst possible way to the life difficulties they experienced. Anthony Sherna's adjustment disorder meant that he was unable to cope with the challenging aspects of his relationship with Susie Wild and the associated frustration and loneliness. He was also unable to cope after he killed

Susie, acting irrationally in burying her body in the backyard and taking his dog to a pet resort. He would have found it difficult to no longer have his job and be forced to go to jail. Liao also found it difficult to cope with and adjust to what she perceived to be Brian Mach's 'betrayal' when he refused to marry her and returned to his wife. She became hysterical when her plans to marry Brian and gain Australian citizenship were thwarted, and would also have found it difficult to adjust to being in jail.

Dissociation

Other killers in this book, including Arthur Freeman and Chamari Liyanage, claimed they were in a state of 'dissociation' when they killed, in Freeman's case his daughter Darcey and in Liyanage's case her husband Din. During and/or after a stressful or traumatic life event, some people experience some degree of 'dissociation', which has been described by mental health professionals as a feeling of numbness or a sense of being outside yourself and watching what you are doing and what is happening to you as if you were a stranger looking on. It has also been described as acting like an 'automaton', or like 'having an awareness of what you are doing but feeling disconnected from the reality of what is happening'.

Everyone has an occasional small experience of dissociation. One common example is when we suddenly realise that we have safely driven our car for several minutes over a familiar route but have no memory of the landmarks and roads we have passed, what we have seen or what we were thinking at the time. After an individual has experienced dissociation there may be significant gaps in their memory of their own involvement in what happened or how they responded to what happened. Liyanage claims she doesn't remember killing Din, so if she is telling the truth she may have experienced an episode of dissociation.

Many people also find it difficult to recall all the specific details of a traumatic experience, such as the funeral of a close friend or family member, often because the experience is so distressing that it feels unreal and can lead to some degree of 'dissociation'. It is less common for someone to kill and not be aware of what they were doing and what they have done. But there have been some cases where people have used the defence of 'dissociation', insisting that they have no recollection, or only a limited recollection of what they did. They argue that the behaviour was not conscious, voluntary or intentional. But dissociation is almost impossible to measure accurately or objectively. In some situations, it may be a protective defence mechanism in that it may reduce the stress of a traumatic or emotionally overwhelming experience so that we can cope with it.

In Arthur Freeman's case, Professor Graham Burrows gave evidence that he believed the accused was suffering from severe depression and, as a result of that, fell into a state of 'dissociation' so that his acts were not conscious, voluntary and deliberate, or intentional. Two other experts disagreed, however, and believed that Freeman was suffering from mild to moderate depression, and that if there was any dissociation, it was not sufficient to have removed his capacity to act consciously, voluntarily and deliberately, or intentionally. Freeman's attempt to claim mental impairment failed and he was convicted of murder.

What to look out for

If someone has a personality disorder it does not mean that they will commit a criminal act, let alone kill someone. The cases outlined in this book illustrate how complex personality disorders can be, and how factors such as trauma, abuse, health problems, broken relationships, family separation and work pressures can combine with a personality disorder to produce tragic results.

Violent behaviour is extreme aggression intended to cause serious harm to another person. Both personal and situational factors converge to enable a violent act to occur. Therefore, the answer to the question, 'Why did someone commit this murder?' is nearly always an equation rather than simple cause and effect. Each additional personal or situational factor increases the likelihood of the outcome. If we are to learn from the cases in this book, we need to look at the whole equation and how a range of factors contributed to the outcome. The cases in the book that did not involve personality disorders can be just as complex, and possibly even more so, as the reasons may be less obvious and hence more difficult to identify.

*At the end of this book, after the references, you will find a list of books where you can find out more about domestic violence and the various personality disorders.

PART I

FILICIDE AND FAMILICIDE

KILLING YOUR OWN FAMILY

What possesses someone to kill their own children, and in some cases their partner as well? While rare, such cases are becoming all too familiar. A parent, more often the father, suddenly kills one or more of their children and often suicides as well, leaving behind devastated and usually shocked extended family, friends and local community. Few have seen it coming, and the actions are usually described as completely out of character for the killer. Because the thought of a parent knowingly taking their own child's life is just too awful to contemplate, the crimes are often explained as an act of madness or coming from a position of intense pain that no one else understood.

The fact is, most fathers who kill their children do so deliberately and while unaffected by psychosis or any other kind of mental illness. They are sane men who have irrationally decided that, for whatever reason, their children and in some cases their partner as well, are better off dead or do not deserve to live. In some cases, they take their loved ones with them because they think that those left behind may not be able to cope without them. It could also be an act of revenge against an ex-partner. Whatever the reason, these killings are inexcusable.

If the men described in this book had killed their neighbour's wife and children, they would have been branded vicious mass murderers and ostracised by the media, family and friends. For some reason, however, those who kill their own children are often seen differently, and their actions explained as an aberration or, in some cases, an 'act of love'. But these killers are extremely selfish and see their family as theirs to dispose of. When South Australian tradesman and football coach Damien Little killed his sons Koda, four, and Hunter, nine months, before taking his own life, his wife, family and friends all said that although Little had been feeling somewhat depressed, he had refused to seek medical help or counselling because it would make him look weak. The young father was described as a popular and respected member of the local community who should be remembered as such. Little must have been in a terrible amount of pain, they reasoned, to have acted as he did. But it isn't that simple.

The same pattern occurred when Geoff Hunt, a NSW farmer, shot dead his wife, Kim, and their children Fletcher, ten, Mia, eight, and Phoebe, six, before shooting himself on their property. Hunt, who came from a respected farming family, was eulogised as a pillar of the local community who may have been struggling to cope with his wife Kim's physical and emotional issues after she was seriously injured in a car accident. This book argues that no amount of pain, or mild to moderate depression, excuses killing those closest to you. It is never justified, and the perpetrators should be called what they are – murderers.

A common myth about these crimes is that parents who kill their children do so out of love and that the extreme love they feel for their child/children means they can't bear to be separated from them. This is not the case. Both these men were murderers who killed their own children in the most violent of ways. Loving fathers and husbands don't kill their kids. And unless the public's perception of these murderers changes, other men will continue to feel that if life gets too tough they, too, can take this option and be eulogised by their loved ones in the media rather than condemned as they should be.

When Geoff Hunt killed his wife and children, he was described in the media by many as a devoted father and loving husband who was under a great deal of pressure from family responsibilities. Friends said he was a respected farmer and a lovely guy who was easygoing, and seemed happy and completely normal – with the perfect family. He was generous, kind-hearted, sociable, hardworking, supportive, gentle, thoughtful, kind, patient . . . the list went on. When Damien Little killed his sons and then himself, it was more of the same. Little, who had been struggling with some degree of mild depression, was remembered as a loving husband and father who was a popular and talented football player and coach. Friends and loved ones spoke fondly about him and, as a mark of respect, some left cans of his favourite alcoholic drink on the pier from which he drove his sons to their deaths.

The reality is, the Hunt and Little children spent their final moments absolutely terrified as one of the two people closest to them, whose main role was to protect them, used a gun to shoot each of them, and, in Little's case, drove off a Port Lincoln pier to 'finish them off' if they weren't already dead. A lovely guy does not shoot his young daughter in the face as she cowers on a bed, as Geoff Hunt did when he shot his daughters, wife and son, or do what Damien Little did to his sons, who thought they were simply going on an outing to McDonald's. The NSW Coroner described Hunt's actions as 'inexcusable' and the 'absolute worst of crimes'. This is how he should be remembered, regardless of the circumstances leading up to his crime. Hunt and Little were murderers, and no one should feel sorry for them.

Shocking and uncomfortable details of these crimes, such as the way Hunt's daughter Mia's body was positioned, which indicated that she was almost certainly awake when her father killed her, are often omitted from news stories. They do not conform to the less threatening and more comfortable narrative of a parent who supposedly acted 'out of love' and was trying to spare their children the pain of living without them. Research by Johnson and Sachmann (2014) suggests that in fact the most likely motivation of those who murder their children is more often related to a sense of ownership, an obsessive need to control and, in some cases where marital separation is an issue, a desire to inflict harm on their ex-partner for leaving them or threatening to do so.

In some cases of family breakdown, the fathers kill their child/children as well as themselves to save the children from having to 'suffer' having a substitute parent if the mother re-partners. There is also evidence that for months before killing their children and themselves, many perpetrators had been searching the internet for media information about examples of parents who killed their children, to reassure themselves that they were not alone in their views or intentions. The positive way many of those who kill their children are described in the media has the potential to influence others to commit the same crimes. Such coverage also detracts from the victims' suffering and makes the crimes seem less horrifying. It implies that nothing can be done about these killings because they are neither predictable nor preventable. This would not be the case if, as a society, we accepted the hard reality about these crimes and focused more on identifying potential warning signs (O'Hagan, 2014).

The following are the most commonly used terms and definitions used in the research literature in relation to killing members of one's own family.

Filicide

'Filicide' is the term used to describe a situation in which a parent intentionally kills one or more of their children. If the parent also suicides, it is most often described as a 'filicide–suicide'. Arthur Freeman, who murdered his four-year-old daughter Darcey by throwing her off Melbourne's West Gate Bridge, committed filicide, while Damien Little committed filicide–suicide. Freeman left his two sons unharmed but killed Darcey, who was about to start her first day of primary school. Minutes earlier he had been on the phone to his ex-wife and Darcey's mother, Peta Barnes, telling her to say goodbye to her children.

Familicide

'Familicide' and 'familicide–suicide' are the two terms most commonly used to describe a situation in which one family member kills or attempts to kill all members of their direct family, i.e. their spouse and their children, and then (usually) suicides (Liem, 2010). Familicide–suicide is more often premeditated and involves the perpetrator making extensive preparations, such as purchasing weapons, stockpiling substances to sedate children, setting up pipelines for running carbon monoxide into a car, and making sure that they will have uninterrupted access to their children.

In their meta-analytic review, Panczak et al. (2013) concluded that a previous history of domestic violence was less common among men who committed familicide and then suicided. In their review, which compared Australian murderers who killed one or more members of their family but who didn't suicide, with those who killed one or more family members but also suicided, McPhedran et al. (2015) concluded that those who also suicided were also more likely to carry out the murders and suicide within a residential setting, such as the family home.

Geoff Hunt is a classic example of familicide–suicide. Hunt committed his crime on the family farm in Lockhart after a period of family stress due to health and relationship problems. He gave no hint of what was about to happen, and while he and his wife Kim had some relationship issues, there was no history of emotional or physical abuse. But he decided that the only way to solve his problems was to kill himself and take his whole immediate family with him. In another NSW case, Darren Milne killed his wife, Susana Estevez Castillo, and their son Liam, eleven, by intentionally driving their car at speed into a tree on a rural road. Their other son Ben, seven, who was also in the car, was seriously injured but survived. Milne had meticulously planned the killings for weeks, possibly prompted by his despair about caring for two sons with an intellectual disability.

Family annihilation

Fox and Levin (2005) have described 'family annihilation' as a subcategory of mass murder, defined as the killing of four or more members of the one family, in one location and during one event. Yardley et al. (2014) have defined 'family annihilators' as individuals (mostly men) who intentionally set out to kill their child/children. They may or may not also attempt to kill the mother of their children, and may or may not attempt to kill themselves. Wilson et al. (1995) identified that in their review of 109 cases of familicide, half of the male perpetrators suicided immediately after they murdered their family.

While all murders by family annihilation are also filicides, they are not necessarily filicide–suicides nor familicides. Geoff

Hunt was a family annihilator who killed all three of his children, his wife and then himself. He could also be described as having committed familicide. The trauma of filicide and familicide is enduring and far-reaching, not only for any survivors in the immediate family but also for members of the victims' extended family, their friends and the local community (Johnson, 2005). This was certainly the case with the Hunt murders, as the family was respected throughout the Lockhart district. The killings affected the wider community and shocked all involved.

Associate Professor Carolyn Harris Johnson, a leading expert in filicide and familicide and the author of *Come with Daddy: Child Murder–Suicide after Family Breakdown* (2005), points out that the media frequently 'romanticises' (saying 'they acted out of love') and sanitises this type of crime, to soothe the anxieties of the audience because the subject matter of child murder is taboo, or too confronting for most people. But this approach distorts the public's understanding of why these events occur and the extent of the perpetrator's responsibility. This makes it much more difficult to identify actions that can be taken as early warning signs and prevent such child murders in the future.

Statistics

Men commit nearly all familicides and filicides (92–97 per cent), and there is evidence that such mass murders are increasing (Websdale, 2010; Wilson et al., 1995; Wilson, 2009; Yardley et al., 2014). Flynn et al. (2013) identified that only in 23 per cent of cases of filicide–suicide was a severe mental illness a contributing factor.

TAXONOMIES (CLASSIFICATION SCHEMES)

1 Filicide taxonomy

Resnick and his colleagues have developed and elaborated on a taxonomy based on the motivation of the parents who commit filicide (Resnick, 1969; Friedman and Resnick, 2007; West et al., 2009). (See also the chart on pages 41–2.)

The '**altruistic killer**' aims to protect their child/children by murdering them. They may believe that their children would be unable to cope with a family breakdown that has occurred or may be about to occur. If their main motivation is in fact to end their own life, they may irrationally feel that murdering their children as well will save them from the pain of being motherless and/or fatherless. Canadian-born Brisbane teacher Jason Lees, 40, may have killed his two-year-old son Brad because he had a very close bond with him, and he appears to have irrationally concluded that his child would not be able to cope if his wife ended their relationship and he would no longer be living with them.

When Lees jumped from Brisbane's Story Bridge with Brad in his arms in 2012, he was remembered as a great dad and respected Year 6 teacher and sporting coach. Lees had given little indication of his intentions, but may have acted due to relationship problems with his wife, who requested privacy after the tragedy. Those who knew Lees were shocked by his actions and paid tribute to him as a person. His school's principal said Lees, who had given no indication of personal problems, was a team player admired for his passion and commitment. He was also a successful international rugby sevens referee. A Gold Coast and District Rugby Referees' Association spokesman described Lees as a gentleman who was always friendly and a genuinely nice bloke. Others described him as compassionate and placid, yet he committed a shocking, violent crime.

The '**partner revenge killer**' murders their child/children to cause extreme pain to their partner and remind them for the rest of their life that it was their fault they died. Arthur Freeman, who killed his daughter Darcey to 'get back at' his ex-wife, fits into this category. Freeman had no other motive than to hurt Peta Barnes, who had received favourable custody news from the Family Court the previous day. Robert Farquharson, who drove his three boys into a dam outside Winchelsea on Father's Day in 2005, also did so to hurt his estranged wife, Cindy Gambino, who had ended their relationship (see *Why Did They Do It?*).

In another case, Perth man Jason Headland was jailed in 2017 for at least 31 years after the 2016 murders of his daughter, Zaraiyah Lily, five, and son Andreas, three, which were to 'punish' his former partner after their marriage broke down. After calling his ex-wife, Anatoria Takiwa, to tell her he was going to break her heart into 50 million pieces, Headland drugged his children by mixing antihistamines into their juice before almost certainly asphyxiating them; the cause of death could not be fully determined. Headland also stabbed himself but survived. He left a note saying he had fought for his family but could take the pain no longer. In court, his defence counsel claimed that he had strong family values and was an active community member, but prosecutors claimed he had shown no remorse, was self-centred and lacked insight or empathy. Headland pleaded guilty to murder, but Justice Lindy Jenkins questioned the extent of his remorse and pointed out that he had not even been prepared to explain how the children died.

The '**unwanted child killer**' is a parent who kills one or more of their children, whom they regard as a hindrance in some way. Akon Guode's murder and infanticide of her three children is an example of this type of killing. She felt overwhelmed and unable to cope after the birth of her seventh child. The possibility that the father of four of her children was intending to return to live with his wife appears to have been one of the triggers for her attempting to kill four of her children by driving them into a suburban lake. One child survived, but three of them drowned.

Mornington father John Myles Sharpe killed his pregnant wife and daughter simply to avoid the responsibility of his growing family. In May 2004, almost two months after they were last seen, Sharpe appeared on Melbourne television pleading with his wife, Anna Kemp, to return home with their nineteen-month-old daughter Gracie. Sharpe told police that Anna had left him for another man and insisted that he had not hurt his wife and child. That story soon began to unravel as police investigated his movements and the awful truth began to emerge – Sharpe had killed Anna and Gracie, because he didn't want a second child (see *Why Did They Do It?*).

2 Familicide taxonomy

Professor Neil Websdale (2010) analysed the cases of 196 men and fifteen women who committed familicide, which he defines as 'the deliberate killing, within a relatively short period of time, of a current or former spouse or intimate partner and one or more of their children, followed in many cases by the suicide of the perpetrator' (page 1). Professor Websdale used data from these case studies to propose a different type of taxonomy. His classification system focuses more on the emotional styles and self-perceived gender roles of the murderers. He highlights what he argues are the key roles of strong negative emotions such as shame, rage, fear, anxiety and depression, in the lives and decisions of those who kill their families.

Professor Websdale concludes that many of these men killed their family members in a state of what he describes as 'humiliated fury' in which shame had 'gone into overdrive'. Their decision to murder their family is triggered by their perception that they have failed in their work, their family and/or their intimate relationships. One or more specific situations leads them to irrationally conclude that overall, they have failed to live up to the definition of masculinity promoted in the society in which they live. Other researchers (e.g. Liem and Nieuwbeerta, 2010; Logan et al., 2013; Roma et al., 2012) have also highlighted the role that strong feelings of failure, humiliation and shame play in the irrational decision of many men to kill their family and themselves.

Websdale has proposed two main categories of men who commit familicide, the 'livid coercives' and the 'civil reputables'.

The livid coercives

The men in this category are usually working class (e.g. have a blue-collar, manual or service job), and may be struggling to earn a living. They tend to be chronically angry, over-controlling, often threatening and/or physically abusive towards family members, and use alcohol to self-soothe. They perceive that they are losing power and have been humiliated in some way by the person upon whom they are dependent, leading them to feel depressed and angry. In many cases, the killing is revenge on their partner for wanting to leave them or for having already done so.

The civil reputables

These men are more likely to be white-collar or technical workers, public servants such as teachers and guidance counsellors, or owners of small businesses who live out their assigned gender roles with traditional division of labour between men and women.

They are usually shy, respectable, responsible and hard-working, conform to community values and are good providers, have good social standing in their community and perform their perceived social roles. When they commit familicide, the community responds with surprise and shock. They rarely have a history of harming their partner or children and are emotionally guarded, usually secretive and constantly worry about the future. The trigger for murdering their family is a significant reversal of fortune of some kind, which they perceive as leading to a sense of current or impending loss of social status, financial status and/or power. They fear they can no longer meet the needs of their family. This leads to strong feelings of shame, humiliation, helplessness and despair, which they keep to themselves. They also obsess privately about how the current situation will adversely affect their partner and children. They don't consider seeking help as an option.

Before they murder their family, these perpetrators seldom have a history of being violent towards their intimate partners.

Most keep their feelings of shame and humiliation secret, not just from the public but also from their families and friends. While they work hard to present an image of their family as happy and stable, they are usually enduring a great deal of emotional suffering, which they feel unable or unwilling to share with anyone else. They are likely to act with considerable preparation and planning, and are more likely to kill their victims while they sleep, perhaps in an attempt to minimise their fear and pain. Geoff Hunt, Darren Milne and Damien Little all fall into this category. They were all respectable, contributing community members who were highly regarded by their peers, family and friends. There is no suggestion that they physically or emotionally abused their partners or children before they committed their violent crimes. Their surviving loved ones and acquaintances were shocked and stunned when they discovered what had happened, as none of them thought them capable of hurting anyone.

3 Taxonomy of family annihilators: Yardley, Wilson and Lynes (2014)

Yardley et al. (2014) developed a taxonomy based on an overview and analysis of 59 British male 'family annihilators' who committed their mass murders between 1980 and 2012. (See also the chart on pages 44–5.) They define 'family annihilators' as those who intentionally kill their child or all their children. Some of the men in the study also killed or attempted to kill their spouse, who was the mother of the children, and some attempted to kill themselves. All their cases were filicides but not necessarily filicide–suicides or familicides, although many were.

They identified that:

- 81 per cent of family annihilators suicided, or attempted suicide.

- 47.5 per cent also killed their partner or ex-partner.
- In all cases, the child victims were the murderer's biological children.
- Most murders happened within the home.
- Most murderers killed using a single method.
- The most common method of murdering family member(s) was stabbing, followed by carbon monoxide poisoning from a car exhaust.
- Survivors of family annihilations were rare, with about only one in ten victims surviving the attack.

The four categories of family annihilator that Yardley et al. (2014) identified from their analysis are:

1. **The self-righteous killer:**

- seeks to blame their partner or ex-partner for their own killings, holding them responsible for any breakdown of the relationship or damage to the family
- has been controlling and possessive within their family in the past
- engages in overly dramatic behaviour and comments
- may attempt suicide to avoid facing the criminal justice system.

2. **The disappointed killer:**

- concludes that their family has let them down and prevented them from creating a successful family
- perceives their family to be an extension of their own needs and aspirations; self-obsession prevents them from seeing their children as separate entities and leads them to conclude that if their life should end, so should their child(ren)'s.

3. **The anomic killer:**
- perceives that they have damaged their family's income or lifestyle
- perceives that they have lost their economic status (e.g. by losing their job or not being successful in their own business).

4. **The paranoid killer:**
- perceives that there is an external threat (real or imagined) that will destroy their family (e.g. social services may take their children away) and kills them to save them from this supposed 'threat'.

Yardley et al. (2014) point out that the common link between all four categories is that the male annihilators believe their masculinity has been threatened in some way and they attempt to exert power and control to try to regain it. For many of these men, their role as the father is a fundamental component of their masculine identity. They feel lost and ashamed when circumstances change and their family ceases to perform its 'masculinity-affirming' functions for them. Annihilating their family becomes a way of exerting their masculinity when other strategies have failed. Geoff Hunt and Darren Milne felt their masculinity was threatened by the situations they found themselves in. They believed that they had lost control of their family situation and their lives, to the point where they irrationally and selfishly thought they had no alternative but to kill their children and their wives.

Leggett (2000) has speculated that many male family annihilators initially intend to suicide, but then decide to kill their spouse and children as well because they believe they will be unable to function without him as head of the household. This killer also wants to protect his family from the shame of having a parent who has suicided. He has a proprietary attitude towards both his partner and his children, and assumes he has the right to decide their fates. He can't conceptualise them as having an existence separate from his (Johnson, 2005). Given their drastic action, Geoff Hunt, Damien Little and Darren Milne almost certainly thought this way. They could have simply taken their own life, but instead decided to kill most or all of their immediate family.

FILICIDE AND FAMILICIDE TAXONOMIES

Resnick's taxonomy of parents who commit filicide

(Resnick, 1969; Friedman and Resnick, 2007; West, 2007; West et al., 2009; Resnick, 2016)

The first and most influential classification system to explain the motivation that leads to a parent murdering their own child or children was developed in 1969 by Dr Phillip Resnick. He reviewed 131 cases of filicide committed by men and women that had been discussed in psychiatric literature dating from 1751 to 1967. Many researchers have applied his model to specific populations in research studies and/or developed it further.

Altruistic filicide	• The parent perceives that the breakdown of their family unit is so catastrophic that they must spare their child/children the pain of that breakdown. They conclude that their child/children would be better off dead. • If the parent is motivated mostly by their own desire to suicide, they may feel that they need to kill their child/children as well to save them from having to deal with being fatherless or motherless. • Examples include Jason Lees and Damien Little.
Partner revenge filicide	• The parent murders their child/children to inflict the ultimate injury on their partner or former partner, conscious that they will have to live with that loss for the rest of their life, knowing that they were the trigger for the death of their child/children. • Examples include Arthur Freeman, Robert Farquharson and Jason Headland.
Unwanted child filicide	• The parent kills the child/children because they are regarded as a hindrance in some way. • Examples include Akon Guode and John Myles Sharpe.
Acutely psychotic filicide	• The parent has a serious mental illness and kills their child/children while experiencing a severe psychotic episode accompanied by hallucinations and being unable to differentiate what is real from what is not.
Fatal maltreatment filicide	• The child dies as a result of abuse or neglect by a parent.

Websdale's taxonomy of men who commit familicide (Websdale, 2010)	
Livid coercives	• Are more likely to come from a working-class background and be relatively socially isolated. • Tend to disguise or mask their sense of shame and humiliation through violence, hostility and intimidation. • Kill with vengeful, explosive violence.
Civil reputables	• Are more likely to be white-collar or technical workers, professionals, public servants (e.g. teachers or counsellors) or small independent businessmen who live in economically aspiring families. • Are usually very responsible and well respected in their community. • Have lived out the expected social and gender roles within their family and community. • Feel nervous and ashamed, both for themselves and the members of their family, at the prospect of being humiliated and/or losing social status. • Shock and surprise their family and community with their aggressive behaviour because they are often seen as 'pillars of their community'. • Tend to be 'emotionally guarded' and not self-disclosing about their feelings. • Are more likely to kill with considerable preparation and planning. • Examples include Geoff Hunt and Damien Little.

Taxonomy of male British 'family annihilators' (Yardley et al., 2014)	
Self-righteous (most common category)	• Seeks to blame his partner or ex-partner for the killings he has committed and, if he doesn't kill her as well, ensures she will experience pain and suffering from the deaths of her children. They often contact the mother just before they commit the murders to tell her what they are about to do, knowing there is nothing she can do to stop it. • Perceives the 'failure' of his often 'idealised' family to be the result of the breakdown of the relationship with his partner, for which he holds his partner responsible. • Is usually controlling and possessive within their family in the past. • Is overly dramatic and narcissistic in terms of the method by which he commits his murders and in his comments in any spoken and written communication beforehand. • Will often attempt suicide to avoid facing the criminal justice system. • Examples include Arthur Freeman, Robert Farquharson and Damien Little (although this remains uncertain, as at the time of publication there had been no inquest).
Disappointed	• Perceives that his family has let him down and prevented him from creating and maintaining his view of what a family should be. • Sees his family as an extension of his own needs and aspirations and a reflection of his own social status. • Example: Geoff Hunt.

Anomic	• Perceives that he has damaged the family's income and lost his economic status e.g. by losing his job, failing to run a successful business, etc.
Paranoid	• Perceives that there is an external threat (real or imagined) that will destroy his family (e.g. from social services who will take his children and place them in care). His distorted perception is that killing his family is a way of protecting them from that threat.

CHAPTER 1

GEOFF HUNT

The cast

Geoff Hunt: Father from Lockhart, New South Wales, who killed his wife, their three children and himself
Kim Hunt: Hunt's wife, whom he shot
Fletcher Hunt, ten, Mia Hunt, eight, and Phoebe Hunt, six: Kim and Geoff Hunt's children, who were killed by their father
Lorraine Bourke: Disability support worker who helped Kim with daily tasks after Kim's car accident
Kerry and Heather Blake: Kim's parents
Jenny Geppert: Kim's sister
Jane Blake: Kim's cousin
John and Lynette Hunt: Hunt's parents
Doug, Allen and Ian Hunt: Hunt's brothers; he was the second oldest
Renae Hunt: Hunt's sister-in-law
Cr Rodger Schirmer: Lockhart Mayor

The motive

Geoff Hunt killed his wife and three children because he couldn't cope with his family responsibilities and the changes in his wife, Kim, after she was seriously injured in a car accident. Rather than leave or seek additional help, he chose to kill his immediate family and himself.

Introduction

When well-to-do NSW farmer Geoff Hunt brutally shot dead his family and himself in September 2014, those who knew him were shocked. They described the respected member of the local community as a devoted father and an all-round good guy. Most reasoned that Hunt, 44, who hailed from an upstanding and prominent farming family, must have been in incredible pain to kill his wife, Kim, 41, and their three children, Fletcher, ten, Mia, eight, and Phoebe, six.

None of Hunt's family, friends or acquaintances could understand what had happened. There had been no obvious warning signs, as the family, which had been through some difficult times following a serious car accident in which Kim had been injured, seemed to be doing relatively well. Hunt's farming friends were also perplexed when they saw that he had driven through a canola field bursting with bright-yellow flowers to get to the dam where he ended his life. In the farming world, disturbing a crop is something a farmer would never do, no matter what.

As a former farmer, Lockhart Mayor Councillor Rodger Schirmer, who was Deputy Mayor at the time, noticed the discrepancy on the television news, as did other locals. 'Geoff drove through the canola crop to get to the dam,' Rodger says. 'That's not something a farmer would do. You wouldn't roll down a crop. This was a high flowering canola crop, and he drove in a direct line through the crop to get to the dam. You just don't.

There must have been a steely determination to do what he chose to do. It struck a lot of farmers, not just me.'

Regardless of the circumstances, nothing excuses the way Geoff Hunt killed those closest to him on the family farm, Watch Hill, outside Lockhart in New South Wales. The local community's stunned reaction highlights just how difficult it can be to comprehend the actions of men who choose to kill their entire family rather than deal with the problems that led them to that point. But if we want to at least try to prevent such tragedies happening again, it is essential to look at the full picture.

Consider how the Hunt children died.

If she was awake, the last thing little Phoebe Hunt would have seen was her father pointing a double-barrelled shotgun at her face. The man who was meant to protect his daughter instead chose to shoot her at point-blank range. Phoebe was in the bedroom her father shared with her mother, Kim, whom Hunt had already shot above the right eye and left for dead on a path outside the house. Phoebe somehow ended up in her parents' bedroom, where Hunt shot her in the face.

Mia suffered the same fate in her own bedroom. Wearing her pyjamas, she was found sitting partially upright in her bed, leaning on her left side against the wall. Her bottom was on a pillow that rested against the bedhead. Mia may have been sitting up in bed, or she could have sat up when Hunt entered the room. Either way, her father shot her in the middle of the forehead. The girls' brother, Fletcher, was also found slumped in his bedroom, lying on his right side in his pyjamas. While Fletcher was also shot at close range, for some reason he was hit in the back of the head and not the front. When he was found, the bedside lamp he usually left on as he slept was still emitting its soft light.

The shocking scene was discovered by disability support worker Lorraine Bourke, who helped Kim with household chores following her car accident, when she arrived for work at about 2.45 pm on Monday, 9 September 2014. Lorraine was surprised to see Kim's car in the driveway, as Kim had agreed to pick Fletcher up from cricket practice after school that afternoon.

The family dog, Ellie, was barking loudly and running back and forth. As Lorraine walked towards the house, she saw Kim lying on the paved pathway with a blue jacket over her head. Lorraine thought her client must have fallen over, but as she approached she saw blood on the ground near her head. Lorraine immediately ran inside and called an ambulance. It turned out that Kim was covered in two jackets, both work coats owned by her husband. As she frantically called for help, Lorraine saw a handwritten note on the dining-room table.

It read, 'I am sorry. It's all my fault. Totally mine.'

The first ambulance arrived at 3.04 pm. After confirming that Kim was dead, the paramedics waited for police to arrive. At that stage, Lorraine thought the children were at school and due to arrive home soon. When three police officers drove up the driveway, they headed about 450 metres to the farm dam, where Hunt's white Mitsubishi utility was parked. They found the keys in the ignition and shotgun shells in the front seat. Hunt was nowhere to be seen.

The officers searched the yard and sheds before entering the house. At around 4.30 pm, they found the bodies of the three Hunt children. A day later, police divers searched the dam and found Hunt's body in the water with a shotgun wound in the roof of his mouth. It is common knowledge in rural areas that a reliable way for those who live on farms to suicide is to shoot yourself when you are standing in a dam, so that if you don't die immediately you will probably fall into the water and drown anyway.

On the surface, it appeared to be a most unlikely crime. But when all the circumstances are considered, and with the benefit of hindsight, we can begin to understand what drove Geoff Hunt to kill his whole family and then himself.

The lead-up to the crime

In 2012, Kim Hunt almost died in a serious car accident. Phoebe was in the car with her mother and escaped with minor injuries, but Kim was left in a critical condition when their car flipped twice on the Lockhart Boree Creek Road. Kim was rushed to Wagga Wagga Base Hospital and then airlifted to Canberra Hospital, before being transferred to Sydney's Prince of Wales Hospital the next day in a serious but stable condition. Hunt stayed by Kim's side as she lay in a coma battling a traumatic brain injury. When she did wake, her recovery was long and slow. Kim had also suffered cervical fractures, and the movement of her right arm was severely affected. She was in hospital for almost eight months.

The family dynamics changed dramatically after the accident, partly due to Kim's physical and psychological issues. She was unable to work at all for a long time. Her physical impairment made it difficult for her to run the household, even though she spent more time at home than she had before the accident. Hunt probably also had to take over some of the physical tasks she had previously done, such as hanging out washing, when the assistance worker was not present. To help deal with her changed circumstances, Kim saw a psychologist who helped her with acceptance and adjustment. Her dosage of the antidepressant Cipramil (citalopram) was doubled from 20 to 40 milligrams.

The Hunt family may have had some experience with depression. The Coroner's report indicated that one of Geoff's brothers had referred to feeling depressed in the past. But their mother,

Lynette, denied any family history of depression, and the Coroner found no evidence of Geoff Hunt being treated for mental health issues. In mid-2009, Hunt did make some comments that the Coroner later considered could indicate suicidal ideation when he told his sister-in-law, as they were discussing marriage difficulties, that he didn't care if he lived any more. In mid-2010, Hunt told his brother Ian, 'If I die, I hope Fletcher dies with me, because I would hate for him to be trying to run the farm with Kim telling him what to do.'

Despite everything, Kim remained enthusiastic about a project she had started before her accident to build her family a dream home. She had sold her property in Wagga Wagga to fund it, and continued with the plans. Other aspects of her life, however, deteriorated after the accident. Issues had arisen in the Hunt family over a shared family trust, which caused conflict between some of the Hunt brothers. In the end, Geoff continued to work with his brother Allen on their farms and did so up until his death. Another brother, Ian, however, described Geoff as a 'very dominant and calculated person'. 'It was either Geoff's way or no other way . . . Geoff was extremely controlling to the point there was no reasoning with him about anything' (NSW State Coroner's findings, 9 October 2015).

The situation worried Kim, who talked about it in counselling and to others. She was convinced that one of the brothers had acted with impropriety in relation to the family trust, and became obsessed about her belief, often raising it with her husband. The brother denied any wrongdoing, but in Kim's mind it was a real issue. Her outlook improved when she returned to work for eight hours a week as a nurse educator in April 2014. But she continued to suffer from significant mood swings and found it difficult to handle their son Fletcher's hyperactive behaviour, which had worsened, perhaps due to his mother's accident. Fletcher was diagnosed with attention deficit hyperactivity disorder (ADHD) and prescribed Ritalin. He also had seven sessions with a child psychologist, who tried treating him by using cognitive behaviour therapy, but this approach was largely unsuccessful.

At Hunt's insistence, he and Kim started seeing counsellor Clive Murphy in June 2013 for marriage counselling. While alone with Clive, Kim said several times that she wished she had died in the accident and she would take her own life if she could. She revealed that she was stressed by her belief that one of Hunt's brothers had defrauded the family business, and by not being able to do things like waterskiing any more. That month, Kim told a telephone counsellor she'd had suicidal thoughts and there were guns in the house, so they sent police around. Kim insisted she was okay, but the police took Hunt's two guns to be safe – a .22 calibre rifle and a W. Cashmore double-barrelled 12-gauge shotgun. Two months later, after Hunt reassured police that all was fine, the guns were returned.

Meanwhile, family and friends noticed that Kim's personality had altered and that due to the brain injury she was struggling to filter her thoughts and information. This could be frustrating for her and sometimes cause her to be aggressive in conversation. She would also criticise Hunt in public. During one car trip to Sydney in June 2013, Kim suddenly became upset and yelled at him for 45 minutes. When they returned home she was referred to a psychiatrist, Dr Stephen Rosenman, who reported that she had increasing difficulty with angry outbursts, disinhibition and loss of empathy, and was finding it difficult to understand the impact of her anger on other people.

Dr Rosenman did not, however, believe that Kim was depressed any more, and recommended that she be weaned off the antidepressant, emphasising the need for her to continue to be cared for by someone who had experience in working with people who had brain injuries. Kim's GP also referred her to neuroscientist Dr Patricia Jungfer, who concluded that her depression had returned and suggested that Kim should keep taking her antidepressant medication. She also suggested seeing a specialist psychologist who had more experience with brain injuries, and Kim was referred to Paula Olymbios. In August 2013, Ms Olymbios diagnosed an adjustment disorder (see page 408) with depressed mood, and concluded that this was directly related to Kim's car accident.

Hunt saw Clive Murphy again in September 2013, and disclosed that he lacked motivation, was avoiding people and was not enjoying being with his children, even though he rated them as the people most important to him. Hunt said his worst fear was being on his own. By April 2014, Ms Olymbios found that Kim was progressing well but feeling unsupported by her husband. The antidepressants were helping, and while she still struggled to cope with Fletcher, things were improving. In June, however, when Kim and her husband spent a week with Kim's cousin Jane Blake, Kim told Jane she felt no love for her husband and was not attracted to him any more. Hunt's mood appeared low and Jane encouraged him to return to the counsellor for further treatment.

Two weeks later, Ms Olymbios spoke with Hunt and Kim, and noted that Kim sounded more positive, although Hunt mentioned that Kim had had 'an episode' that lasted about two weeks. When Kim had her last appointment with Dr Jungfer in September, she was functioning well, and her mood was stable. She was still enjoying her part-time work. Her home life was going well, and the family was socialising more. Kim was, however, still wearing a forearm splint to improve her finger positioning following surgery on her right hand, and this meant her hand strength was still severely limited.

On Sunday, 7 September, Fletcher played in a community junior Australian Rules football game that saw his father abused by parents from the opposition team. Hunt was acting as a goal umpire, and when the scores were close he gave the opposition team one point for a behind, believing the kicker had missed the goal. But some people from the opposition team were sure it was a goal and that Hunt should have awarded six points. After the game, some opposition supporters verbally abused Hunt and had to be shepherded away from him. Hunt, Kim and the kids later had lunch at a local vineyard with his brother Allen and his wife Renae and kids and another family. They all went to a park to play afterwards. Allen did not notice anything wrong. Kim made a few terse comments to Hunt, but others attributed them to her crash injuries.

The murders

On Monday, 8 September 2014, the children went to school, Kim attended her part-time job and Hunt spent most of the day working at one of the properties he and his brother farmed about 10 kilometres from his home. Renae Hunt spoke to her brother-in-law during the day and noted that Hunt sounded 'exceptionally happy'. They did discuss some difficult issues and Hunt confided that he was worried about Fletcher's future. Renae later said he seemed relieved when she gave him examples of farmers with ADHD who had done well in life.

At around noon, Hunt's friend Craig Fletcher called to see if he was okay following the football incident. Hunt told him he was shocked and upset by it, but said nothing to make Craig feel concerned about his welfare. At 4.13 pm, Hunt called local Luke Trevaskis to see if he could play tennis two days later. He told Luke he would prepare a tennis roster and send it around in the next day or two. When Lorraine arrived for her shift at

Watch Hill between 2.30 and 3 pm, Kim was tidying up and using the ride-on mower. After picking the kids up from the bus stop, Kim helped Fletcher with his homework. He was distressed and told her he had been teased at school about Hunt's umpiring issue the day before and that he had been called an expletive that rhymed with his surname. Others had called his father a cheat.

Hunt returned home at about 5 pm, wrapped some Father's Day presents for his dad, John, and took the kids to visit their grandfather. John later said that his son appeared normal, but his mother, Lynette, did notice that he seemed less happy than usual and 'had no smiles'. Hunt mentioned the disputed football goal, but did not seem too concerned about it. They left at about 6 pm.

While that was happening, Kim and Lorraine watered the garden and picked some fruit at a neighbour's property they were looking after. When they returned, the kids were eating a dinner that Hunt had prepared. Kim complained about what he was serving them for dinner. Lorraine later described her as 'cranky'. They went into the backyard and she attempted unsuccessfully to calm Kim, who offloaded about Hunt being lazy and again mentioned how some of her in-laws had allegedly stolen money from the family trust.

When they returned to the house, the children were either having their bath or were already in their pyjamas. Hunt was making school lunches for the next day. Lorraine noticed that he was quieter than usual and asked Kim if he was depressed. Kim said he wasn't and she was angry with him because he had played golf on Saturday, leaving her to mind the kids. At 7 pm the children were watching *Home and Away* on television, with their father lying on the couch with them. Kim and Lorraine sat at the dining table, with Kim complaining about Hunt being lazy and doing nothing. Lorraine later said it was so tense, 'you could cut the air with a knife'.

When Lorraine left, Hunt said, 'Goodbye, Lainie, thanks, see you tomorrow.'

At about 7.30 pm, Hunt spoke to Allen on the phone. It was a general catch-up, so they would know what each other was doing on the farms the next day. Allen said his brother seemed a bit rushed, like he had to go. Hunt told him he was going to attend a grain marketing meeting in Lockhart. The call only lasted about three minutes.

Sometime after that, Geoff Hunt killed his entire family and then himself.

When word of the tragedy spread, the whole community was shocked. No one had noticed any obvious warning signs, and it appeared that Hunt had not revealed the full extent of his troubles to anyone. Cr Rodger Schirmer, who did not know the family well but knew Hunt to say hello to and helped his extended family after the deaths, says what happened was 'a total shock'. Despite experiencing some problems, to most people who knew them, the Hunt family appeared to be well supported, financially secure and popular.

Rodger says many locals saw the deaths as a tragedy that did not change their view of Geoff Hunt as a good bloke and a good father who belonged to a nice family. 'I think people have decided that it wasn't Geoff,' he says. 'He was a very good father, they were involved in the football club. He couldn't have been a better dad. There was no harshness in him or anything like that. Everything seemed quite normal. And that's why it's so shocking.'

The Coroner's report

Sitting at Wagga Wagga in October 2015, the NSW Coroner, Michael Barnes, investigated the deaths. He found that Geoffrey Francis Hunt, 44, Kim Jeannine Hunt, 41, Fletcher Austin Hunt, ten, Mia Isobel Hunt, eight, and Phoebe Amelia Hunt, six, all died on 8 or 9 September 2014, at their home, Watch Hill Farm. NSW Police Force Behavioural Science Team manager and senior forensic psychologist Dr Sarah Yule prepared a psychological autopsy on Geoff Hunt, which is an indirect assessment based on available information. She found that Hunt had probably experienced depressive symptoms over some time. Coupled with his tendency to internalise cognitive and emotional distress, this escalated into his decision to kill his family. Marital and family stressors, including Kim's permanent injuries, probably contributed to his feelings of hopelessness about the future.

'In contrast to other cases of family murders and suicide where the deaths are preceded by custody disputes and sometimes a history of family violence, in this case it appears Geoff could not contemplate separating from Kim or his children,' Mr Barnes wrote. 'In Dr Yule's opinion, the children were likely killed because Geoff believed they could not cope without him. These distorted beliefs may have included that he was ending Kim's misery, particularly given that her recovery was believed to have reached its maximum expectation. Therefore, Dr Yule concludes that Geoff's primary intent was suicide, and his decision to kill the remaining members of his family had a pseudo "altruistic" motivation. His distorted thinking resulting in this action was likely associated with symptoms of depression and feelings of hopelessness for his and his family's situation' (NSW State Coroner's findings, 9 October 2015).

The Coroner found that the communities of Lockhart and Tumbarumba (where Kim grew up) had suffered due to the deaths of the Hunt family members, who were well known and respected. 'Generally, family and friends thought Kim and Geoff Hunt were both leading largely happy, stable and successful lives, overcoming or at least coping with the adversity dealt to them,'

Mr Barnes wrote. 'The manner of their deaths demonstrates the truth was far different . . . it is unavoidable the focus of the inquest is on indicators of dysfunction, disharmony and mental illness. But that should not obscure the fact that both Kim and Geoff had done much in their lives to be proud of and had many very admirable qualities. They were both successful in their chosen careers, and, perhaps more importantly, they were both engaged and caring parents who undoubtedly loved their children dearly. Geoffrey Hunt was the scion of a prominent local grazing family. He was well liked in the area, charismatic, an excellent sportsman and a tertiary educated and skilful farmer. He was sociable and hard working' (NSW State Coroner's findings, 9 October 2015).

The Coroner found that while farming success was weather- and market-dependent and could be stressful, the Hunt family was very well established in agribusiness and held large, productive parcels of land. 'Geoff and his brother had relevant tertiary qualifications and a work ethic that equipped them to succeed in primary industry,' Mr Barnes found. 'There is no basis to suspect financial pressure played any part in these deaths.'

Mr Barnes found that financial tensions within the family (he had seen no evidence of wrongdoing by Geoff's siblings), Kim's accident, her mental health issues, lack of empathy and increasing criticism of her husband, all of which were beyond her control and a result of injuries sustained in the crash, had strained their marriage. Hunt had also shown some indicators of mild depression, such as lack of motivation and avoiding people, but kept any signs of not coping well hidden. Mr Barnes ruled that the crime was 'clearly' not premeditated, as Hunt had made plans for the following day and the children's school lunches. 'We also know that Kim was in a very bad mood,' he said. 'Despite Geoff having fed the children their dinner, made their lunches for the next day and supervised their bathing she had been openly and constantly critical of Geoff throughout the evening . . . Further, she had heard that Fletcher had been abused at school for something Geoff was alleged to have done wrong the day before at the football' (NSW State Coroner's findings, 9 October 2015).

The Coroner also dismissed rumours that Kim may have killed her children. There was no evidence she had shot a gun, and her physical limitations would have made it impossible for her to do so accurately three times. 'I reject any suggestion that Kim Hunt killed the children prompting Geoff to kill her then himself,' Mr Barnes found. 'I accept the evidence of the forensic psychologist that Geoff's primary intention was to end his own life. It is well recognised that people at risk of suicide frequently act impulsively, with little planning or premeditation. For some reason, that night Geoff came to act on the view that he could not go on, that his life was not going to improve and that he was better off dead. Because of his emotional dependence on his wife and essential self-image of his position as the head of a family that he believed was dependent on him, his distorted logic led him to conclude that the children and his wife would not cope without him. He then set about systematically and cold bloodedly killing each of them, before killing himself.

'What Geoffrey Hunt did was inexcusable; the absolute worst of crimes. It wasn't premeditated; it wasn't motivated by malice or to cover up other wrongs but it was completely unnecessary. It was the result of an egocentric delusion that his wife and children would be better off dying than living without him. The financial resources and family supports that were available to the Hunt family would have readily facilitated a marital separation whereby Geoff could have continued to work the farm, Kim could have continued to work part-time and both would have had extensive contact with the children they so deeply cared for. It is unfathomable why Geoff Hunt would not have actively explored those options before taking the outrageous actions he did' (NSW State Coroner's findings, 9 October 2015).

Geoff Hunt's background

The second of four sons, Geoff Hunt was born in March 1970. He grew up on the family farm before completing an agricultural science degree and returning to work in farming with his brothers Doug, Allen and Ian. Hunt was a talented sportsman who excelled at tennis, football and golf. He was popular in the local community. His friends later insisted that he was a devoted husband and father, easygoing, outgoing and positive. One described him as a bit of a closed book, but said he tried to put a positive spin on everything.

Kim Blake was born in December 1972, and had a younger sister, Jenny. They grew up on the family farm in Tumbarumba, about 160 kilometres south-east of Lockhart. Kim studied nursing at Wollongong University and worked in several hospitals before moving to the Wagga Wagga Hospital Intensive Care Unit. She sometimes also worked at Lockhart Hospital. Kim was a determined, knowledgeable and driven person, but also quite highly strung. She set high standards for herself and those around her, but was also described as very generous, warm and community-minded. She loved helping people, cooking, gardening, waterskiing and horseriding. Kim appeared to have boundless energy and took on double and even triple shifts at work if needed.

Geoff Hunt met Kim Blake at the Lockhart Picnic Races in 1996 and they married in October 2001. Fletcher was born in 2004, Mia in 2006 and Phoebe in 2008. Fletcher was a boisterous and loud child with lots of energy. His behaviour was sometimes challenging, most likely due to his ADHD. Fletcher liked playing Australian Rules football and riding his motorbike. Mia was the quietest of the siblings, and suffered some anxiety when her mother was unwell. She responded well to counselling with a psychologist, and enjoyed reading and her own company. She often did Fletcher's homework for him. Phoebe was more like her brother – lively and talkative.

The family lived at Watch Hill, a 1215-hectare farm about 20 kilometres from Lockhart. It was one of several properties jointly owned by the families of Hunt and his brother Allen. Geoff and Kim were outwardly happy, but in 2009 a relative noted that the marriage seemed to be becoming strained. They said Hunt appeared dispirited and unsure if they would make their tenth wedding anniversary. In 2010, Kim saw a psychologist three times for symptoms of anxiety and depression. At that point, she had no previous diagnosed mental health history. She was prescribed an antidepressant. Kim told the psychologist that her son Fletcher was causing her grief with his cruelty to animals and aggression, symptoms of his ADHD. She also discussed the severe drought that was affecting much of New South Wales that year, and issues she was having with some relatives. Kim then started a program of cognitive behaviour therapy, relaxation strategies and time-management techniques. The antidepressants appeared to work well.

The family continued to have its ups and downs, and in December 2011 Kim left home for the night after an argument, telling a family friend that she was fine and just needed to cool off. But generally speaking, the Hunts were a well-liked and respected family whose members enjoyed their involvement in the local school, hospital and farming communities.

While her physical health slowly improved after her accident, the brain injury changed Kim's personality. She also remained physically impaired, with general weakness on her right side and restricted strength and movement in her right hand. From that point, some people noticed that Kim could sometimes be unpleasant to people, particularly her husband, and that she became fixated on issues that worried her. She was frustrated by her physical limitations and lost her ability to 'filter' information, often speaking her mind without considering how her comments might be taken by others. This was not Kim's fault, as it was entirely due to the brain injury from the accident, and most of her friends and family understood this. But it did not make life any easier.

Friends and family noted that due to these involuntary behaviour changes, Kim also became more critical of her husband. Hunt seemed to let it go, but the Coroner later found that over time this caused him deep distress. His usual reaction was not to respond, but remove himself from the situation. While Hunt made offhand comments doubting his relationship would last, he did not appear to take active steps at that time to end his marriage or to seek additional counselling.

Domestic violence does not appear to have been an issue. Kim's sister Jenny, who had always been close to her, said Kim had never mentioned any violence, 'whether it be physical, mental or psychological'. Jenny was also close to Hunt, who never indicated to her that he would take his own life, although she did think he felt it was essential that he needed to be around to care for his wife and children. Hunt made a significant contribution to running the house and caring for the children, even before the car accident when he and Kim were both working full time.

After the accident, Kim tired easily and needed periods of sleep most days to avoid aggravating her mood and frustration levels. She struggled to adjust to her changed circumstances. Kim had returned home from hospital in February 2013, under the care of the South West Brain Injury Rehabilitation Service

Outreach Team, and needed daily help to cope with household activities such as cooking meals, cleaning and getting the children ready for school. When Phoebe started school in 2014, Kim's weekday hours of support were reduced to 3 pm to 8 pm. Things seemed to be improving for Kim, but her husband clearly did not think so.

Why did he do it?

There are reasons why Geoff Hunt killed his family and himself, but none of them excuse his actions. The family was under significant personal stress. Kim, who was an energetic high achiever before her car accident, was still struggling physically and mentally. Although she had returned to work part time and was helping to run the household, she lost her temper easily and was often critical of her husband, sometimes aggressively and at times in front of others. Due to her brain injury, Kim could be negative in her outlook, and continually raised accusations of alleged impropriety regarding the Hunt family trust.

There was also Fletcher's ADHD, which can be difficult to manage. Having a child with such a condition in a household that is already under strain would not have helped. Kim was much physically weaker than she had been and would have found it difficult to keep up with any of her children, let alone one who was also impulsive and inattentive. All of this would have been distressing for Hunt, who appeared to be doing his best to keep his family functioning as normally as possible and together as a unit.

Being accused of cheating after his controversial goal umpiring decision during Fletcher's football game would have caused Hunt additional distress. This possibly would have been compounded when Fletcher said he had been called names at school because of it. As a respected farmer and community member, this type of slight would have been keenly felt, and could have contributed to Hunt's overall feeling of shame and despair. It may even have been the last straw after several challenging years. While some can shake off snide comments, others who pride themselves on their reputation and/or position in the community would be horrified to be accused of cheating. Geoff Hunt probably fell into the latter category.

Hunt may have had a mild degree of depression when he killed his family, but there is no evidence that his thinking was impaired by any kind of mental illness. He chose not to seek additional professional help apart from earlier brief marriage counselling. Many families face similar problems, some much worse than what the Hunt family endured. Coping with them is difficult, but such situations can be dealt with and Hunt knew this. But for some reason, he appears to have felt that the shame or embarrassment of asking for help would be worse than murdering his whole family. At this point, someone could possibly have intervened to help him find another way – but only if Hunt had shared the depths of his despair or shown signs that things were turning deadly. Unfortunately, he didn't.

As we have seen, when a murderer kills some or all of their immediate family members, it is called familicide (see pages 29, 411). In some cases it is an act of revenge, while other family murders are sparked by a warped belief that those family members are better off dead and would be unable to survive without them. Hunt may have surmised that if he killed himself, his family could not cope without him. He perceived that life wasn't working well, so in his mind he was putting his family out of its misery. Either way, his reasoning was irrational and selfish, and disregarded the lives of those who depended on him. Such thinking isn't necessarily a sign of mental illness. Many assume that in cases like this the perpetrator must have been psychotic or severely mentally ill. Geoff Hunt was neither, and even though he may have had mild depression it is no excuse – even people with *severe* depression know right from wrong.

A mentally ill person who murders is most often psychotic and has lost their grip on reality. For example, they may believe that the devil has told them someone is evil and must be killed. Hunt's irrational thinking involved believing that his family was better off dead. He was not psychotic. This was a man who wasn't coping with life and felt sorry for himself. His situation was not ideal, and clearly difficult, but Hunt had a responsibility to his family to at least try to deal with his problems. Instead, due to an egocentric, irrational and misplaced belief that his wife and children had to die with him, an entire family was lost. It was an extremely brutal crime, but the media coverage after Hunt killed his family seemed not to want to go there. Friends were quoted describing him as a terrific family man and a pillar of society. If Hunt had done something so drastic, they reasoned, life must have been intolerable. But this wasn't the case.

Given that Geoff Hunt suicided when he killed his wife and three children, no one will ever know why he took such drastic action. But one thing is certain: there is no excuse for it. No matter how good a bloke he was, or how much he helped or cared for his family, nothing justifies the fact that he decided to murder them all. Geoff Hunt had choices. He could have taken a resilient and rational approach to managing his concerns by seeking additional counselling or medical treatment for any underlying mild depression, or confiding in friends or family about how concerned he was about the overall situation. He was financially stable, so he could afford to separate from Kim if needed and still provide any help she might need in running the household.

Hunt had once confided to counsellor Clive Murphy, however, that his worst fear was being on his own. In that case, it could also be speculated that, as her health improved and she returned to part-time work, Kim may have been talking about a possible separation, and this may also have influenced Hunt's decision. If this was the case, he could have arranged for either him or both of them to participate in additional marriage counselling. He did none of those things. Instead, he decided to shoot Kim, Fletcher, Mia and Phoebe before shooting himself. Hunt's actions fit into several categories of men who kill their children or families as identified in several taxonomies (see pages 41–5) such as those described at the start of this section.

ALTRUISTIC KILLERS

(Resnick, 1969; Friedman and Resnick, 2007; West et al., 2009)

A father who kills family members in an 'altruistic' filicide believes that the breakdown of his family unit is so catastrophic that he must spare his children the pain by killing them and himself. This self-obsession prevents him from seeing his children as separate entities rather than being 'owned' by him, so he decides that if his life should end, so should theirs. Hunt had spoken about not wanting to leave his son Fletcher behind if he died, as he would not want him to have Kim telling him what to do. He saw himself as the family's rock, and if he was no longer there, especially given Kim's physical issues, he was convinced that they could not cope without him. Hunt did help around the house and was widely considered to be a good farmer and father, but that did not mean his family could not cope without him. In this sense, his thinking was irrational and self-focused.

CIVIL REPUTABLE KILLERS

(Websdale, 2010)

These killers are often professionals or independent businessmen from aspirational families. They are usually responsible and well respected in their community, and follow typical social and gender roles within their family and community. The idea of being humiliated and/or losing social status makes them feel nervous and ashamed for themselves and their family. When they act, their aggressive behaviour comes as a shock to most if not all who know them, as they are often seen as 'pillars of their community'. This is partly because they tend to guard themselves emotionally and not discuss their feelings. Geoff Hunt was certainly a pillar of the local community and came from a highly respected family. He placed a high value on maintaining this image, even if he was crumbling underneath. In the end it became too much, and rather than face what he perceived to be the humiliation of admitting he was struggling, he killed himself and took his family with him.

DISAPPOINTED KILLERS

(Yardley et al., 2014)

A disappointed parent who kills his family is more likely to put considerable preparation and planning into their final act. They believe that their family has let them down and prevented them from creating and maintaining their view of what a family should be. To them, their family is an extension of their needs and aspirations and a reflection of their social status. Hunt was disappointed in his family, which was not living up to his expectations of what it should be. To him, Kim was no longer the vibrant, high-achieving professional he had married, and she even struggled to physically care for her children. He was also concerned that Fletcher's ADHD would prevent him from become a productive and community-minded adult like him and his immediate family members. While his fears were unfounded, in Hunt's eyes those around him had let him down and were preventing him from maintaining the status he believed he deserved at home and in public.

In the end, the choices that Geoff Hunt made destroyed his family. There may not have been a history of domestic violence, but this was the ultimate act of family violence. While it is painful, cases such as this need to be discussed, as they can raise awareness about potential warning signs for others. These signs can be extremely difficult to spot. While he and Kim had taken part in some earlier marriage counselling and he occasionally spoke in a way that suggested he may have considered suicide, Hunt gave few hints about what he was thinking in the lead-up to his crime. Those wondering 'what if' did not have much to work with.

In Hunt's case, few if any people who cared about him could have done anything differently. His immediate family was well supported by family and friends, and he and Kim had earlier sought marriage counselling and help for their children when they had problems. They were active and respected community members who appeared to make the most of the cards that life dealt them. It was clear that things were not perfect and Kim's anger issues were causing Hunt some distress. But she was dealing with this by seeking professional help, and those close to the family understood why she acted the way she did.

If anything, the only possible warning sign was when Hunt said he hoped that if he died Fletcher would die with him. This type of talk is not common, so on its own was probably seen as morbid. Generally, Hunt appeared to be coping – if not perfectly. Regardless of whether there were any overt signs, no one is to blame for what happened to his family other than him. Hunt refused to seek further help and did not give those people who cared about him and his family a chance to help him change his self-focused and irrational mindset.

In other cases, there may be warning signs that a person is considering drastic action. If you think a loved one is displaying a significant amount of negative talk, such as life being all too hard, talk with them, ask how they are coping and discuss options for help. If someone does not appear to be coping with life, reach out and encourage them to seek help while offering personal support, such as being there to talk at any time or minding the children so that they can take some time out. If something seems wrong, don't wait for them to ask for your help – ask them if they are okay and, if necessary, support them in seeking professional assistance. If appropriate, share stories of some of your own difficult or challenging times, without making it about you.

While Geoff Hunt's crimes both shocked and shattered the Lockhart community, they galvanised locals and helped boost awareness of mental health issues. Riverina Bluebell, a mental health promotion group, links people to local support groups, services and helplines, while promoting educational activities. Since the Hunt family tragedy, it has stepped up its efforts to promote local wellbeing events and community activities. In late 2016, Riverina Bluebell partnered with the Rural Adversity Mental Health Program, Centre Stage Scripts, Murrumbidgee Local Health District, the Department of Primary Industries and the National Disability Coordination Officer Program to tour a live theatre show across the Riverina. *Carpe Diem* addresses mental health in rural communities and stresses the importance of professional care in times of crises. Starring actor John Wood, it also highlights the importance of mateship and looking out for each other. Geoff Hunt's brother Allen spoke at one of the performances, which were well attended and much appreciated.

Cr Rodger Schirmer says local awareness and acceptance of mental health issues has improved. There is still a way to go, but he says more men are being encouraged to access services and talk to others when they feel that life is becoming difficult. Some of those who organise Riverina Bluebell events have experienced mental health issues, giving them great empathy and an insight into this growing issue. Schirmer says it can be difficult to identify serious problems, as many men, like Geoff Hunt, find it hard to confide in others. But the growing number of local support groups and an increasing willingness to discuss mental health is helping.

The Spirit of the Land Festival, a colourful celebration of the land through sculptures, fine art, photography, markets, boutique stalls, food, open gardens, entertainment and vintage vehicles, has also continued to grow and galvanise the local community. The festival started in 2006 during the worst drought in Lockhart's recorded history as a tribute to the resilience of those who live and work on the land. It was inspired by those who saw the inner strength, courage and determination of a community battling an invisible foe. 'Some people are doing it tough, and the pressures that people are under are real and manifest themselves in different ways,' Rodger says. 'Mental health is a problem that so many people are suffering with. If treated, and you get on the right medication to make things better, then there's potentially good outcomes.'

Predicting actions as drastic as Geoff Hunt's is not easy. But it doesn't hurt to offer a sympathetic ear or help to find suitable professional help for someone who is in trouble. There is no doubt Hunt was in a difficult position, some of which was not of his own making. Many men will relate to his feeling of helplessness and of being unable to confide in anyone about how hopeless it all seemed. This tragic case should be held up as one that demonstrates there are always better options, no matter how difficult life seems.

Australia has a comprehensive health system with a range of outlets for those who feel they cannot cope, from confidential helplines to subsidised sessions with psychologists and psychiatrists. Men and women in need must be encouraged to access them. Friends and family should also be encouraged to look for signs that someone close to them might not be coping during and/or after major challenges and changes to their life circumstances, and to offer ongoing non-judgemental support.

CHAPTER 2

ARTHUR FREEMAN

The cast

Arthur Freeman: Killed his daughter, Darcey
Peta Barnes: Freeman's ex-wife and Darcey's mother
Darcey Freeman: Died aged four when her father, Arthur, threw her from West Gate Bridge
Darcey's brothers: Darcey had two brothers, who were aged two and six when she died

The motive

Arthur Freeman murdered his daughter, Darcey, four, to take revenge on his ex-wife, Peta Barnes, after they had been to court and his access to his three children had been reduced.

Introduction

A Melbourne scorcher was forecast as parents prepared to send their children back to school on 29 January 2009. The hot weather often hits when the holidays finish and kids are confined to crowded classrooms for the new school year. In this case, hot was an understatement. Temperatures would soar well above 40 degrees Celsius around the city that day. At Laverton airport, outside Geelong, the mercury would climb to 45.8. The temperature had not quite begun its steep ascent when four-year-old Darcey Freeman and her two brothers climbed into their dad's car for the 130-kilometre trip from their grandparents' holiday house at Aireys Inlet, south-west of Geelong, to school in Melbourne. A bright little girl with a gorgeous smile, Darcey was looking forward to her first day at St Joseph's Primary School in Hawthorn.

The murder

The siblings and their father, Arthur Freeman, 37, had stayed overnight with his parents, and the plan was to leave bright and early so he could get them to school in time for the morning bell. As they cruised past Laverton, the traffic began to thicken, as it always did on a busy weekday morning. Geelong is an attractive place to live, with affordable real estate and proximity to Victoria's beautiful surf coast. As a result, thousands of workers commute between Melbourne and Geelong each day along the Princes Freeway, guaranteeing traffic gridlock. The budding development of housing estates between the two cities at the time didn't help, with thousands of extra cars joining them along the way. Today was no exception, and a long line of vehicles snaked its way up onto the West Gate Bridge.

Melbourne's largest bridge stretches almost 2.6 kilometres across the Yarra River, connecting the CBD with the western suburbs. The distinctively curved, cable-stayed girder structure stands 58 metres from the river at its highest point and sees up to 200,000 vehicles cross each day. One of Melbourne's most recognisable landmarks, the West Gate Bridge opened in

1978 amid much fanfare that was also tinged with sadness. On 15 October 1970, a section collapsed while under construction, killing 35 workers, so its momentous opening was also a chance to remember those who were lost. The gateway to Melbourne's west has since become an iconic part of life in Melbourne, but also a source of endless frustration during peak hour and roadworks, and after accidents.

As Arthur Freeman approached the West Gate Freeway with his children on that busy summer morning, the traffic was predictably clogged. Motorists resigned themselves to a slow crossing as they crawled towards their air-conditioned offices. The delay meant Freeman had more time to consider the Family Court access and custody proceedings in which he and his ex-wife, Peta Barnes, were embroiled. Consent orders had been made the previous day. After some debate, arrangements were changed from equally shared custody to Freeman having only three days' custody every second weekend. He would also have custody on the afternoon and early evening of the Thursday in the other week.

Freeman was not happy with his treatment by the court and found the experience unpleasant. But he had told his friends that he was glad it was over and did not express any dissatisfaction with the result. Freeman had called his mother and reached his parents' Aireys Inlet home around midnight. By that time, he was distressed and didn't want to talk about the proceedings. Freeman then had an unsettled night and was still upset when they all got up the next morning. His father suggested that he could go with them to Melbourne as the driver. But his son declined.

Instead, Arthur Freeman now found himself approaching the West Gate Bridge in heavy traffic as his frustration mounted. At some point, he had a long phone conversation with Elizabeth

Lam, a friend in England. Upset and crying, he described the result of the Family Court proceedings as having lost his children. He vowed to continue his fight through the court.

Not long after that conversation, the mother of Freeman's children, Peta Barnes, called. They spoke twice. In the first conversation, Freeman told Peta to say goodbye to her children, and in the second, he said she would never see them again. He then drove to a point at or close to the top of the bridge, pulled into the left-hand emergency lane and turned on the hazard lights. After the car stopped, Freeman told Darcey to climb over into the front seat. He then reached over from the driver's side, pulled his daughter from the car and led her over to the parapet, where he lifted her up and threw her over the edge into the river below.

Darcey fell more than 50 metres into the water. Her brothers, aged six and two, were still in the car. Freeman showed no emotion as others frantically tried to save his little girl, who died later that day from her injuries. He returned to his car and drove off as if nothing had happened. When one of his sons asked if he could move into the front seat, Freeman stopped the car so that he could. The boy was aware of what had happened and asked his father to return to help those who were working hard to retrieve his sister from the river because Darcey didn't know how to swim. Instead, Freeman drove into the city and parked in La Trobe Street before entering the Commonwealth Law Courts building where his case had been held.

As he entered the building, Freeman carried one of his sons and led the other by the hand. He tried to hand one to a security official, who declined. Freeman became distressed, cried and was unresponsive to his boys and court officials. A counsellor tried unsuccessfully to console him, after which Freeman told police officers to take him away. Freeman later told health professionals that he was very worried about running late for school. Once he approached the West Gate Freeway, he said he had a feeling of being trapped and that he was never going to make it. As traffic crawled onto the bridge and it felt like they were not moving at all, his sense of anxiety and hopelessness rose. Instead of dealing with his frustrations by hitting the dashboard or yelling, as others might, this man decided to throw his only daughter to certain death in one of the most horrifying ways imaginable.

As Melbourne came to grips with the tragedy, people were left shaking their heads. They simply could not understand how a parent could do this to their child. Few could believe this was possible without the perpetrator having some sort of serious psychotic episode.

But was that the case?

The trial

Arthur Phillip Freeman pleaded not guilty to the murder of his daughter Darcey due to mental impairment. Following a nineteen-day trial in 2011, a jury convicted him of murder. It did not accept his mental impairment defence. Expert opinion, which generally agreed that Freeman had some degree of depression, was divided on the seriousness of that condition. During the trial, Freeman said he could not remember what he had done but accepted he was responsible for Darcey's death. His defence claimed that he was mentally ill. Psychiatrist Professor Graham Burrows gave evidence that he believed the accused was suffering from severe depression and, as a result of that, fell into a state of 'dissociation' so that his acts were not conscious, voluntary and deliberate or intentional. Other experts disagreed.

In sentencing Freeman, Justice Paul Coghlan quoted Professor Burrows as saying Freeman was 'acting somewhat like an automaton'. Addressing himself to Freeman, he continued:

'He expressed that opinion based on the history given by you on examination, your father's description of events on the night of 28 January 2009 and the morning of 29 January 2009, the description of how you appeared at least to some of the witnesses on the West Gate Bridge, and the fact that he found you highly hypnotisable,' Justice Coghlan said. 'He added that people who are highly hypnotisable are more likely to dissociate.'

However, two other professionals, Dr Skinner and Dr Bell, believed Freeman was only suffering from mild to moderate depression, and if there was any dissociation, it was not such as to have removed his capacity to act consciously, voluntarily and deliberately or intentionally. 'In any event, the jury rejected your defence of mental impairment,' Justice Coghlan said to Freeman, 'and once that defence was rejected, it was inevitable that you be convicted of murder' (*R v Freeman* [2011] VSC 139).

In deciding whether to impose a life sentence, the judge considered a number of matters of aggravation, including that:

- This was the killing of an innocent child.
- The circumstances in throwing his four-year-old daughter from a bridge more than 50 metres above the ground 'could not be more horrible'. 'What Darcey's last thoughts might have been does not bear thinking about, and her death must have been a painful and protracted one,' Justice Coghlan said.
- The conduct was 'a most fundamental breach of trust and it is an attack on the institution of the family which is so dear to the community'.
- Darcey's brothers, aged two and six, both witnessed the killing.
- Any motive had nothing to do with the innocent victim, who was used to hurt her mother 'as profoundly as possible'.

- The crime scene was remarkably public and had 'the most dramatic impact'. This brought the broader community into this case in a way that had been rarely, if ever, seen before, offending the collective conscience.
- The boys would have heard the threats made to their mother over the phone (*R v Freeman* [2011] VSC 139).

Justice Coghlan received victim impact statements from relatives and friends of the family. In hers, Peta Barnes revealed she had suffered from PTSD and that she would never get over what happened. 'Where to start is a challenge as this statement brings to the surface all of the raw emotions I live with daily,' she wrote. 'Since the loss of Darcey I grieve on a daily basis and realistically do not see how that can ever change. The saying "time heals all wounds" is not true for myself and I don't ever expect it to be. Not a day goes by where I do not constantly think of Darcey, where I don't miss her and wish with all my heart that she was with me.

'I can feel her little hand holding mine when I walk down the street or drive in the car. I lie in bed at night and hold her in my arms. I talk to her and think of her daily wishing she was participating in the activities that were happening at that time. No words could ever truly describe the loss of a child to a parent. The emptiness that sits within you, the piece of you that no longer exists, the fact you no longer go on in life as a complete person. Seeing little girls who have similar traits or looks to Darcey heightens my already active emotions. Holding myself back from giving the child a hug is always a struggle of self-control.

'Not a day goes by where I don't flashback to the emotions I felt when I was told by my ex-husband that I would never see my children again. The panic and fear these words set off inside me resonates within me even today. I feel them now in incidents of my daily life that would not have impacted me prior to Darcey's passing. I notice that I have heightened anxiety in everyday situations and have to manage myself carefully to control this.

'The events of the day of Darcey's passing are all horrific in their nature. To articulate the impact of this day and the ensuing future it has brought cannot truly be expressed in a Victim Impact Statement. No one can erase the thoughts and associated feelings I have of sitting in the hospital and having to tell the hospital staff that they were allowed to turn the life support machine off. Of holding Darcey in my arms as she passed away and knowing that this decision would take her from me again and knowing that there was no other option available to me' (*R v Freeman* [2011] VSC 139).

Others who witnessed the crime were also severely traumatised, and at least one female police officer involved in the recovery of Darcey's body developed PTSD and major depressive disorder.

Items put to the court in mitigation on Freeman's behalf included several reports by health professionals and written references from some of Freeman's friends, a neighbour, a family friend and his grandfather. 'They all speak well of you and give you their support,' Justice Coghlan said of the references. He said Freeman had not had any treatment for or experienced any mental illness, and had had no problems with alcohol and drugs before the tragedy. 'You have had a long-term interest in racing cars,' the judge said. 'You were a social tennis player. You are now being prescribed the anti-depressant drug, Effexor, but that may be subject to review. You are being held in Exford Unit, where there is provision for suicide watch.'

Freeman's defence argued that impaired mental functioning at the time reduced culpability and should be considered in sentencing. One expert, Dr Bell, said Freeman's depression was moderate, but there was little evidence that mental impairment had affected his actions: 'There is minimal evidence of more pervasive and severe depressive cognitions such as thoughts of hopelessness, futility, self-recrimination and despair or other neurovegetative symptoms of severe depression such as loss of libido, anorexia [loss of appetite] and diurnal mood variation. The observations of Mr Freeman's friends and family of him in the hours following the handing down of the Family Court judgement on 28 January suggest that he was in a heightened state of distress and agitation, expressing an inconsolable feeling that he had lost his children.

'All of the observations of witnesses regarding his behaviour on the morning of Darcey Freeman's death suggest that he knew the nature and quality of his conduct. Mr Freeman continued to demonstrate that he was able to think purposefully about his situation and to continue to make reasoned judgements about both his own behaviour and the behaviour of others. Unfortunately, we do not know what Mr Freeman was thinking at the time he threw his daughter over the rail of the West Gate Bridge. Nevertheless, there is minimal evidence to support a conclusion that at the time of engaging in conduct constituting the offence Mr Freeman was suffering from a mental illness that had the effect that he did not know that his conduct was wrong, that is that he could not reason with a moderate degree of sense and composure about whether the conduct as perceived by reasonable people was wrong' (*R v Freeman* [2011] VSC 139).

In their earlier reports, psychiatrists Dr Lester Walton and Professor Paul Mullen described Freeman as suffering from a depressive illness, but neither concluded that he was mentally impaired. Dr Skinner believed that Freeman was quite distressed and suffering from some anxiety and mild to moderate depression, but disagreed with Professor Burrows' diagnosis of severe depression. Dr Walton's most recent report had said: 'Arthur Freeman remains in the grips of what is becoming an increasingly chronic depressive disorder. As best I can judge, this condition seems not to have been of psychotic proportions at any stage and certainly is not at present. It is entirely appropriate that Mr Freeman undergoes quite close psychiatric monitoring at present as he is a meaningful suicide risk. He also requires active treatment for his depression and he is receiving that, although it will be timely in the near future to review his current drug regimen. I believe it is fair comment that this man's depression may well have made at least some contribution to the offending as it is well recognised that depressive disorders do erode a person's capacity to consistently exercise proper social judgement.

'The condition is potentially treatable and even reversible, although I suspect that Mr Freeman may well be left with long-term depression as he comes to terms with the nature of his offending. Depressive disorders are quite common and I imagine that the mitigation of general deterrence would be modest' (*R v Freeman* [2011] VSC 139).

Justice Coghlan said none of the psychiatrists mentioned above believed that Freeman was suffering from a psychotic illness when he killed Darcey. 'Given the relative lack of seriousness of your condition and the grave seriousness of the offending, I have given weight to your condition, but not significant weight as it relates to moral culpability, denunciation and general deterrence,' he said.

Justice Coghlan accepted that Freeman's offending was not premeditated but related to his increasing anger towards his former wife over the Family Court proceedings, exacerbated by his being late for Darcey's first day of school. 'I have no doubt that the resentment you bore your wife had been building up for some time,' he said. The judge also accepted that Freeman had shown some regret, but not remorse. 'I accept that it does demonstrate that by that time you appreciated the enormity of what you had done and there was some aspect of regret,' he said. 'I am not satisfied that it does show remorse. Your behaviour through the whole of this period of your life was self-centred, with a strong tendency to blame others. You are yet to say sorry to anyone for what you have done.

'There is a passage in the most recent report of Dr Walton which is illuminating: "Mr Freeman indicated that he had a strong desire to be able to meet with his surviving children and explain to them all the circumstances surrounding the death of their sister. However, when I asked him to provide me with such an explanation nothing emerged other than peripheral issues." I have come to the conclusion that the passage shows that your attitude to this matter is still self-centred. I am satisfied that you continue to lack any insight into your offending and I regard your prospects of rehabilitation as bleak' (*R v Freeman* [2011] VSC 139).

Prosecutors called for a life sentence without parole, as intentionally killing a child without psychiatric illness and motivated solely by spousal revenge was in the worst category of murder. Justice Coghlan said a non-parole period was appropriate, as Freeman, then 37, was not beyond redemption. 'I have had regard to your mental illness and although I do not regard it of such significance relative to the seriousness of your offending, then [sic] to lead me to fix a sentence other than life imprisonment but I have taken it into account in deciding both whether I should fix a non-parole and in deciding what that non-parole will be. I have taken into account your previous good behaviour. I have taken into account the references tended [sic] on your behalf and the support which you have from your direct family. I have taken into account those matters put on your behalf on the plea except where I have indicated that I do not regard it as appropriate to do so' (*R v Freeman* [2011] VSC 139).

Freeman was sentenced to life imprisonment with a 32-year minimum. The earliest date he can qualify for release is 29 January 2041.

The appeals

Soon after, Freeman sought leave to appeal the severity of his sentence. His lawyers argued that 32 years was manifestly excessive when his depressive condition and reference to comparable cases was considered. Justice Chris Maxwell found that with the exception of the defence expert, Professor Burrows, the relevant experts believed Freeman's depression was only of moderate severity. The sentencing judge, Justice Coghlan, had given weight to his condition but not significant weight 'as it relates to moral culpability, denunciation and general deterrence'.

Justice Maxwell found no submissions were made to the trial establishing a causal connection between the impairment of mental functioning and the offending. The defence counsel had also declined the judge's request to state to what extent Freeman's depressive condition reduced his moral culpability. 'No such submission was advanced in this case, presumably because (with the exception of Professor Burrows' testimony) there was no evidence of that kind before the court,' Justice Maxwell said. 'The applicant has provided no account of his state of mind and intentions immediately prior to, or after, putting his daughter over the side of the bridge. He has consistently said that he is unable to recall what happened.

'Professor Mullen, for example, expressed the following opinion in his report: "In the absence of such information, in my opinion, all that can be concluded is that Mr Freeman had a depressive disorder, probably with suicidal preoccupations, at the time he killed his daughter. No clear connection between that depressive disorder and his actions on the West Gate Bridge can be made on the basis of the information available to me"' (*Freeman v The Queen* [2011] VSCA 214 [27 July 2011]).

Freeman's lawyers cited the case of *R v Fitchett*, in which Donna Fitchett killed her two children and was sentenced to seventeen years on each of two counts of murder, with a total effective sentence of 27 years and a non-parole period of eighteen years. Justice Maxwell found the case was 'very different', as the presiding judge had accepted that there was a causal link between Fitchett's mental state and her offending. She was also found to be 'profoundly remorseful', whereas no such finding was made in this case.

The tragic 2005 case of Robert Farquharson (*R v Farquharson*), who was sentenced to 33 years in jail after intentionally driving his three boys into a dam and allowing them to drown, was also cited. Justice Maxwell found there was nothing in Farquharson's sentence to suggest that Freeman's was outside the range open to the judge. Freeman also contended that the sentencing judge gave inadequate weight to his remorse and rehabilitation prospects. But Justice Maxwell cited Dr Walton's report, which found that while indicating a strong desire to meet his surviving children to explain the circumstances of their sister's death, when asked to provide such an explanation 'nothing emerged other than peripheral issues'.

Justice Maxwell refused leave to appeal. 'Your attitude to this matter is still self-centred,' he said. 'I am satisfied that you continue to lack any insight into your offending and I regard your prospects of rehabilitation as bleak. No arguable basis has been established for appellate intervention in this sentence. Leave to appeal is accordingly refused' (*Freeman v The Queen* [2011] VSCA 214 [27 July 2011]).

Freeman's legal team then made an application to the full bench of the Court of Appeal. They again compared the case to others of spousal revenge and contended that the original judge erred in his assessment of Freeman's psychological illness and rehabilitation prospects. Justice Geoffrey Nettle delivered the ruling, which backed the previous decisions. 'We see no error in that aspect of the judge's reasoning,' Justice Nettle said. 'It appears to us to represent an accurate summation of the weight of the psychiatric and psychological evidence which was before him and adequately to support the conclusion that the applicant's mental condition was relatively lacking in seriousness compared to the gravity of the offending. Contrary to submissions advanced on behalf of the applicant, in our view the assessment of moral culpability required the judge to have regard to both the extent of the applicant's mental dysfunction and the gravity of the crime in question and to consider each in light of each other.

'That is to say, if an offence is but venial, a lesser mental condition may go a significant way to reducing the offender's moral culpability. But if an offence is as serious as this was, a relatively insignificant mental condition is likely to weigh less in the scale of assessment of moral culpability. It requires a substantial degree of mental disability to result in a substantial reduction in moral culpability for this class of offending. Under Ground 3, it was contended that the judge erred in equating the applicant's post-offence self-centredness and blame of others with an absence of remorse and that the judge was unfair in effect to criticise the applicant for failing to apologise for his actions. We reject that contention' (*Freeman v The Queen* [2011] VSCA 349 [9 November 2011]).

The judges again rejected all grounds and dismissed the application.

Arthur Freeman's background

By all accounts, Arthur Phillip Freeman had a relatively ordinary childhood. Born in Geelong in June 1973, he grew up there with a brother and two sisters. His father was a schoolteacher and his mother a school crossing supervisor. Two of his siblings became teachers.

Freeman's primary education was unsettled because he was bullied and received some counselling because of it. But his family life was later described in court as unremarkable. High school was less difficult. Freeman attended Newcomb High School, where he did not experience the problems he'd had at primary school. He studied aquatic science at Deakin University, but transferred after a year to information technology and graduated with a Bachelor of Computer Science.

While at university, Freeman lived in various share houses with other students. His first job was in computer programming and data collection, which he did for several employers and eventually at Colonial First State, where he met Peta Barnes. They married in December 1999. The young couple moved to the United Kingdom in early 2000, where both worked. They purchased a flat in Maida Vale, in London's north, and had three children. The marriage was regarded as happy. Peta wanted the children to be educated in Australia, so they returned in 2006, renting a house in Hawthorn.

Peta worked while her husband stayed at home to care for the children, apart from a period during which he worked in late 2006. The marriage ended in March 2007, despite several attempts at counselling. The couple divorced in June 2008. Freeman moved to Geelong for some time but continued to care for the children during the day. When Peta and the children moved out of the first house in Hawthorn, Freeman rented a flat nearby in Power Street, Hawthorn. They shared custody of the children. In August 2008, Freeman returned to the United Kingdom in an unsuccessful attempt to obtain a British passport. He stayed in England for several months and then returned.

Why did he do it?

Until he separated from his wife, Arthur Freeman did not appear to have any serious psychological issues, unless he hid them well. His marriage was described as relatively happy for at least part of its eight years, but it failed when Darcey was about two. Freeman may have had some underlying anxiety or dissatisfaction with how his life had played out in recent years, as he had found it difficult to find work and was unable to stay in England long term after his marriage broke up. But none of this was anything worse than the ups and downs faced by many people dealing with separation and caring for children across two households. These situations play out in thousands of families across Australia each year, with varying degrees of success or otherwise.

Peta Barnes had reportedly told three doctors of her concerns and fears about Freeman harming her children. She also told a doctor that she believed he was vengeful enough to kill the children to get back at her. In another alleged incident, Barnes saw what she considered to be signs of potential violence, when she was about leave the house with her baby son and Freeman grabbed him out of her arms and acted as though he was going to smash the baby against the fireplace. Barnes's mother was reportedly present and they both had to physically fight him when he wouldn't let go (Norris 2016). Freeman also reportedly (Anderson 2011) made threats at a 2008 social function that his ex-wife would regret it if she prevented him from having access to his children.

On the day Darcey died, Freeman acted in an even more callous way. During family break-ups, some people say and do things in the heat of the moment that they may later regret. They might tell their children negative stories about their ex-partner to poison their thinking about them. Or they might make threats to physically harm either each other or their loved ones. Such talk is clearly unacceptable, but rarely acted upon. In this case, Freeman carried out the threat he made to Peta as he was driving his children to school that morning. In one phone conversation, he told her to say goodbye to her children, and in another he said she would never see them again.

The fear Peta Barnes would have felt at that moment is indescribable, and Arthur Freeman would have known it. Peta would have been hoping and praying that this was just a threat and that her children would soon be at school. The next few minutes were sheer torture for her. Then, to find out that her ex-partner had thrown his daughter off the bridge, in full view of peak-hour morning traffic, would have been more than any mother could take. Yet Arthur Freeman was able to calmly stop his car in the middle of a busy freeway and, as his sons sat in their car seats, pick up his young daughter and literally discard her, knowing that she would die a terrifying, public and painful death that would also traumatise everyone who saw what he did.

Many people who heard about this terrible act assumed that Freeman must have been psychotic. Surely, no one in their right mind could do such a thing. As we have seen, Freeman did try to argue in court that he was not guilty due to mental impairment, but that argument was rejected. One expert found he was severely depressed, but two others disagreed and found his level of depression to be only mild to moderate. Very few people who are depressed commit murder. It is an insult to everyone who at some time has suffered from depression to suggest that it automatically turns them into violent criminals.

They are no more likely to commit a serious crime than anyone else in the community.

Freeman was certainly upset, agitated, distressed and felt painted into a corner. The Family Court decision had made him feel wronged, anxious and helpless. But he still knew right from wrong, and his actions at the time of the crime were those of a man who could function and interact with others. The court found that he was not suffering from a mental illness that distorted his thinking process; he knew what he was doing. Freeman was clearly motivated by anger, revenge, spite and a need to inflict pain on his ex-wife. To do so, he was prepared to end the life of his precious daughter in the most public, horrific way possible. Darcey's death did not just traumatise her own family. Everyone who was on the West Gate Bridge that day or heard about the killing afterwards was horrified. Many families felt some of Peta Barnes's pain as the case was covered extensively in the media.

Freeman's callous and murderous behaviour clearly placed him in the 'partner revenge' and 'self-righteous' categories as defined by various experts (see the chart on pages 42–4).

The '**partner revenge killer**' (Resnick et al.'s taxonomy) murders their child (or children) to cause extreme pain to their ex-partner and remind them for the rest of their life that the death was 'their fault', although clearly it wasn't. They often call their ex-partner just before they murder their child, as Freeman did, to ensure they cause maximum pain and distress.

The '**self-righteous killer**' (Yardley et al.'s taxonomy) seeks to blame their ex-partner for the killing they committed, holding them responsible for any breakdown of the relationship or damage to the family. They usually engage in overly dramatic behaviour, as Freeman did by throwing Darcey off the West Gate Bridge during peak-hour, knowing that his ex-wife and many others would be traumatised. His is one of the worst possible examples of this type of killing.

Freeman's decision to murder his daughter so publicly, which may have been made on the spur of the moment or could have been planned as he drove towards Melbourne that morning, or even earlier, came from a place few of us can contemplate. He must have known that Darcey and his two boys would be terrified, and that his actions would be roundly condemned and would make him a pariah for the rest of his life. But he did it anyway. Freeman may have surmised that no one would believe that a person of sound mind could do such a thing, and that he'd be declared not guilty on the grounds of mental impairment. If so, he didn't count on experienced health professionals who would be able to see through that act.

Mild depression aside, this was one of the coldest, most calculated acts of brutality committed by someone entrusted with the care of their children. You could not imagine a worse breach of that trust. And for what? In the end, it appears that Arthur Freeman was prepared to commit one of Australia's most shocking murders simply to get back at his wife, without a thought as to how it would impact on his two sons who were also in the car, or the rest of their family and friends. He was not mentally ill. He was just determined to hurt his ex-wife because he was angry about the court's decision to reduce his access to the children. He chose a path that would not only deprive Darcey of any future, but would also damage the lives of his two sons and destroy his own future.

CHAPTER 3

AKON GUODE

The cast

Akon Guode: Killed three of her seven children after driving the four youngest into a lake
Hanger, Madit and Bol Manyang: Guode's three children, whom she killed
Alual Chabiet: Guode's daughter who survived the crash
Akoi Chabiet: Guode's oldest child, who gave evidence in court
Ayan and Elei Chabiet: Guode's other daughters
Nhial Chabiet: Guode's first husband, a soldier in the South Sudan rebel army, who died in the civil war. Father of Akoi and Ayan.
Nhial Chabiet's younger brother: Guode's second husband and father of Elei
Joseph Tito Manyang: Father of Alual, Hanger, Madit and Bol. He was married to Aziw Deng Yel but had also been having a longstanding and very public affair with Guode. When the children died, he was living separately from both women, but was rumoured to be about to return to his wife.

Aziw Deng Yel: Joseph's wife
Makok Kuol: An adult cousin of Akon Guode's children, who lived in Morwell where there was a strong Sudanese community
Abook Kon: Guode's aunt who lived in Morwell

Akon Guode's children **Killed by their mother*	**Father**	**Age when killings occurred on 8 April 2015**
Akoi Chabiet	Nhial Chabiet	19
Ayan Chabiet	Nhial Chabiet	14
Elei Chabiet	Nhial's younger brother	11
Alual Chabiet	Joseph Tito Manyang (Alual was given the surname Chabiet, possibly to cover up her real parentage)	5
*Madit Manyang	Joseph Tito Manyang	4
*Hanger Manyang	Joseph Tito Manyang	4
*Bol Manyang	Joseph Tito Manyang	17 months

The motive

The reasons why Akon Guode drove four of her children into a lake and watched as three of them drowned are complex. Guode was struggling to raise her seven children alone, had suffered traumatic experiences during the civil war in South Sudan, almost died giving birth to her youngest child, and was in serious debt. Joseph Manyang, a married man with whom she had four children, was rumoured to be about to return to live with his wife and their children, and may have been planning to take the children that he'd had with Guode with him. After she killed three of her children, Guode was also diagnosed with major depressive disorder and PTSD. All these factors probably contributed to her actions, but do not excuse them.

Introduction

The seemingly endless expanse between Melbourne's CBD and Geelong is fast being filled by developments offering affordable new homes for those priced out of city markets. Melbourne's outer west is flourishing as new estates compete for the first-homebuyer dollar by promoting family-friendly parks, playgrounds and lakes. Their residents can commute to Melbourne or Geelong while enjoying a semi-rural lifestyle in a new home.

The outer suburb of Wyndham Vale lies 31 kilometres south-west of Melbourne's CBD. Its housing estates are close to local attractions like Werribee Open Range Zoo and natural features such as Lollipop and Cherry creeks, which meander through it towards Port Phillip Bay. Wyndham Vale is also close to where scenes from the original *Mad Max* were filmed, leading some to dub it '*Mad Max* country'. The area is dotted with lakes, some designed as an estate's focal point. Among them is Lake Gladman, a shallow wetland on Manor Lakes Boulevard, near the local Manor Lakes College. Home to swans, ducks, geese and other birds, it also features a popular children's playground.

During the week, Lake Gladman lies peacefully as busy residents drive past on their way to work or to drop children at nearby childcare centres and schools. Enclosed by Manor Lakes Boulevard, Balcombe Drive and Pedder Street, the area is an attractive and usually safe space for those living and working nearby.

The killings

The afternoon of 8 April 2015 was a typical Wednesday in Wyndham Vale. The temperature was a mild nineteen degrees

Celsius as parents headed for school pick-ups, looking forward to hearing their children's stories about their day over an afternoon snack. For those driving near Lake Gladman, that regular routine was shattered just before 3.40 pm when they saw a grey 2005 Toyota Kluger, which had already driven past the lake several times, perform a U-turn, mount a kerb, make three deliberate steering turns to navigate the only open access point and drive into the lake at full speed. As the car veered off Manor Lakes Boulevard, it passed between trees on the grass reserve.

The vehicle continued down the bank and hit large rocks before landing in the lake. Initially the car was not very far in, the water only rising to bottom of the door seal. Rather than get out, however, the driver gunned the engine, taking the vehicle another 20 metres into much deeper water. Witnesses thought they were seeing things. Why would a car drive straight into a lake in the middle of the day, in full view of everyone driving past?

Once over their initial shock, they realised the situation was deadly serious.

A local schoolteacher who called triple 0 did not seem too concerned initially. The witness told the operator that she saw the car deliberately mount the kerb, drive along the grass area and then 'full bolt' into the water. Describing how the lake was shallow and unlikely to swallow up the car, she became slightly more concerned when it sank to the point where the windshield was under water. The witness then became distraught when she saw through the window a toddler disappear under the water. At that point, she realised that there were children in the car and in a distressed voice told the triple 0 operator that there were children under the water and floating, trying to get out of the car but unable to swim.

When the car finally stopped, Akon Guode climbed out of the front driver's side. When her four children who were trapped inside tried to escape, Guode did nothing. She stood nearby, watching as three of them drowned and another, who finally escaped the car, struggled to swim ashore. While the witness called triple 0, other passers-by leapt into the lake to help the children, who clearly could not swim. With Country Fire Authority (CFA) members who had quickly arrived at the scene, they frantically tried to determine who was in the car and how to get them out. One witness later described seeing a small child floating on its back and trying to keep its head afloat before sinking into the water. Another used a steel-capped boot to smash the rear window and free a toddler from his car seat.

Guode did not answer when a witness tried to ask her what had happened and how many people were in the car. Nor did she ask how her children were as others tried to save them. Instead, she stood still and let out a strange wailing noise. As it turned out, four of her seven children were in the car. Three of them, four-year-old twins Hanger and Madit, and seventeen-month-old Bol, had drowned. Their older sister, Alual, five, was rescued and made a full recovery. It later emerged that as Alual tried to escape the freezing water, the panicked little girl thought there might be crocodiles in it. CFA members who quickly rescued Alual took her to the edge of the lake. Bol was removed from the car, but he was not breathing and died later in hospital. Hanger was found beneath the water and pronounced dead on the bank of the lake. When rescuers realised there had been four children in the car, they conducted a foot sweep and found Madit lifeless at the bottom of the lake.

Several paramedics attended to Guode and took her to the Royal Melbourne Hospital. At 4.19 pm, she told them she had felt dizzy while driving to the Manor Lakes shops and could not remember anything until she was in the back of the ambulance. A neurological assessment found no abnormalities. Guode also told a police officer that she was shopping at Coles, became dizzy and wanted to go home. She later told hospital staff she had been feeling dizzy for a month and had seen doctors about it. During a police interview, Guode claimed that she was not feeling well and felt like she was going to faint. She said she had a history of dizziness after receiving an injection in her neck while giving birth to Bol.

The situation was unbelievable to the good Samaritans who attended in those first frantic minutes. It had to be a terrible accident, they thought. But, to their mounting horror, what they saw indicated otherwise.

Guode and her youngest children had left home at about 1 pm. All four were fathered by Joseph Manyang, who'd had a long-term affair with Guode while he was married to Aziw Deng Yel. Joseph had lived by himself for the last few years but there were rumours within the Sudanese community that he was planning to return to live with his wife, leaving Guode alone to raise Alual, Madit, Hanger, Bol and her three older daughters, Akoi, nineteen, Ayan, fourteen, and Elei, eleven. Guode had told Akoi that she was going to visit a grandparent on the day her children died, but that never happened. Instead, Guode spent two and a half hours in the car with the four children, repeatedly driving past Lake Gladman. She tried several times to call Joseph, but he didn't answer. About fifteen minutes before she drove into the lake, Guode was seen parked at the side of the road with her head in her hands. The children appeared hysterical. CCTV footage later emerged that showed the car near the lake, shortly before Guode's car entered it. She then appeared to steer her car past several obstacles, before ploughing into the water at full speed.

A few days later, Guode attended her children's funeral at St Andrew's Church in Werribee, sitting in the front pew with

Joseph by her side. Melbourne's South Sudanese community offered its support, singing songs from the Dinka culture. Makok Kuol gave the eulogies for his cousins, describing them as 'three beautiful angels'.

The sentencing

Despite her repeated claims of innocence, on 10 August 2015 Guode was charged over her children's deaths. She initially blamed her actions on a dizzy spell and later the effects of witchcraft, which she claimed was used against her by Joseph's estranged wife. During her committal hearing in June 2016, Guode broke down several times and begged for bail. She sobbed and wailed loudly, prompting her defence lawyer, Julian McMahon, to ask that she be excused for part of the hearing. At one point, he said his client had sobbed uncontrollably for fifteen minutes and shook like she was freezing. Prosecutor Michele Williams told the court, however, that Guode should not be able to leave simply because she did not want to hear the evidence.

The court heard that Guode had suffered from depression-like symptoms for several years as she struggled to cope with the backlash from the Sudanese community regarding her affair with Joseph, who remained married to Aziw Deng Yel, although he was now living alone. Guode had started the relationship after arriving from South Sudan as a refugee in 2006 with her three oldest children. Her first husband, Nhial Chabiet, had been murdered in the civil war and Guode had been violently raped.

The situation in the local South Sudanese community was tense, and Guode claimed she was too scared to leave the house for fear of what would be said to her about her relationship with Joseph. He told the court that he and Guode loved each other and she would never intentionally harm their children. He continued to visit her in jail. Guode also said she was under a spell cast by

Aziw, and accused Aziw of threatening her when the twins were born. Guode said Aziw had rung her and also approached her at home and at the shops to verbally abuse her, but Aziw denied all of this. Another witness claimed to have overheard Guode say on the day her children died that she would rather end her life and theirs than see them live with Joseph and his wife. In another twist, a witness who had allegedly heard Guode admit to killing her children refused to give evidence, claiming she feared for her life.

Akoi, then twenty, told the court that her mother had been so unwell after having her youngest child, Bol, that she had to help feed and bath her baby brother. She said people looked at her mother 'funny' if she attended a social event, and that those who used to talk to Guode wouldn't any more. Her mother had also been distant with her children, watching television or staying in her room. After giving birth to Bol, her mother started getting headaches and dizzy spells but never sought medical help, according to Akoi. The dizziness would strike randomly, sometimes accompanied by a headache. Akoi told her teachers that she was worried about her mother, and she had noticed that overdue bill notices and letters from debt collectors had started to arrive. An aunt said Guode had seen a doctor about the headaches and been prescribed medication.

Guode initially pleaded not guilty to the murders of Hanger and Madit, the infanticide of Bol and the attempted murder of Alual. While murder in Victoria carries a maximum penalty of life in prison, infanticide carries a maximum five-year sentence. It is defined as a woman's conduct that causes the death of her child in circumstances that would constitute murder but, at the time, the balance of her mind was disturbed due to not fully recovering from the effect of giving birth to that child in the past two years, or developing a disorder in the child's first two years. In

January 2017, Guode changed her plea to guilty. During a March 2017 plea hearing, she wept uncontrollably as details of Bol's death were outlined. Her barrister, Marcus Dempsey, said Guode had been under enormous stress, which was compounded when her youngest child was born. The birth had been traumatic, and she had lost a lot of blood, after which her mental health declined.

Forensic experts said the ongoing affair with Joseph, Guode's subsequent ostracism by the South Sudanese community, and her growing debts had also contributed to her distress. At the time of the deaths, Guode was being chased by debt collectors, and rumours were circulating that due to community pressure Joseph was going to move back to live with his wife. At the time, he had been living alone and visiting both of his families regularly. The deaths rocked Melbourne's Sudanese community, and many could not believe that an apparently loving mother would kill her children. Joseph told the media that Guode was happy and loved her children 'very well'. But others were not so sure.

The awful situation brought back memories for many people in the general community of Winchelsea father Robert Farquharson, who drove his sons, Jai, ten, Tyler, seven, and Bailey, two, into a dam outside town and left them to drown after an access visit on Father's Day in 2005. After two trials, Farquharson was found guilty of murder and sentenced to 33 years' jail. Farquharson blamed the 'accident' on a coughing fit, but, like Guode, did not help rescuers trying to save his children. On the night, several of those present instinctively knew that it was not an accident. Eventually it emerged that Farquharson had murdered his three sons in an act of revenge against their mother, Cindy Gambino, who had recently separated from him. Farquharson had played the role of 'poor Robbie' around Winchelsea, to the point where many locals continued to believe his innocence even after he was convicted and jailed. In Guode's case, she faced social isolation due to her affair with Joseph, as well as financial pressures and lingering memories of her traumatic life in Africa.

In the end, Justice Lex Lasry found there was nothing involuntary about Guode's actions, which her guilty pleas acknowledged. 'It also appears that for some time at least you had thought about what you were going to do – at least in the two hours or so before you did and possibly for longer than that,' he said. Justice Lasry did not treat Guode's failure to help as an aggravating circumstance, however. He was more interested in the fact that it took at least three turns to drive into the lake, making the act of driving into the lake deliberate rather than accidental. Justice Lasry thought Guode's actions after driving in could also be explained by shock. 'I could not be satisfied beyond reasonable doubt that your conduct represented a continuing intention by you to kill your children,' he said. 'Whilst you obviously had such an intention on entering the water in your vehicle, in my opinion by this stage you were shocked by what you had done and had no real ability to deal with it' (*R v Guode* [2017] VSC 285).

Justice Lasry said that before she killed her children, Guode had not been involved in any form of criminal activity in Australia and was not known to have a propensity for violence or other antisocial conduct. He said the murder charge in relation to Bol had been replaced with infanticide, and outlined the pressures that Guode had described to forensic psychiatrist Dr Danny Sullivan, which included caring for seven children with inconsistent support from Joseph, and significant and ongoing financial problems on top of the trauma she experienced in Sudan during the period of civil war. Dr Sullivan had diagnosed a major depressive disorder that was 'mild to moderate in severity' and linked to Bol's birth. It involved some degree of impairment in functioning.

'What specifically led you to do what you did on 8 April 2015 is not within Dr Sullivan's ability to identify, as he accepted,' Justice Lasry said. 'However, importantly your condition remained at the time of these offences and in his opinion impaired your ability to exercise appropriate judgements, think clearly, make calm and rational choices and appreciate the wrongfulness of your conduct. In his last report . . . Dr Sullivan reported another conversation with you in which you acknowledged that you did see your husband killed and that you had been raped. Dr Sullivan offered the opinion that there is evidence of post-traumatic stress disorder. What happened to you in South Sudan may have contributed to the mood disorder he diagnosed' (*R v Guode* [2017] VSC 285).

Justice Lasry found there was a realistic connection between Guode's mental state and her offending. 'In particular, those principles apply so as to reduce but not eliminate the moral culpability of your conduct,' he said. 'They also apply to significantly moderate the role of specific deterrence in the sentence to be imposed on you as well as general deterrence. Your symptoms and their severity were described by Dr Sullivan in his reports and evidence. Those symptoms were severe and had been for some time.' Justice Lasry acknowledged that the guilty pleas negated the need for a trial, but was unsure about the extent to which Guode was remorseful. 'Certainly, you are suffering significant grief and you have accepted criminal responsibility for your actions,' he said. 'However . . . though you have pleaded guilty to these offences, you do not accept that you intended to kill them. It seems clear enough that you know that by pleading guilty to these offences it is implicit that you admit your intention to kill. To actually say that in [those] terms is, I suspect, too painful for you.'

Guode's life, Justice Lasry accepted, had been one where 'out of an instinct of self-preservation you have not dwelt on the misfortune that has happened to you. I agree with your counsel that your reaction does not make you irredeemable. Your rehabilitation during and after your time in custody will be complicated. You will have to deal with the pressures within the prison in which you are held. On your release, you may have to cope with deportation, the loss of the rest of your family and the difficulties of somehow re-establishing your life. How that will all turn out is beyond my ability to estimate. All I can conclude is that there is no real prospect of your becoming involved in any further criminal activity. I do not believe that in the future you are a person from whom the community will need to be protected. I hope you will be treated with compassion' (*R v Guode* [2017] VSC 285).

Justice Lasry sentenced Guode to 26 years and six months in jail with a minimum of twenty years. 'The sentence I am about to impose is, in some respects, inadequate to reflect the gravity of what you have done, yet at the same time excessive given your mental state as well as your background of hardship and desperation,' he said. 'In my opinion it is a case where principles of both totality and mercy are significant. These are obviously grave offences. Offending against children, particularly where a homicide occurs, shocks the public consciousness because invariably the victims are very young and innocent of any wrong doing or contribution to their fate. These children trusted you as their mother as they were entitled to do. Your betrayal of that trust was catastrophic in its consequences whatever the true reasons were for your actions. This case is an all-encompassing tragedy. It is a tragedy for your family with three children deceased through your actions. It is a tragedy for you because you have destroyed the life you had started here in Australia and it is a tragedy for the community. But above all, your actions amounted to an horrendous crime on innocent children and a gross breach of trust and a betrayal by you of your obligation to protect your children' (*R v Guode* [2017] VSC 285).

Akon Guode's background

In sentencing Akon Guode, Justice Lasry acknowledged her difficult life, one that most Australians could not imagine. She was born on 10 June 1979 in the South Sudanese town of Wau. For religious reasons, her father had sixteen children with three different wives, including her mother. They all lived within the one family. Guode completed the equivalent of Year 10 at school and spoke more than one language, but her reading and writing skills were limited. Her early life was 'settled and positive', and she started dating her husband, a soldier in the rebel army of South Sudan, in 1996.

When civil war broke out, things became chaotic. In 2001, Guode took her two young daughters, Akoi and Ayan, to Eritrea. Justice Lasry found that there was some suggestion her husband was killed in front of her and their children, but she had denied this. 'Consistent with your approach to dealing with issues in your life, you seemed reluctant to in any way rely on this incident preferring to say that you were not present,' he said. Guode later told health professionals, however, that she did see her husband shot dead and his body burnt, after which she was raped until she was unconscious. She later displayed mild PTSD symptoms, which overlapped with a mood disorder (*R v Guode* [2017] VSC 285).

After her husband died, in accordance with Sudanese custom, Guode married her husband's younger brother and had another daughter, Elei. The relationship did not work out. In 2003, Guode lost several other family members and left her second husband, walking to Uganda and foraging for food on the way. She and her children survived attacks by hiding in the bushes. When they arrived, they lived in several refugee camps. With assistance from the United Nations, Guode applied for refugee status in Australia and became a permanent resident after arriving in 2006. She moved from Sydney to Melbourne and lived in the suburb of Sunshine. Guode met Joseph in 2008, and gave birth to Alual in 2009, twins Hanger and Madit in December 2010, and Bol in 2013. At some point, Joseph separated from his wife and lived alone.

Life in Melbourne was difficult, and Guode accumulated debts due to everyday expenses associated with a family that included seven children. She relied on Centrelink payments and some contributions from Joseph, although it is unclear how much he supported her financially. Guode worked for a year at a daycare centre and reportedly sent some money back to her family in South Sudan, but then returned to welfare payments, which at one point were stopped due to overpayment. By 2015 she was being chased by debt collectors for unpaid debts of thousands of dollars.

When Bol was born in 2013, Guode bled heavily and needed a life-saving blood transfusion. She suffered increasingly from depression, complained of migraines and dizziness, was often tired and would sleep during the day. That year, Guode had considered moving and starting afresh in Morwell, which had public housing and a growing Sudanese community. She also had an aunt, Abook Kon, there who was supportive and encouraged her to move. In late 2014, Guode again raised the idea, complaining that she was lonely in Melbourne and felt uncomfortable about the rumours and nasty comments being spread about her in the local Sudanese community. Guode discussed her Morwell plans with Joseph and had planned to travel there by train on the day her children died.

In the end Guode's remaining children were left without a

mother for at least 26 years. Initially Akoi, who was nineteen in 2015, deferred her Deakin University commerce degree to care for her younger siblings Ayan, Elei and Alual, who has diabetes. A local driving instructor also started a public campaign to help Akoi secure her driver's licence so she could drive her sisters to school and activities. Akoi had already spent a lot of time with her siblings. When her mother almost died giving birth to Bol, she did much of the cooking, cleaning and housework while juggling her Year 12 studies.

Why did she do it?

Known as filicide, killing your own child/children is a highly emotional crime that few people can understand. Why would anyone want to take the life of an innocent child, let alone their own? The reasons why Akon Guode made a conscious decision to kill some of her seven children are extremely complex and depended on a range of factors. The six main ones were:

1. her major depressive disorder
2. the likelihood that she was also suffering from PTSD as a result of the horrific experiences she endured during the Sudanese civil war
3. ongoing stress and humiliation arising from the nastiness and ostracism directed at her by some in the local Sudanese community
4. an attempt to prevent Joseph from taking the children to live with him and/or to make him suffer for a perceived lack of support and commitment
5. coping with the stress of caring for seven children
6. the fear and stress of being tracked down by debt collectors over the significant amount of money that she owed.

If we apply Resnick's taxonomy of filicide motivations (2016), Guode's actions place her in the category of 'unwanted child filicide' (see page 42). She had struggled physically and emotionally since her youngest child, Bol, was born. She nearly died afterwards due to massive blood loss and would have been severely traumatised. After being discharged from hospital as a single mother, she had seven children to care for. The older children, particularly Akoi, helped her, but day-to-day life would have been challenging. Finding herself ostracised by some members of the local South Sudanese community due to her affair with Joseph would not have helped, and her financial situation was precarious. In a nutshell, Guode was not coping with her parenting role and had very little support. At the time of the killings, rumours were also circulating that Joseph planned to return to live with his wife, taking the children that he had fathered with Guode with him. This would have ended Guode's hopes of moving to Morwell with the children, where her relative could introduce her to a thriving Sudanese community.

The pressure was indeed intense, but it appears that Guode did not form the intent to kill until later in the day. Although there was some premeditation, given she drove around the lake several times, perhaps looking for the best spot to drive in or building up the courage, her actions earlier in the day had given no indication that she planned to end the lives of her younger children. That morning, Guode had shopped at Aldi, spending $78.70 on, among other things, twelve litres of long-life milk, two packets of baby wipes, three loaves of bread, six litres of fruit juice, a kilogram of rice and a kilogram of peanut butter. Someone who was already planning to kill their young children a few hours later would be unlikely to do this.

It is not surprising that Guode was diagnosed with major depressive disorder after the killings, although it is not known how much the deaths themselves contributed to this. It is also highly likely that Guode had PTSD due to the trauma she experienced in South Sudan. Before coming to Australia, she was viciously raped, probably saw her first husband killed and experienced an unhappy second marriage when custom dictated she marry her husband's younger brother. Guode and her older daughters also spent time in refugee camps after walking to Uganda and foraging for food, evading attacks along the way by hiding in the bushes. PTSD does not directly cause violence, but being caught up in a war zone, raped and witnessing terrifying and life-threatening events would have been extremely traumatic for Guode and made her feel very unsafe at times.

Some of the effects of PTSD include:

- intrusive and painful memories and flashbacks of the traumatic experiences
- the loss of the assumption that the world is a safe place
- a tendency to assume the worst will happen
- being anxious, watchful and constantly on guard in case something bad happens
- difficulty sleeping
- depression and a sense of numbness
- tiredness and loss of energy.

All of this could have contributed to Guode simply crumbling under the pressure of trying to parent seven children in undoubtedly stressful circumstances. But it does not excuse her actions, as she is far from the first person to experience trauma, depression and a stressful family situation. Thousands of parents face trauma, tragedy and depression – sometimes all three – without deciding to kill their children. Part of her problem may have been her reluctance to seek help. When she almost died giving birth, Guode had initially refused a life-saving transfusion. She was also reluctant to seek help or confide in others about her problems and/or her PTSD. This and her social isolation would have contributed to her inability to cope.

Even if we can, to a point, understand why Guode 'cracked', many people find it inexplicable that she would or could, having driven into the lake, stand and watch Hanger, Madit and Bol drown while Alual fought for her life. Like Robert Farquharson, Guode did not help rescuers or attempt to save her children. Lake Gladman was quite shallow, and she could easily have waded towards them. No one but Guode will ever know why she did not do this, but she was clearly prepared to let her children die. She knew they were under the water and unable to get themselves to safety, but did nothing.

FAMILY DESTRUCTION: DAMIEN LITTLE AND DARREN MILNE

Filicide–suicide and familicide–suicide

As we have seen, when a parent intentionally kills one or more of their own children and then themselves, it is known as filicide–suicide. Familicide–suicide is the term most commonly used to describe a situation in which one family member kills all members of their immediate family – their spouse and their children – and then takes their own life (Liem, 2010). The term 'family annihilator' is also sometimes used by some researchers to describe those responsible for this type of murder–suicide. Perpetrators are almost exclusively male (Johnson, 2005; Websdale, 2010). Familicide–suicide is more often premeditated and involves careful preparation, such as purchasing weapons, stockpiling substances to sedate children, setting up pipelines for gassing, and making sure they have sole and uninterrupted access to the children. Damien Little killed himself and his two sons, while Darren Milne tried to kill his whole family. Yet both were portrayed in the media as upstanding citizens.

Damien Little (filicide)

The new year had just dawned in sunny Port Lincoln, west of Adelaide in South Australia, as local families enjoyed their Christmas holidays on the beach. But for those with financial and relationship problems, the summer brought with it added pressures and dark thoughts of having to deal with them. Damien Little was battling depression as he struggled to keep his young family going. He and his wife, Melissa, were living in a shed while they built their dream home overlooking the water outside town. The one-hectare block would be perfect for their sons Koda, four, and Hunter, nine months, to grow up on.

The project had already taken several years, and there was some concern among others that Little's relationship with Melissa was becoming strained. Rather than seek help, Little kept his worries to himself, refusing to seek counselling or medical help. Instead, the 34-year-old truck driver, labourer, local football star and 'all-round good guy' took the weakest route possible to deal with his problems. He decided to kill his two young sons and himself, leaving his wife to pick up the pieces.

On 4 January 2016, the young father purchased a coffee at a Port Lincoln McDonald's drive-through window. He then drove to the nearby pier in Boston Bay and shot his two boys before turning the gun on himself and driving his white station wagon at high speed into the ocean, in water up to 30 metres deep. Australians were shocked as footage was aired of Little's car being winched from the sea, not far from where he and Melissa were building their new home. A makeshift memorial quickly emerged at the scene, overflowing with flowers, teddy bears, loving notes from friends and relatives, and bottles of their lost mate's favourite Johnnie Walker Red Label scotch – as if he might come back for a sip.

The sad scene summed up a shocked community's attempt to come to grips with an unimaginable tragedy inflicted by one of their own. Those who knew Damien Little struggled to understand how a seemingly caring family man and popular Australian Rules footy coach could take his sons' lives in such a horrific way. Good guys don't just kill their children. Little had lived a life that gave no hint of what was to come. He grew up on a farm in Port Kenny, west of Adelaide on the Eyre Peninsula, the second youngest of five brothers – Nathan, Shannon, Kynan, Damien and Aaron. They were active boys and enjoyed going shooting. All played Australian Rules football, and had last taken the field together in 2012. Little and Melissa, a teacher, met at a local high school and married in March 2007. They ran a floor-covering business, and in his spare time Little played for and coached at Lincoln South Football Club.

When Damien Little died, Melissa led the chorus of praise for her husband, whom locals remembered as a loving father, a great sportsman and a good mate. His family said the popular local footballer and coach had been battling depression for three years but, because of his pride, had refused to seek help, despite their pleas to do so. Several media sources reported that he was described by those who knew him as a 'top bloke' and a 'family man'. In some reports Little was even cast as the victim of a terrible tragedy. One pub owner summed up the thoughts of many when he described the child killer as 'just a normal, everyday Australian bloke'.

Melissa made several touching statements. On the Friday after the tragedy, she described her pain in a heartfelt statement and vowed to remember her precious boys every day. She said that while she was in incredible pain, Damien had been a wonderful husband and father who loved his children. She said he enjoyed being part of the local community and always put his family first, spending quality time with his boys. Melissa still loved her late husband and wanted him to be remembered as a respected and valued family and community member. Her boys would also be terribly missed – Koda for his big heart, hugs and enthusiasm to help; and Hunter for being such a happy and contented baby whose personality had been starting to emerge.

How does a popular sportsman and father turn on his family like this and cause his wife a lifetime of pain? Like Geoff Hunt, Damien Little tried to battle his demons on his own, and few people realised the extent of the pain he was in. Relatives told the media that Little had struggled with depression for a few years but had not been prepared to seek medical assistance or consider taking antidepressants. Even if Little was depressed, however, that does not excuse what he did. Rather than seek help when he felt down, he allowed the situation to fester and, in the end, chose a course of action he knew would devastate those left behind.

Darren Milne (familicide)

Caring for children with disabilities is not easy. Darren Milne, 42, and his partner, Susana Estevez Castillo, 39, had two boys with fragile X syndrome, a genetic condition that results in varying degrees of intellectual disability and autism-like symptoms. The condition of Liam, eleven, was slightly more severe than that of Benjamin, who was seven. Susana, who had diabetes, was 29 weeks pregnant after IVF treatment to ensure their third child did not have fragile X syndrome. Friends said later that she and Milne hoped the child would be able to help care for their boys when they got older. The family was financially secure, and Milne had a good job as an electrical engineer. Susana came from a wealthy family in Mexico, and had investments of almost $200,000. She and her husband appeared to be making the most of a tough situation.

Then, on 1 February 2015, apparently without warning, Darren Milne deliberately drove the family car into a tree at Fountaindale in rural New South Wales. Milne, Susana and their unborn baby died instantly, and Liam passed away before emergency crews could get him to hospital. Ben suffered multiple injuries but survived. A witness told police the Toyota Corolla was travelling at about 90 kilometres per hour and did not attempt to miss the tree. No brake lights were observed.

Investigators later found extensive evidence that Milne had carefully planned the crash to ensure that no one survived. He had spent months meticulously scouring the local area to find a suitable crash site, taking photos and filming dash-cam videos along country roads to make sure of it, driving up and down the proposed route numerous times to work out the best place to hit a tree. Each time he cruised along that stretch of road, Milne must have contemplated how he and his family would most likely die. Rather than rethink his actions and seek help for his problems, he then used his engineering skills to rig up two petrol bombs designed to ignite upon impact. Milne wanted to leave nothing to chance, and even disabled the driver's side airbag. Thankfully the bombs failed, which enabled Ben to survive.

Notes found on an iPad in the car offered some clues about Milne's motives: 'It's not worth it, neither of us have the skills to make it work. We have both given it our best shot over a long period of time. There is too much conspiring against us. G got the calculation wrong, it's that simple. L and B are both happy, B doesn't know it yet, it is a good time to go. It's only going to get tougher as time goes on. We have been completely Sd over, maybe we can stop it from happening to someone else. They are going to have to manage ADD [attention deficit disorder] and diabetes, it is going to be too much. They need to exercise and manage their health, it is going to be hard to see this fail. Things are going to get progressively harder for Ben, he hasn't seen any malice or bullying yet but it is coming. From this point I need to be totally focussed, forget everything else, need to source comfort from the fact. See if A bags can be disabled. Finalise medical records, disks and leave copies. Letter to HGA, correspondence. Start cleaning stuff up.'

A second document read: 'Take DVR out of car as to not raise suspicion. Carry out recon after daylight savings, full day on RDO. Look at Old Pacific Highway to Central Coast. Stay until dark. Practise at least 10 times. Memorise all markers, learn the road backwards. Copy all work, personal stuff to portable disk. Start taking personal stuff home. Leave credit cards well in credit. Leave enough money to pay next phone' (Coroner David Day's findings, 15 July 2016).

Police found the family home in Ryde to be orderly, if a little untidy, which was nothing unusual. It emerged that they had just had a six-week holiday, and friends told police that despite the boys' disabilities, Milne was a loving father who was very good with them. They clearly loved him. Susana struggled at times with the different way of life in Australia, but did her best to cope with her situation. Milne had been treated for depression, both with medication and cognitive behaviour therapy, but he decided to discontinue his treatment in August 2014.

On 15 July 2016, after sitting in Wyong, Coroner David Day found that the crash was a deliberate and preventable act by Milne, who took his own life and in doing so Susana's, Liam's and that of their unborn child. 'I can only conclude that the collision with the tree was not accidental,' the Coroner found. 'It was a deliberate and planned act. Darren Milne took his own life and in doing so took the lives of Susana and Liam. The actions of Darren Milne should attract more than the usual disapproval attached to murder and suicide. He made assumptions about the quality of the boys' lives. He disregarded the boys' fundamental human rights. He disregarded potential advances in medical science potentially beneficial to the boys. He assumed successful execution of his plan without regard to the possibility that the front seat occupants, he and Susana, may not survive, but that one or both the rear seat passengers would survive, terribly injured, disfigured or otherwise, or worse, be conscious, trapped inside the cabin when the car caught fire.

'His [sic] disregarded the excellent services available to persons contemplating self-harm. He had a psychologist. He dropped out of treatment. The telephone directory book lists many registered psychologists in practice who could assist him and others contemplating suicide. Medical General Practitioners are trained with respect to depression and suicidal ideation. Further, the National Fragile X Chromosome Association of Australia offers support for parents and those with the condition. I thank the Association for their interest in this matter and commend their efforts in the field. These persons and organisations can and do help. Their efforts are recommended to the public. Suicide is a preventable death, and in this case, the deaths of Liam and Susana were preventable' (Coroner David Day's findings, 15 July 2016).

Milne and Susana, who studied international economics, had met when he was on a trip to Europe. She moved to Australia a year later to be with him. They did not find out the boys had fragile X syndrome until Liam was eight and Ben was four. It was a huge shock, although Susana had a history of mental impairment in her family. By all reports, Liam and Ben were happy children with some potential to enjoy life. Milne and Susana's marriage was described as strong and, although it did have its moments, Milne did not show outward signs of being unable to cope in the lead-up to his death. Nor did he show any signs of additional stress at work, and was his usual, helpful self. Life was undoubtedly difficult for him, but despite having the financial means, he failed to take advantage of his access to a range of support services.

Milne probably started planning the deaths after he stopped seeing his psychiatrist. If this was the case, he may have been suffering from some degree of depression. But that in no way mitigates or justifies what he did to his family, causing untold pain to the loved ones who were left behind. Milne appeared to believe that life was too hard for him, Susana and their boys, and that they would all be better off dead. This was despite Susana being pregnant with what was believed to be a healthy third child. Like Geoff Hunt and Damien Little, Darren Milne appeared to shun the help of others and did not confide in anyone when things became too much. Instead, he chose a shocking course of action that destroyed his family and would see him remembered as a murderer.

Darren Milne fits into two filicide/familicide subcategories. The first is 'altruistic' family killers. West et al. (2007, 2009) suggest that these parents believe the breakdown of their family unit to be so catastrophic that they must spare their child/children the pain of it. They believe that their children are better off dead. If they are also motivated by a desire to suicide, these killers may feel that they need to murder their children to save them from growing up without a mother or a father. Milne probably felt his family's situation was 'all too hard' for all of them, given that their two boys had special needs that may have prevented them from looking after themselves.

Milne also seems to fit into the 'disappointed' category described by Yardley et al. (2014), who looked at British male family annihilators. These fathers believed that their family had let them down and prevented them from creating and maintaining their view of what a family should be. They saw their family as an extension of their own needs and aspirations, and a reflection of their own social status. Milne may have seen his situation as a failure because his children had impairments that impacted on their day-to-day lives, as well as those of their parents. This belief is often misplaced, as support services and others can usually help if a family is not coping. But Milne obviously decided that it was not worth persevering, and selfishly made the decision for his wife and children as well.

Depression and familicide/filicide

Major depression has been associated with filicide and familicide in some cases, but in most of these there was also a psychosis involved. In the cases outlined in this book, although some of the perpetrators had been diagnosed as having a mild to moderate degree of depression, none was diagnosed as being psychotic, which means they knew what they were doing and were in control of their actions when they committed their murders. In their review of maternal and paternal filicides, Bourget et al. (2007) identified many studies that found parental psychiatric illness was often associated with filicide, and that the most common diagnosis was 'major depression with psychotic features'. 'Major depression' isn't the same as just 'feeling down' or worried and sad. It is more disabling, especially when it occurs with a psychosis, which is characterised by being out of touch with reality and is completely disabling.

Bourget and Bradford (1990) identified that 31 per cent of parents who had committed filicide had a diagnosis of major depression. Similarly, in a review of 131 cases of filicide, Resnick (1969) found that 75 per cent of the parents who committed such murders had displayed psychiatric symptoms, including major depression and schizophrenia, before the offences. In a review of maternal and paternal filicide cases that occurred in Canada between 1991 and 2001, Bourget and Gagné (2002, 2005) found that 85 per cent of mothers and 56 per cent of fathers who had committed a filicide had been diagnosed with major depressive disorder or schizophrenia/other psychosis. Friedman et al. (2005), in their analysis of coroners' files, concluded that 25 per cent of men who had committed filicide had a history of psychosis and 50 per cent of them had a history of major depression.

Campion et al. (1988) identified in their study of twelve men who had committed filicide that eleven of them had psychiatric disorders and seven of them were suffering from an acute psychosis at the time of the offence. None of the killers described in this book had been diagnosed as having a psychosis and none were considered to be mentally impaired to the point where they were not responsible for their actions, which places them outside these statistical categories.

CONCLUSION

When a parent kills their child or children, and in some cases other family members and themselves as well, those left behind are always shocked and horrified. Rarely do they see it coming. Loved ones must then pick up the pieces and ponder what went so wrong and how it could have happened. In many cases, as this book outlines, the perpetrators are remembered as loving parents and upstanding community members who must have been in terrible pain to have done what they did. Surely they must have been psychotic or so depressed that they were not in control of their thoughts or actions.

Such a scenario offers some comfort. To think that a person who killed their children was driven by a mental illness that was out of their control can help to rationalise an act that is unfathomable to most of us. Many people who knew Geoff Hunt wanted to believe that this popular and respected farmer, father and community member was 'not himself' when he killed his entire family. The same goes for Jason Lees, Damien Little and Darren Milne, who killed themselves and their boys and, in Milne's case, his wife as well. It can be simply too painful to contemplate any scenario other than these loving fathers having reached breaking point and genuinely believing they and their family members would be better off dead.

But that kind of rationale lets them off way too easily. Geoff Hunt, Damien Little, Darren Milne and Jason Lees are murderers and should be remembered as such. All knew what they were doing when they chose to take the lives of those closest to them. None of them was suffering from a psychosis or a debilitating mental illness, and unless society and the media starts to change its attitude to such crimes, others will be encouraged to take the same route, safe in the knowledge that they too will be eulogised as 'good people' who meant well but were pushed over the edge by circumstances out of their control. If we are to make inroads in predicting and possibly preventing similar tragedies, we must ask tough questions about why a person would decide to take such a drastic and unacceptable path.

These men all faced tough family situations, but nothing that thousands of others don't have to deal with every day. They had options. They were all capable workers, good fathers and intelligent people who could have sought help, or, if they felt it was all too hard, left their partner to start again. Instead, they felt that the shame of admitting they could not cope or did not want to continue in their current family situation was worse than taking their own lives and those of their children, and in Milne's case of his wife as well. These were not altruistic acts, they were the ultimate acts of selfishness.

Arthur Freeman's actions in killing his daughter in the most public and traumatic way possible were arguably even worse. In throwing his daughter Darcey off West Gate Bridge after telling her mother she would never see her again, Freeman showed that he was prepared to kill his own daughter simply to hurt his ex-wife. Nor did he consider the trauma that would be experienced by his sons, who were also in the car, or the thousands of people on their way to work who would encounter the scene. In the media coverage that followed, no one had any sympathy for Freeman, as his actions were so public and so horrifying – and rightly so. But why should we feel sorry for Hunt, Little, Milne or Lees? Jason Lees did the same thing as Arthur Freeman to his two-year-old son Brad. The only difference was that Lees jumped off Brisbane's Story Bridge with his son. The fact that Lees also died seemed to lessen his crime in the eyes of those who eulogised him as a respected teacher and rugby coach. While Freeman was described in the media as 'evil', Lees was remembered as a positive guy who everyone loved.

Damien Little killed both of his sons in a similar way to Freeman, in that he drove himself and his boys off a Port Lincoln pier to certain death in full view of anyone who happened to be passing by on that warm summer day. Geoff Hunt's murder of his wife and three children was not so public, but equally ruthless. Hunt shot his wife, son and two daughters before turning the gun on himself. The girls, aged just six and eight, were shot in the face. If any of these men had done this to other people's children, they would have been labelled evil mass killers and compared with infamous Australian murderers such as Derek Percy, who has been linked to the deaths of nine children around the country, or 'Mr Cruel', who broke into several Melbourne homes in the late 1980s and early 1990s to kidnap teenage girls and is suspected of murdering thirteen-year-old Karmein Chan. It appears, at least in some cases, that killing your own children is not considered by society to be as bad as murdering someone else's.

Akon Guode's actions were also inexcusable, even though she had suffered terrible trauma in her life as a Sudanese refugee, almost died in childbirth and was struggling to raise seven children by herself. Her situation was challenging and complex, but she had some choices. If she was not coping, Guode could have sought assistance from Victoria's health services and crisis lines, which would have helped her deal with her physical, emotional and financial problems, and possibly offered some respite from the children. But she did not exercise these options. Instead, she drove her car into a lake and watched as three of her young children drowned.

All these situations are extremely tragic, regardless of who was at fault. Predicting them is incredibly difficult, as people who kill their children and sometimes themselves usually offer few clues before they act. Some face difficult circumstances, which Guode did in attempting to raise her children alone while being shunned by her local Sudanese community for having an affair with a married man. Hunt was dealing with physical and emotional changes in his wife Kim, who was still recovering from a life-threatening car accident that had impacted on their relationship, Freeman was dealing with a marriage breakdown, Milne was raising two boys with an intellectual disability, and Lees was reportedly having relationship problems. Little had been dealing with mental health issues and possibly feeling the strain of not being able to build their dream home as quickly as he had hoped.

None of these situations was ideal, but all had potential solutions if the perpetrators had fully confided in those closest to them and/or sought more help if they were not coping. There is not much that those close to them could have done to prevent their actions. The men all had family and/or friends who would have helped had they known the full extent of their pain. Guode's situation was more difficult, as she had few friends and relatives in Australia, but she could have reached out to local authorities or perhaps her relative in Morwell. The fact that none of them sought help when they most needed it shows that as a society, we need to take a more holistic approach if we are to identify and prevent similar tragedies. For a start, we need to be more honest in discussing these killings and calling them what they are – murder. If the media stopped describing these killers as 'good blokes' and 'loving parents', and their crimes were reported and talked about in the same way as other murders, it might discourage others who may be considering a similar course of action.

Familicide and filicide can be extremely difficult for loved ones to predict, but here are some of the behaviours and/or situations that, often in combination, can be difficult to cope with for some people who might need additional support:

- an unexpected significant life change, such as a child with special needs, a partner with a chronic serious illness or their own serious health concerns
- growing financial pressures
- showing signs of being depressed, such as withdrawing socially, lack of motivation, inability to meet commitments, constant negative talk but not doing anything about it or denying that anything is wrong
- withdrawing socially if they are usually involved in family events and/or community events such as sporting activities
- becoming less engaged or reliable at work, such as taking more sick leave without having a recognised illness
- dealing with a family break-up in which they feel aggrieved about the custody arrangements or their treatment by their ex-partner
- repeatedly and unfairly criticising a current or ex-partner who has done nothing to deserve it.

If someone you know is experiencing these sorts of issues, it does not mean they will take drastic action or become violent. But it could be helpful to talk to them or approach someone who can. Even if the situation is not serious, they would probably benefit from a sympathetic ear or referral to a health professional who can help them deal with a problem that cannot be solved by a friend. Some mental health services are covered by Medicare, so it might also pay to research their availability and show your friend or loved one that they can afford to seek professional help. Someone with a problem may believe that the cost of such help is prohibitive, but most Australian states and territories offer a range of free or low-cost mental health services, including Medicare rebates for visits to private psychologists.

Monitoring the wellbeing and mental health of colleagues, friends and loved ones, and offering support if you think it is needed can make a positive difference, regardless of how mild or complex their issues are. In more serious cases, such as a family experiencing serious conflict or potential violence, you may need to encourage those affected to seek professional help. If you are extremely concerned about potential violence, contact the police.

*A list of support services for those experiencing relationship problems can be found on pages 403–7.

PART II

NARCISSISTIC PERSONALITY DISORDER AND MALIGNANT NARCISSISM

ARROGANT, DANGEROUS AND SOMETIMES VULNERABLE

What is a narcissistic personality disorder?

The term 'narcissism' comes from the Greek myth of Narcissus, a handsome young man who fell in love with his own reflection. Thanks to the explosion of social media and the selfie, 'narcissistic' is now a commonly used term. Many people – young, middle-aged and old – photograph themselves at concerts, sport, special events and home, then post the images on Twitter, Facebook, Instagram and the like. Some people obsess over their selfies and how many 'likes' they will attract, spending hours achieving the right outfit, 'look' and pose. But this doesn't make them all narcissists. Most people will act in a narcissistic way at some point, whether it's posting that selfie, jumping a queue or saying something negative about someone they perceive as a threat. But that doesn't necessarily mean they have a narcissistic personality disorder (NPD).

Most people have some mild narcissistic traits, such as keeping fit, fussing over our appearance and displaying a healthy degree of self-confidence. This might include telling the world about our workplace promotion on social media, or taking 'time out' to pamper ourselves. In some cases, those who achieve a high degree of success may appear to be even more narcissistic, lapping up the attention, encouraging their admirers and enjoying their social media followers hanging off their every word. None of this necessarily means someone has an NPD. But if a person displaying those traits is repeatedly inflexible, boastful and self-promoting, vindictively puts others down and causes problems or distress in personal relationships, the workplace and everyday life, they may have an NPD.

A person with NPD displays a pervasive pattern of grandiosity, a constant need for admiration, attention and/or status, and a relative lack of empathy for others. This may involve nasty behaviour, often publicly displayed on social media, towards anyone perceived as a threat. It begins by early adulthood and is evident in a variety of situations. In our first book, we looked at several killers who had an NPD. Retiree Peter Caruso bludgeoned to death Rosa, his wife of almost 50 years, when she finally challenged the narcissistic hold he had exerted over her for most of their marriage. Gerard Baden-Clay murdered his high-achieving wife, Allison, after she stood up to him and his philandering ways. Baden-Clay's real estate business was in debt and he had the added motive of securing a life insurance payout.

Keli Lane and Roger Dean also had an NPD. Lane killed her two-day-old daughter Tegan after hiding the pregnancy from family and friends, simply because the baby was an inconvenience. Dean, a nurse, started two fires at the Quakers Hill Nursing Home that eventually killed fourteen residents and injured many more in order to cover up his theft of prescribed medications, knowing that few elderly residents could escape a burning building. The callous disregard these killers showed for the lives of others is consistent with the behaviour of many of those with an NPD who put their own interests first, no matter how badly those around them are harmed by what they do. In this book, we investigate several cases involving 'malignant narcissism', a subtype of NPD that is especially dangerous to others.

Recognising someone with an NPD

Diagnosing a personality disorder is difficult and requires professional knowledge. You can, however, get an idea of the key characteristics of someone with an NPD by looking at the criteria identified by key professionals in the fields of psychiatry and psychology. The DSM-5 (APA, 2013) says a diagnosis of NPD can be made when an individual displays a pattern of behaviour that is evident by early adulthood and occurs across a range of contexts. The pattern is characterised by a belief that he or she is more talented or worthy than they are in reality, a desire to be admired by others, a quest for influence and status, and a relative lack of empathy in most situations.

A diagnosis of an NPD can be made when at least five of the following behaviours are present. He or she:

- has an inflated view of their own abilities, status and importance, and expects others to recognise and acknowledge their superiority, even when there is little or no evidence to support these perceptions
- focuses excessively on their desire to be more successful, influential, good-looking, talented, wealthy or admired than other people

- has a strong belief that they are better and more special than other people and therefore prefers to keep company with high-status individuals and be connected with high-status organisations
- desires, needs and constantly seeks admiration from others
- expects special treatment because they perceive that their superiority entitles them to always get what they want
- is prepared to exploit others to achieve their own goals
- demonstrates low levels of empathy towards other people and is unconcerned about and unresponsive to their feelings and needs
- often feels envious of others but may also believe that other people envy him or her too
- demonstrates behaviours and attitudes that are egotistical, arrogant, vain, snobbish and/or self-important.

Individuals with a narcissistic personality disorder are more likely than other people to behave in some or all of the following ways. They:

- have an inflated (and often unwarranted) perception of themselves as being smarter, of higher status and more successful than others
- expect others to meet their needs and treat them as being important
- constantly seek attention, praise, compliments and admiration from other people because of their self-perceived and often self-inflated sense of superiority
- often boast, exaggerate or lie about their achievements to create an image of themselves as highly successful and 'special' even when, in reality, this may not be the case
- tend to gravitate towards jobs, careers, businesses, friends

and partners with the potential to provide them with power, status, celebrity and/or wealth
- have a strong sense of entitlement and perceive that they deserve and have a right to privileges, honours and special treatment
- often selfishly use others for their own ends
- are less likely than other people to accept responsibility for their own behaviour and more likely to blame others when things go wrong
- often devalue the contributions of others and put them down in order to feel more powerful than them
- tend to be unsatisfactory partners because of their self-focus, need for admiration and assumption that others will cater to their needs.

Those with an NPD often gravitate towards careers and businesses that have the potential to provide them with wealth, status, power or celebrity, such as business, finance, the military, the entertainment industry and politics.

Typical behaviours of people with an NPD

As with other personality disorders, the severity of an NPD can range from mild to extreme. Two people with an NPD may also behave differently in some ways, depending on which criteria they meet, other factors in their lives and which subtype they fit into. Four main subtypes of NPD have been identified – elitist, amorous, compensatory and unprincipled (Millon et al., 2004) – and help to explain some of the small variations in the behaviour of those who have an NPD. A person may fall entirely into one subtype, or have a combination of traits from several.

1. **Elitist:** Characterised by a narcissistic pattern of behaviour that arises from a desire to be seen as superior to other people,

plus their fear of being ordinary. They strive to find ways in which they are better than others, drawing on aspects such as their family background, their wealth, and what school or university they went to. They self-promote, boast and lie about or exaggerate their achievements, and often exploit others while doing so. Many are 'social climbers' who will do whatever it takes to be seen as having high status. Their belief in their own superiority often results in them ignoring the suggestions, advice or concerns of others.

2. **Amorous:** Characterised by a narcissistic pattern of behaviour that arises from a constant need for admiration and a sense of their own superiority that makes them feel entitled to the sexual favours of others. They usually engage in multiple sexual conquests as a way of reinforcing their over-inflated self-image. They often play their game of sexual and romantic seduction with several people simultaneously. They usually exploit and discard each conquest, moving on to the next one. They often falsely imply the possibility of an exclusive relationship but have very limited capacity for genuine intimacy and connection.
3. **Compensatory:** Characterised by a pattern of unstable, narcissistic behaviour that arises from an underlying sense of insecurity and weakness rather than genuine feelings of self-confidence and high self-esteem. They strive for recognition and prestige to compensate for their basic lack of a feeling of self-worth. They usually have ongoing aspirations for status and prestige, a tendency to exaggerate and boast, and are hypersensitive and overreactive to criticism or slights.
4. **Unprincipled:** Characterised by a pattern of unscrupulous and antisocial behaviour in an arrogant way. This subtype is very similar to the subcategory of malignant narcissism (see pages 139–44, 413).

Initially many people with an NPD may appear charming and appealing. Their seemingly buoyant mood and optimistic outlook is interpreted as them being cheerful and carefree. But their true colours eventually emerge when they do whatever it takes to preserve their 'superior' status, often harming others in the process. Many men with an NPD are misogynistic, seeing women as sources of admiration and support for them and their self-image rather than individuals with their own rights and needs. Both men and women with an NPD may often dress in a way that attracts attention and admiration. For example, they may wear expensive brand-name clothing or jewellery, or 'extreme' clothing that shows off biceps, cleavage and tattoos. They may not be as good-looking as they think they are, but their way of dressing, coupled with their self-belief, can make them seem more attractive, confident and charming. They often enjoy being photographed or having their children photographed, and enthusiastically share these pictures on social networking sites, where they work to boost their self-image by developing many contacts and online 'friends' rather than creating a sense of intimacy with real friends. They will find as many ways as they can to promote themselves positively (Buffardi and Campbell, 2008).

The approach of someone with an NPD is often more like a 'fantasy' of success than a realistic process. As a result, aspects of their life are like a 'house of cards' that in some cases is easily knocked over or simply 'falls down'. Someone with an NPD may:

- look for friendships or romantic relationships with people they believe can potentially contribute to their success and their 'successful' public image
- have limited capacity to love anyone but themselves, and their relationships are based mostly on *their* wants, needs

and expectations. They have very little sensitivity to, or concern about, the needs of their partner or children, and are usually not interested in participating in a mutually nurturing and supportive intimate relationship. In many cases the role of the other people in their life is simply to act as a 'mirror' for themselves.

- use emotional and/or physical abuse to establish power and control over an intimate partner. This may involve pushing, shoving or punching, mocking, belittling and humiliation, sulking or withdrawal. They hide this abuse to preserve their public image. Their victim may get used to the abuse and see it as less controlling than it actually is, gradually losing trust in their own perceptions and judgement.
- lack realistic insight into their own behaviour and tend not to learn from mistakes. They often blame other people when things go wrong and excuse their own shortcomings by claiming that others were pressuring them or imposing unrealistic expectations. They tend to cover up any 'failure' when they are able to do so.
- act in ways that are arrogant, rude and patronising, especially towards those they perceive to be of 'lesser' status
- attempt to present an image of themselves as omnipotent and omniscient. They often overestimate their abilities, exaggerate their accomplishments, minimise their limitations and seem boastful and pretentious. They assume that others see them as they see themselves, and are surprised and sometimes shocked when this isn't the case. They get irritated when others choose not to assist them with their 'very important work'.
- act vengefully against people whom they think have not supported them or have acted against them

- use charm and confidence about their future success to convince people to lend them money or invest in their ventures. This money is often lost.
- insist on having the 'best' of everything, such as the best (and most expensive) car, house, computer, clothing brands and school for their children
- play up their self-assessed abilities while dismissing and undervaluing the abilities, work, successes and contributions of others, looking for opportunities to undermine those they see as competition
- be a rather boring conversationalist as they are not very interested in what others have to say. They often monopolise the conversation, talk about themselves, show off and interrupt to regain control of the conversation.
- hurt family, friends and colleagues with insensitive or unkind remarks
- be oversensitive to what they perceive as slights from other people and quickly take offence.

Beneath the grandiose and self-promoting behaviour of an individual with an NPD is what has been described by Sheehy (2017) as 'a pit of fragile self-esteem'. They often have difficulty coping with feelings of embarrassment and shame, and with the frustration that arises when they can't have what they want. They tend to be oversensitive to criticism and may struggle to cope when their self-image is threatened by their own actions or someone whose words or actions make them feel powerless, ashamed, embarrassed, defensive or exposed. This can happen if they make a mistake or a wrong move, or if someone they rely on as part of their 'public image', such as a partner or business associate, criticises them, disagrees with them or threatens to leave them. Many avoid working in teams, unless they can manipulate the situation to make it look like they are the star performer, even if they are far from it.

When a person with an NPD believes that something or someone has threatened their inflated view of themselves or their positive public image, they may suffer what has been described as a 'narcissistic injury'. For example, a shop assistant may rebuke them for trying to jump the queue and tell them to wait their turn, or their partner may stand up to them after years of emotional abuse. A 'narcissistic injury' can then spark a 'narcissistic rage' (Kohut, 1972), an angry verbal and/or physical attack on the person whom they perceive has 'injured' them and their self-image. They might direct verbal abuse at the shop assistant for daring to challenge them, or physically attack their partner for daring to criticise them. Depending on the nature of the 'narcissistic injury', these 'rages' can vary from short and minor to prolonged and severe.

Prevalence of NPDs

It is estimated that up to 6.2 per cent of the population has an NPD (Dhawan et al., 2010) and 50–75 per cent of them are male (DSM-5, APA, 2013), but there is some evidence that NPD rates may be increasing, at least in the United States. Researchers such as Professor Jean Twenge, co-author of *The Narcissism Epidemic* (2010), have identified a general trend in which today's young people are developing more narcissistic traits than earlier generations. Professor Twenge suggests that this is due to a combination of more permissive parenting, an over-focus on developing children's self-esteem by stressing how 'special' they are, the development of celebrity culture, the internet and social media. In line with these findings, a study by Stinson et al. (2008) found that only 3.2 per cent of those aged over 65 had experienced an NPD during their lifetime, compared to 5.6 per cent of people aged 45 to 64, 7.1 per cent of those aged 30 to 44 and 9.4 per cent of those aged 20 to 29.

Comorbidity (other disorders that often occur with NPDs)

About 21 per cent of people with an NPD also have an antisocial personality disorder (ASPD) (Blackburn et al., 2003), while 37 per cent also have a borderline personality disorder (Stinson et al., 2008). These disorders are explained in detail elsewhere (see pages 127, 336–7). The combination of ASPD and NPD is further discussed on pages 139–44.

Heritability of NPDs

Genetic and environmental factors combine to create an NPD. The heritability – the degree to which genetics plays a role in developing a disorder – is estimated to be .77 (Torgersen et al., 2012). This means that 77 per cent of the differences between those in research studies who had an NPD and those who didn't, were most likely due to genetic differences between them. But research has not yet clearly identified exactly what specific genetic predispositions are inherited. Some studies have suggested that some people with an NPD have a deficit in serotonin, a brain chemical that regulates moods. A serotonin deficit can also lead to depression and sometimes aggression.

Other contributing factors to NPDs

It seems likely that limited capacity for emotional empathy might be one of the genetic factors (see pages 411–12). Although results from studies into NPD and empathy are mixed, they have generally found that people with an NPD display lower levels of emotional resonance (feeling the feelings of others) but normal levels of emotional recognition, also called cognitive empathy – i.e. reading and understanding the feelings of others (Ritter, 2011; Baskin-Sommers et al., 2014). A study by Baskin-Sommers et al. (2014) concluded that people with an NPD are *capable* of responding emotionally to the feelings of others, but are more able and willing than others to switch off this 'emotional empathy' when it suits them, or they perceive that it isn't in their best interests. For example, they may use this type of self-serving 'empathic disengagement' when they don't want to respond emotionally to the distress of someone they are mistreating or trying to control, or when they themselves are trying to stay in control and not appear vulnerable.

Many people with an NPD develop and talk about a mythical 'perfect childhood' as part of their self-image. Parenting does appear to play a role in the development of an NPD, especially when parents give a child excessive praise, fail to set clear behavioural boundaries or let their child misbehave without consequences. This type of parenting can give a child unrealistic messages about who they are and what is acceptable behaviour. If children don't experience and learn to manage 'moral emotions', such as compassion, embarrassment, humility, guilt and shame, it is more difficult for them to be resilient, respect the rights of others, develop behavioural boundaries and behave well.

If they easily get almost everything they ask for, children don't learn that setting realistic goals, working hard and making sacrifices are the keys to success. If a parent gives a child what they are demanding to calm them down during a temper tantrum, the child learns that they can use negative emotional pressure to extract things from others. Overindulgence and/or a lack of parental supervision can also send the child a message that they can do and have whatever they want, and denies them opportunities to learn to tolerate the frustration of not always being able to get their own way.

Parents have an important role to play in helping children learn about their ability strengths and character strengths, but they also need to help their child understand their limitations. A child raised in a family that rates status and success extremely highly learns that the types of qualities that contribute to a grandiose self-image are highly valued, and learns to prioritise them in their own life. Telling a child too often how 'special' he or she is and how everyone expects them to excel and outshine others can also contribute to an unrealistic sense of self. Such self-illusions are difficult to maintain in the world outside the family and as they become independent young people. It is also important for parents to teach their child to respect the strengths of others and to value teamwork.

Treatment of NPDs

Individuals with an NPD rarely seek treatment. They are usually unwilling to acknowledge the disorder and unable to admit that their weaknesses have had a negative impact on others. Some try to manipulate the therapist into acknowledging their superiority. Many of those who do agree to undertake treatment, often at the urging of a partner, soon drop out, as they usually find the process too exposing to cope with and most are not genuinely interested in changing. Treatment, which usually involves cognitive behaviour therapy, is more likely to be successful if they have also developed depression. Taking SSRI medication, which is primarily used to treat depression and anxiety, may be helpful under these circumstances in some cases.

The malignant narcissism subcategory

Malignant narcissism is a pattern of behaviour that combines most of the core features of an NPD with many of the features of an ASPD. The features that are part of an NPD (DSM-5, APA,

2013) that are also likely to be found in malignant narcissism include:

- an exaggerated sense of their own importance and cleverness
- fantasies of unlimited power and success
- a belief that they are special and unique
- a strong need for admiration
- a sense of entitlement
- a willingness to take advantage of others to meet their own needs
- a lack of empathy
- feelings of envy towards others who are successful.

The features of ASPD (DSM-5, APA, 2013), some of which are likely to be found in individuals who fit into the subcategory of malignant narcissism, include:

- physical aggression and sometimes violent and/or sadistic behaviour
- preparedness to lie, con, exploit, manipulate, steal, cause injury or murder to gain control and/or achieve their goals; these intentions are more often a specific part of their planning when they seek specific goals rather than behaviours that occur incidentally during the execution of those plans
- lack of remorse for the harm they cause to others
- lack of preparedness to admit what they have done
- an extreme lack of empathy.

The syndrome of 'malignant narcissism' was first identified by social psychologist Erich Fromm in 1964–65. He described it as embodying 'the quintessence of evil' and described those with it as 'human monsters'. Fromm (1965) further described malignant narcissism as 'the most severe pathology and the root of the most vicious destructiveness and inhumanity'. It is probably best perceived, however, as a spectrum rather than an all-or-nothing disorder, and it can range from low to high severity depending on the specific combinations of the two personality disorders (Malkin, 2017).

There are a range of typical behaviours of individuals with malignant narcissism. They are usually motivated more than others by an intense need for recognition, admiration and power, and are prepared to do whatever it takes to achieve those outcomes (Goldner-Vukov and Moore, 2010). They seek to cultivate an external image of being powerful and successful, but internally their self-evaluation may be surprisingly fragile, fluctuating between over-confidence, superiority and showing off, concern about inferiority, vulnerability, insecurity, shame, and hypersensitivity to self-doubt and criticism from others. Malignant narcissists believe that they are uniquely superior, omniscient and omnipotent compared to others, and hence entitled to more wealth, power and control than others. This belief encourages them to ignore the rights of others, often in dishonest, destructive and violent ways. They sometimes behave sadistically towards others.

The behaviour of people exhibiting malignant narcissism is likely to be even more extreme and dangerous than the behaviour of those who just have an NPD. They are determined to have what they want, and often become furious and potentially violent if thwarted. These individuals tend to be nastier, more vindictive and more likely to use aggression, deceit or illegal behaviours to achieve power, success and wealth. They are also more likely to bully people and disregard social norms and laws. Many are skilled in avoiding detection (Gunderson and Ronningham, 2001; Kernberg, 1992), and are not hindered in their pursuit of power, status and adulation by the scruples or inhibitions that develop in most people who have a healthy conscience and empathy for others. This lack of empathy and conscience enables them to lie, cheat, manipulate, harm and destroy others more easily.

Although some people with malignant narcissism or just ASPD can 'parrot' words that sound like they are being empathic, it is usually an illusion. Several studies have suggested, however, that many individuals with an ASPD or malignant narcissism are capable of 'predator's empathy', which enables them, like a lion stalking its prey, to sense fear in another person and detect other small signs that enable that person to be successfully manipulated or exploited (Malancharuvil, 2012).

Individuals with malignant narcissism can become dangerous when they are so addicted to feeling powerful and admired that they are prepared to do almost anything to achieve their 'high', including lying, cheating, stealing, physically or sexually assaulting, using, hurting, conning, betraying and, sometimes, murdering others. They regularly distort and falsify the truth in order to embellish and support their story of the brilliant and successful person they believe themselves to be. If they are forced to confront the unpleasant reality that they are not as special or clever as they claim they are, and would like to be, they can become even more dangerous (Malkin, 2017).

Although the term malignant narcissism is widely accepted in the fields of psychology and psychiatry as a subcategory of NPD, it is not currently a specific diagnostic term used in the *Diagnostic and Statistical Manual of Mental Disorders* (DSM-5). But it is increasingly used to describe people who exhibit extreme characteristics associated with NPD behaviour combined with those of ASPD. Several researchers and authors have concluded that dictators such as Adolf Hitler, Joseph Stalin and Mao Zedong have demonstrated malignant narcissism (e.g. Burkle, 2016; Glad, 2002; Goldner-Vukov and Moore, 2010; Montefiore, 2007; Yang and Halliday, 2007). These leaders were all prepared to let countless people suffer to achieve their goals, and demonstrated no empathy or remorse as they did so. They saw themselves as superior, unassailable, more intelligent than those around them, omniscient, all-powerful and justified in their actions, despite the immense pain and suffering they caused.

Man Haron Monis, who was responsible for Sydney's fatal Lindt café siege in 2014, is clearly someone whose behaviour fits into the malignant narcissism subcategory. Monis spent his adult life lying, deceiving, manipulating and abusing people with whom he was associated. He had an inflated view of his importance, called himself a spiritual healer when he had no qualifications, and even tried to join a bikie gang. When his lies and criminal activity were about to catch up with him, Monis created fictional links to terrorist organisations that he knew would attract media attention, took hostages and killed one of them, Tori Johnson, as he died in a hail of gunfire that killed another hostage, Katrina Dawson.

Megan Haines, a nurse who killed two nursing home patients after they complained about her rude and unprofessional behaviour, also has malignant narcissism. Haines worked in nursing homes despite her dislike of older people and decided to kill two elderly NSW nursing home residents to prevent her already tarnished nursing record from being further sullied.

Sydney based Robert Xie is another malignant narcissist who resorted to extremes to promote his self-image. Xie killed five members of his wife's extended family because he was jealous of his brother-in-law's status in the family. He was also sexually abusing a young relative and thought he would have easier access to her with her family 'out of the way'.

These people felt no guilt for their actions or empathy for their victims. In their minds, they were simply doing what needed to be done to improve their own situation. Having malignant narcissism does not mean someone will become a killer, but it does mean that they are prepared to go a lot further than others to achieve their own ends.

DONALD TRUMP

US President Donald Trump's controversial and often confrontational behaviour has led some experts to argue that he has malignant narcissism. Twenty-seven psychiatrists and mental health experts recently published a book *The Dangerous Case of Donald Trump: 27 Psychiatrists and Mental Health Experts Assess a President* (Lee, 2017) claiming that, in their professional opinions, President Trump displays many of the indicators of malignant narcissism in his behaviour. The book challenges the President's fitness for the office, arguing that the key issue is his 'dangerousness' rather than him having a mental illness (Friedman, 2017; Gilligan, 2017). They believed it was their duty to warn people involved in government and the general community of these dangers.

In November 2016, three of the authors wrote to then President Barack Obama strongly recommending that Trump, then President-elect, be asked to undergo a full medical and neuropsychiatric evaluation in preparation for assuming office. In January 2017, all the authors wrote a combined letter to the US Congress recommending an evaluation of President Trump's capacity to fulfil the responsibilities of the presidency. This letter was published in the *Huffington Post* in November 2017, with comments by one of the book's authors, Dr Michael Tansey.

The editor of *The Dangerous Case of Donald Trump* and several authors of its chapters (e.g. Gartrell and Mosbacher, 2017) also made a joint submission to Congress recommending legislation to create an independent, impartial professional panel of investigators to evaluate President Trump's fitness to fulfil the duties of the presidency but also to assess future sitting presidents and vice-presidents annually, as well as evaluate future presidential and vice-presidential candidates for their fitness to fulfil their potential duties.

What has caused such consternation among professionals? We all know Donald Trump has always had a healthy ego and been brash, bold, boastful and uncompromising in his public comments and actions. But concerns have arisen about this behaviour being extreme, nasty, self-centred, exploitative and part of a long-term pattern of narcissistic behaviour that is a danger to the presidential office, the future safety of the United States, the future of democracy and anyone who gets in his way. President Trump has displayed numerous dangerous traits and behaviours consistent with someone who has malignant narcissism, including boasting and grandiosity. He constantly claims to be the best and that he is surrounded by the best people. Before he took office, he said, 'I will be the greatest jobs President [sic] that God ever created.' In an interview with CNN, President Trump claimed he had an uncle who was a top professor and it was in his blood to be 'really smart'. He has boasted that his IQ is much higher than that of presidents Barack Obama and George W. Bush, and once claimed he could stand in the middle of New York's Fifth Avenue and shoot somebody and he wouldn't lose any votes. (See the Media Today reference on page 422 for a link detailing some of Trump's many boasts.)

Those with malignant narcissism lie with ease and invent a universe of 'alternative facts' that support their exaggerated grandiosity. Trump is a classic example of this. He constantly accuses the media of presenting 'fake news' when much of it is substantiated. He even started denying the existence of a tape in which he said he could grab women's private parts with impunity, after earlier admitting it was real. Others also verified its existence. Political observers comment that President Trump appears to be indifferent to the truth and simply talks about what he wants to be true (Sheehy, 2017).

A good example of President Trump's lies is his exaggeration about the size of his inauguration crowd. He claimed it was the largest in history, and that there were 'a million, a million and a half people in the mall' listening to his speech (Zaru, 2017), when photographic evidence clearly showed otherwise. He also falsely claimed that President Barack Obama was a Muslim born in Kenya and not an American citizen, had a Hawaiian bureaucrat murdered to cover up the truth about his birth certificate and also wire-tapped President Trump's building (Dodes, 2017; Gartner, 2017). Fact-checking website Politifact estimated that 76 per cent of Donald Trump's statements were either false or mostly false (Holan and Qui, 2015), and *Politico Magazine* estimated that he told a lie every three minutes and fifteen seconds (Cheney et al., 2016).

Others go even further in what they have to say about President Trump's alleged dishonesty. New York State Attorney-General Eric Schneiderman concluded that Trump University was 'a straight-up fraud from beginning to end' (Gass, 2016). Gartner (2017) has also highlighted dozens of law suits initiated in response to President Trump's pattern of not paying contractors he has hired. He has also been exposed as allegedly engaging in serial sexual assaults that he then bragged about, arguing that because of his celebrity and power he was able to get away with it. When a dozen women who had been victims of these assaults came forward, he called them 'liars' (Dodes, 2017; Gartner, 2017).

Many health professionals are concerned that President Trump's malignant narcissistic behaviour could put his country at risk. He regularly mocks and insults North Korean dictator Kim Jong-Un in the press and online, calling him names such as 'Rocket Man' and describing him as short and fat. President Trump has also repeatedly asked 'if we have nuclear weapons why can't we use them?' (Fisher, 2016). He even urged his followers at rallies to punch and beat up protesters, and suggested that they could always assassinate his political rival Hilary Clinton (Gartner, 2017). Even if he was joking, such actions are entirely inappropriate for someone in his office and potentially dangerous. Taken the wrong way, they could prompt someone like Kim Jong-Un to take drastic action. But President Trump is unfazed by criticism. As someone with malignant narcissism, he believes that he is always right and that those who question him are wrong and 'out to get him'.

Some have even highlighted that Donald Trump gains pleasure from lying about and deriding anyone who gets in his way. This, they argue, is incompatible with running a democracy that requires respect for and the protection of multiple viewpoints, and creates profound danger for America's democracy and safety (Dodes, 2017, p. 91). Psychiatrist Steven Reisner (2017) has pointed out that his impulsivity, threats, aggression, ridicule and denial of reality, and the mobilisation of the mob that Trump used to win the presidency, are not the symptoms of any mental illness but signs of an evil person.

CHAPTER 4

MAN HARON MONIS

The cast

Man Haron Monis: Monis shot dead Tori Johnson in the 2014 Lindt Chocolate Café siege, before he was killed by police

Tori Johnson: Thirty-four-year-old man who was the Lindt café manager and died in the siege

Katrina Dawson: Thirty-eight-year-old barrister and mother who died in the siege

Zahra Bahmani and Mohammad Hassan Manteghi: Monis's parents. He had five older sisters.

Zahra Mobasheri: Monis's first wife in Iran, who divorced him in absentia. They had two girls.

Name suppressed by the courts: Monis's first wife in Australia. They married in 2003 and had two boys. She was murdered by Amirah Droudis in 2013.

Amanda Morsy: Monis dated Amanda briefly in 2003

Irene Mishra: Monis dated Irene for nine years from 2002. She died of natural causes in 2012.

Amirah Droudis: Monis's second Australian wife. In 2016 she was found guilty of murdering his first Australian wife at his behest.

Manny Conditsis: Specialist criminal trial lawyer who represented Monis with regard to his letters to the families of deceased Australian soldiers and the accessory to murder charge

Timeline

May 1964. Mohammad Hassan Manteghi born in Iran.

1983. Meets and marries his Iranian wife Zahra Mobasheri.

1986. The couple's first daughter is born.

1995. Their second daughter is born.

1996. Still known as Mohammad Manteghi, Monis arrives in Australia on a business visa, leaving his wife and daughters in Iran. At some point, possibly in 2002, he changes his name to Michael Hayson Mavros.

August 2002. Monis begins dating his first Australian wife (name suppressed by the courts), who knows him as Michael Hayson.

January–July 2003. Has a relationship with Amanda Morsy.

August 2003. Marries his first Australian wife and they have two sons. From August 2002 and during this marriage he has an affair with Irene Mishra.

2004. After protracted legal issues and still known as Michael Hayson Mavros, Monis is granted Australian citizenship.

Mid-2000s. His first Australian wife divorces him.

2006. Mavros changes his name to Man Haron Monis and begins a relationship with Amirah Droudis. His first wife in Iran, Zahra Mobasheri, divorces him in absentia.

December 2008. Monis proposes to Droudis; a few weeks later she tells her family they have married.

2009. Monis is charged with thirteen counts of using a postal service to cause offence, menace or harass. He eventually pleads guilty after a years-long court fight.
May 2012. Irene Mishra dies of natural causes.
April 2013. Monis's first Australian wife is murdered. Amirah Droudis is later charged with her murder.
November 2013. Monis is charged with being an accessory to his ex-wife's murder.
April 2014. Monis is additionally charged with three counts of indecent and sexual assault relating to his time as a so-called 'spiritual healer', and he is bailed.
October 2014. Police charge Monis with another 37 counts of sexual or indecent assault. Most were allegedly committed between 2002 and 2010.
12 December 2014. Monis learns that his High Court appeal, seeking to challenge the validity of the *Commonwealth Postal Act* so he can apply to overturn his conviction for offensive letters he had sent, has been rejected.
15 December 2014. Monis enters the Lindt Chocolate Café at 8.33 am, before starting the siege at about 9.40 am.
16 December 2014. Monis, Tori Johnson and Katrina Dawson die as the siege ends.
November 2016. Amirah Droudis is convicted of the murder of Monis's first Australian wife.
February 2017. Droudis is sentenced to 44 years' jail, with a non-parole period of 33 years.

The motive

Man Haron Monis orchestrated the Sydney Lindt café siege as a way of attracting attention to himself and gaining public notoriety, following many years of selfish and violent acts designed to inflate his image and his 'importance' in society. The siege had nothing to do with official terrorist organisations, although Monis wanted people to believe that it did.

Introduction

The man responsible for the fatal 2014 Lindt Café siege was widely linked by media outlets to terrorism and Islamic State. Some in the media branded him 'a nutter'. There is no evidence to suggest that he was ever psychotic. But there was a lot more to Man Haron Monis than met the eye – and none of it good. Monis did not have a mental illness that loosened his grip on reality when he manipulated those around him to his advantage, abused government officials and tried to convince people he was 'special'. Rather, this incredibly insecure man of few genuine talents was driven by his malignant narcissism, a potentially dangerous combination of two personality disorders that compelled him to promote himself at the expense of others.

After arriving in Australia from Iran in 1996, Monis caused headaches for a range of Australian authorities and those unlucky enough to be caught in his personal orbit. While he appears to have kept a relatively low profile until 2001, he then began to assume countless identities. Monis racked up traffic infringements, harassed people with threatening letters, changed his religious affiliation when it suited him, and set up spiritual self-help groups that he used to sexually abuse vulnerable women. He was also part of many legal cases that dragged through the courts, and used a website and social media to taunt authorities and make wild claims about imaginary conspiracy theories and terror-related issues. At one point, he tried unsuccessfully to join a bikie gang. Most seriously, he was charged with being an accessory to the 2013 murder of the mother of his Australian-born children.

As his deceitful life finally began to implode, Monis latched onto a terrorism theme that was striking fear into the hearts of people globally, knowing that it would gain maximum media attention for him and could turn him into a 'martyr'. There is no evidence to suggest that he was officially involved with any terrorist group, but Monis tried to give the impression that he was an important 'player'. This blatant attention-seeking was part of a pattern of behaviour perpetuated over many years, and was designed to make this ultimately pathetic man feel noticed and important.

Man Monis was in fact a complete fraud. When one person or organisation saw through his self-aggrandising antics, he moved on to another. In some cases, he took matters into his own hands, his actions becoming increasingly erratic until they involved numerous threats to innocent people and violence fuelled by a narcissistic rage. This man would stop at nothing to be noticed and to promote himself at the expense of those around him. That included allegedly inciting the murder of his first Australian wife, and shooting manager Tori Johnson in the Lindt café siege.

Monis's manipulation of the system began when he came to Sydney from Iran in 1996 and successfully applied for a short-stay visa. In his application, Monis had falsely claimed he was a legal consultant to the managing director of an Iranian manufacturing and engineering company visiting Australia to meet with BHP Billiton. In reality, he was wanted by the police in Iran for stealing up to AU$550,000 from a travel agency where he had been working. Monis then applied for an Australian protection visa, this time falsely claiming to be a political refugee, and was granted a bridging visa. In that application, Monis said that his involvement with Iran's Ministry of Intelligence and the CIA could see him executed if he returned to his home country. In 2000, he was granted a protection visa and he became an Australian citizen in 2004. Monis was interviewed by ASIO several times over this period as part of immigration security assessments, but was not considered a national security risk at any stage (State Coroner of NSW, inquest report, 2017).

Initially known in Australia as Mohammad Hassan Manteghi, Monis formally changed this to Michael Hayson Mavros in or about 2002. Then in 2006, he officially became Man Haron Monis. Over the years, he was also known by several other aliases. Whichever name he used, Monis was high-maintenance in his dealings with Australian authorities. He lived in at least seventeen different locations, mostly in southern and western Sydney. Early on, he spent six weeks in Western Australia working as a Persian rug salesman. After being sacked, Monis successfully sued for wrongful dismissal and the WA Industrial Relations Commission awarded him about $14,000. He racked up four traffic infringement notices in Western Australia, and committed another nine traffic offences in New South Wales, three of them leading to licence suspension in those states.

From 1997 to 2000, Monis worked as a security guard and had access to guns. While presenting himself as a 'spiritual healer' between 2002 and 2010, he set up self-help organisations that earned him up to $125,000 a year. Despite this income, Monis also received government income support for seven and a half of his eighteen years in Australia, including help from the Asylum Seeker Assistance Scheme, Newstart and Austudy.

In 1999, he registered Daftar-E-Ayatollah Manteghi Boroujerdi Incorporated, purportedly to promote spiritual matters through teaching, education and humanitarian, religious and charity work. *The Martin Place Siege Joint Commonwealth – New South Wales Review* (January 2015) found that Monis was also linked to the following companies:

- MHMB, registered in October 1998 and cancelled in January 2001

- Spiritual Power, active July 2001, renamed Spiritual Consultation in 2003 and cancelled in September 2014
- Spiritual Counselling, registered in October 2002 and cancelled in September 2004
- Holy Spirit Counselling, registered in January 2007 and cancelled in August 2012
- Australian United Muslim Clerics Pty Ltd, started in January 2008 and deregistered in March 2010
- Hizbullah Australia, registered in September 2008 and cancelled in December 2011.

In 2011, Monis applied to register a company named IISIO Incorporated to provide humanitarian assistance to mankind, especially women and children, to promote peace and spirituality in society and to encourage people to live in harmony. It was also supposed to research and provide information, intelligence and advice for the development of international Islamic policy-making about spirituality, culture, economy, education, science, technology, politics and security. None of these organisations achieved any of their supposed goals, and in 2014 Monis was charged with more than 40 indecent and sexual assault offences dating back to 2002. These allegedly occurred while he was representing himself as a spiritual healer and clairvoyant, taking advantage of vulnerable women who sought his help and guidance.

Over the years, Monis also claimed a range of religious affiliations and other connections (Martin Place siege review, 2015), including:

- Shiite status of Hojatoleslam, a title provided to middle-ranking scholars within Shiah Islam
- an association with the Ahmadi sect to support his application for a protection visa

- spiritual healing skills, which he used to sell related services, mostly to women
- presenting as a non-religious businessman in his Michael Hayson Mavros phase
- adopting the apparently self-appointed title of Sheikh Haron to increase his standing and appeal in the Islamic community and ultimately (unsuccessfully) to build a following
- purporting to have converted from Shia to Sunni Islam, which is unusual.

Monis travelled overseas 21 times from 2003 to 2007, including ten visits to Bangkok. Some trips lasted only one day, and he twice flew to London and back in less than two days. The joint review could not establish why he took these trips. This period of intense travel was followed by political activism, during which Monis sent about 60 letters, faxes and media releases to people including the Prime Minister, the Opposition Leader, the Federal Attorney-General, the Australian Federal Police Commissioner, Queen Elizabeth II, the Pope and families of Australian soldiers killed in Afghanistan.

The letters to soldiers' families started by expressing sympathy but then asked why similar sympathy had not been shown for innocent people killed in conflicts in Iraq or Afghanistan. He called the dead soldiers evil criminals and murderers, and said they would go to hell, likening one to the 'dirty body of a pig'. In 2009, Monis was charged with thirteen counts of using a postal service to cause offence, menace or harass. At one point, he held a public protest outside the Downing Centre courthouse complex. Monis took the case to the High Court, arguing that the relevant section of the *Commonwealth Postal Act* – sending 'offensive' material in the post – inhibited political free speech.

The High Court was split three to three, so, in effect, the law stood and his trial was to proceed. One of his lawyers, Manny Conditsis, ultimately persuaded him to plead guilty, and he was sentenced to a community service order. After completing it, Monis re-engaged his High Court lawyers to again challenge the *Postal Act* in the High Court, on the basis that no clear decision was made the first time. Manny now understands that on the Friday before the Lindt siege, Monis was told that the High Court had refused his request for special leave to hear his case. 'I think this may be pivotal – as if he had been successful, that would have given him the limelight again, at least for a time,' Manny says. The implication is that if Monis had been given leave to challenge the court's decision, the resulting publicity may have given him enough of the 'attention' he craved and he therefore might not have organised the Lindt café 'siege' as a substitute attention-grabber. Around the time of the postal charges, Monis was prominent on social media and the internet, making inflammatory comments. He used a website, www.sheikhharon.com, to post provocative statements, media releases, copies of his letters and responses. In 2008, he used it to publish a 'fatwa' referring to US, UK and Australian heads of state as war criminals. He also posted a video clip entitled 'Suicide Fatwa' in which a female protégé discussed 'legitimate suicide attacks'.

In 2009, Monis sent a media release to the NSW Police Force warning of a possible terrorist attack in Australia. He regularly sought attention and publicity in these ways. Monis chained himself to the gates of the WA and NSW parliaments, and was involved in several protests. He tried to use events such as the September 11, 2001 terror attacks in New York and the 2009 Victorian bushfires to push his agenda, claiming that the bushfires were really an act of terror. He repeatedly tried to give information to intelligence agencies that was inevitably rejected as not credible. ASIO investigated him four times (Martin Place siege review, 2015).

The making of a siege gunman

By 2010, Monis was well known to security and police agencies. While trying to push his fanciful theories and ideas, he met with police and ASIO many times. Government agencies held hundreds of thousands of pages of information on him. A search of the National Security Hotline database found 41 references to Monis, from 11 May 2004 to 12 December 2014. Some were calls he made claiming knowledge of terrorist activities. From April 2008 to January 2009, ASIO investigated Monis to see if he posed a terrorism threat. He offered to work for ASIO several times, but the information he proffered was considered unreliable. For example, in 1998 he told ASIO's public line that he had information of interest about the upcoming 2000 Sydney Olympics. ASIO interviewed him twice, but decided that despite his claims he in fact had no credible information.

Not content with challenging authorities internally, Monis instigated politically motivated public protests to draw attention to himself. In November 2000, he staged a hunger strike outside Western Australia's Parliament House to convince the Iranian Government to allow him to see his children in Iran. He took that complaint to the NSW Parliament in January 2001. In 2006 he held another protest outside Channel 7's Martin Place headquarters in Sydney, branding celebrity host David Koch a killer and a terrorist. Monis had seen television footage of a UK doctor who blew himself and others up in what was described as a terrorist act, and believed the coverage unfairly targeted all Muslims. Despite the footage coming from the United Kingdom, he directed his protest at David Koch, who is Australian.

Despite countless incidents and investigations, authorities decided Monis was not involved in politically motivated violence and had not tried to incite communal violence. They concluded he had not expressed an intention to commit politically motivated violence, and was not in significant contact with known individuals or groups of security concern. Neither were any of his immediate acquaintances. Australian Federal Police and NSW Police Force criminal investigations found no information to indicate that Monis had either a desire or an intent to undertake terrorist acts in Australia. ASIO's final assessment of Monis was that he was not a threat to national security.

ASIO, police agencies and the NSW Joint Counter Terrorism Team continued to assess new information received about Monis and his social media presence. He was discussed by many joint counterterrorism teams between 2008 and 2014. Several times, Interpol Tehran also contacted Australian authorities to alert them to the fact Monis was wanted in Iran for fraud-related offences. But Australia had no extradition treaty with Iran.

In July 2011, Monis was charged with intimidating his first Australian wife, whom he had married in 2003. Initially, police had taken out a provisional apprehended domestic violence order against him, which was continued on an interim basis. Police later sought a final apprehended domestic violence order against Monis, but the court did not support it. Monis was also charged with stalking and intimidation, charges that went to a defended hearing at Campbelltown Local Court. He was acquitted and at that time had no criminal convictions.

In April 2013, Monis's then wife, Amirah Droudis, stabbed Monis's 30-year-old ex-wife to death before setting her on fire in the hallway of Monis's apartment block in suburban Werrington in western Sydney. Droudis was eventually found guilty of the horrific murder in November 2016. Justice Peter Johnson found she had been 'enthralled' by Monis and committed the murder at his behest. As the frenzied stabbing took place, Monis intentionally crashed his car into a police vehicle outside Penrith Police Station to create an alibi. The following day, he filmed his sons with Droudis in her Croydon unit to portray them living an ordinary suburban life as a family. When Droudis was charged with the murder in November 2013, Monis was charged with being an accessory to his ex-wife's murder. His behaviour had clearly escalated from annoying to criminally dangerous.

One lawyer's story

Monis used many lawyers over the years and was a high-maintenance client. Criminal lawyer Manny Conditsis met him in February 2013, when Monis was facing charges for writing his offensive letters to the families of Australian soldiers killed overseas. Manny, a senior trial advocate and an accredited criminal law specialist of more than 30 years, primarily practises out of Gosford on the NSW Central Coast, about an hour north of Sydney. In 2012, Manny received the NSW Law Society President's Medal for his pro-bono work. At the time, he felt Monis's case was difficult because there would be little or no public support or empathy 'and the media would be all over it'. But he agreed to take it on because Monis was referred to him by another lawyer.

'My first impression of him was that he was courteous, idealistic, passionate about Islam and lobbying against unjust wars, and that he believed that the postal charges were trumped up by the Government and/or ASIO and/or the Australian Army and/or the police,' Manny says. 'Monis's belief in that regard was fuelled by the fact that he was the first and only person ever charged with the offence(s) of sending offensive letters under the *Commonwealth Postal Act*. Monis maintained those characteristics and beliefs the whole time I acted for him. He always referred to me as "Mr Conditsis" although on more than one occasion, I invited him to call me by my first name.'

Among other things, Monis told Manny that he was a cleric in Iran, having studied under his father, a highly respected cleric. Monis claimed that he fled Iran in the mid-1990s because he feared for his life at the hands of the Iranian regime. Monis later said he had carried out 'covert' work for the Iranian Secret Service under threat of his life. Manny's new client said he loved Australia and its people but the Australian Government was corrupt 'and would do anything it was directed to do by America'. Monis told Manny he had been a peace activist since his teen years, and criticised Australia's involvement in 'unjust wars'. Monis used this view to justify writing the letters.

The letters were clearly offensive to the families involved, but Monis claimed they were intended to gain their support while they mourned their loved ones. 'He didn't believe that the families were truly offended by the letters ("How could they be offended? Look at the letters. What part of what I said could have offended them?" he often said) and that they were put up to it by the military/police/government,' Manny says. 'He had no intention of pleading guilty to writing offensive letters, because he contended that he never intended for the families to be offended and he doubted they were, in fact, offended. He considered that jail would be a small price to pay for taking a stand and fighting these unjust wars, and said he was not afraid of going to jail because if that's what happened, then it would have been God's will.'

Monis had surprisingly good English, but at times appeared to lack comprehension of certain words and phrases. 'It appeared to me that he was quite intelligent and had a reasonable understanding of the law in respect of the postal charges and the High Court decision in "rejecting" his appeal,' Manny says. He agreed to act for Monis with regard to the charges related to writing letters to the families of deceased Australian soldiers, on the basis of a legal aid grant. Monis already had a grant from the Legal Aid Commission before Manny was retained. The terms of the Legal Aid grant in effect offer payment of about 30 per cent of the usual private costs of a lawyer with Manny's extensive experience. Monis qualified for legal aid as he was an Australian citizen and was receiving Centrelink benefits.

One of the conditions of Manny's retainer was that Monis refrain from chaining himself outside courts as he had done in the past. Monis agreed and kept his word. At this point, Manny believed his client was misunderstood and his intention in fighting 'unjust wars', while misguided, was, on balance, good. 'But he was so driven by his cause that he could not see or allow himself to see that his letters and their timing would cause offence to the families,' he adds.

Over time, Manny tried to get Monis to understand and accept that his letters would have offended the families, but Monis never acknowledged this before his sentence hearing. 'He would never directly answer the question as to whether he himself would be offended if he was in the position of the families and would go on to refer to each letter, word by word, sentence by sentence, and attempt to explain to me that they were not offensive,' Manny says. 'Monis said on numerous occasions that, it's not an excuse for a soldier simply to say, "I am following instructions" to absolve that solder of criminal responsibility. Monis would refer to the Nazi regime and Hitler's instructions to massacre the Jewish people, and that those soldiers could not be excused from responsibility simply because they followed instructions.'

Monis repeatedly insisted his letters were 'bouquets of flowers', which led Manny to believe that some of the objectively offensive comments may have been lost (to Monis) in the translation. There was no such thing as a casual or easy conversation with Man Monis. He and Manny rarely discussed personal matters or used small talk. Whenever Manny raised the issue of the letters causing offence, Monis doggedly defended himself, which became tiresome and draining. Attempting to persuade his client to plead guilty was 'exhausting'. 'I rationalised the apparent lack of empathy by Monis towards the families as his inability to look past his own obsessed cause (lobbying against unjust wars),' Manny says.

Manny tried hard to understand and empathise with his client. This was tested in the lead-up to the letters trial when Monis repeatedly refused to plead guilty or agree to facts, including that he had intended to cause offence. Eventually, he agreed to plead guilty but refused to apologise or to express remorse during the sentence hearing. 'In my view, and with the benefit of hindsight, his reluctance to acknowledge intent to cause offence may have reflected a delusional belief or personality disorder,' Manny says. 'That is, he could not bring himself to acknowledge that he intended to cause offence by his letters, because he would not have liked such a person; and he believed he was or wanted to be seen as a good person with good motives.'

Monis was full of contradictions. He claimed to be a peace activist but could not acknowledge that his war letters were offensive. He identified as a cleric but hung out with a bikie gang. When Manny challenged Monis about this, he said, 'I like to ride bikes in a group. They never do anything wrong in front of me and they allow me to pray.' Monis also criticised Manny for ordering a glass of red wine when he himself was a smoker. When Manny suggested that Monis was being hypocritical and asked him why he smoked, Monis laughed it off and appeared to acknowledge silently that he did not have an adequate response.

By the time the postal charges trial started in late June 2013, Manny was exhausted by Monis's fluctuating instructions relating to plea negotiations with the Crown. They varied from supporting the Crown's proposed 'agreed facts', to disagreeing and seeking last-minute changes. Throughout, Monis remained relatively calm but was occasionally 'effusive and quite assertive' if the Crown didn't agree with what he proposed. 'I found the process of getting Monis to the point of pleading guilty draining and exhausting,' Manny says.

Even when he did admit guilt, Monis insisted that Manny not make any submission to the court about contrition. The lawyer advised his client to seek an adjournment to allow for a report from a psychiatrist or psychologist, but Monis would not allow himself to be assessed by either, even when told a good report would be favourable for him in the sentencing process. He refused to say sorry just to get a better sentence, as he said it would not appear genuine and he said he planned to apologise to the families afterwards. That way, he explained, they would know he was sincere. Manny had not been instructed like this before, and at the time found it 'refreshing' as most clients would simply have expressed insincere regret just to get a better sentence. But was it genuine regret or just another opportunity for Monis to become the focus of attention?

As the criminal charges surrounding the murder of his first Australian wife loomed, Monis again denied any wrongdoing and accused police of being 'out to get him'. His wife, Amirah Droudis, was charged with, and later convicted of, the actual murder. Manny represented Monis, who was charged with being an accessory before the fact. His reduced fees for the bail application were paid by the family of Amirah Droudis, not by Monis. As the murder investigation began to take up more of his time, Manny complained about Monis's increasing demands and told his client he could not continue to represent him on these terms after the bail hearing finished. Leading up to Monis being charged as an accessory, Manny was representing him in relation to the police murder investigation. As Monis had not at that stage been charged, Legal Aid would not give a grant and, as Monis didn't have the money to pay, Manny generously did not charge Monis for that work.

Monis did not appear to care that he was taking advantage of his lawyer, and at no stage showed empathy for his ex-wife and the vicious way she was murdered. Nor did he show any feelings or concerns about his children being left without a mother, whom he ordered killed because he said she had wronged him and 'deserved God's vengeance'. After he was charged, Monis spent time on remand and complained bitterly about his treatment in prison. Manny had never seen him in such an emotional and physical state. 'It appeared to me that he was completely broken,' he says. 'He began to cry and sob uncontrollably, with "snot" running out of his nose. It took quite some minutes for Monis to compose himself. I was taken aback because I would never have anticipated that I would ever see Monis in such a state.'

Manny believes the prison experience may have changed Monis and instilled in him a hatred for authorities that he had not felt previously. 'To him, such mistreatment would have been most unjust and personal, and fitted his perception that he was being victimised by authorities, leading him to even greater isolation,' Manny says. At the bail hearing, Manny was infuriated when his client suddenly yelled out, 'I am guilty, Your Honour.' As it turned out, he was referring to stealing some food while in prison due to the authorities allegedly not feeding him breakfast.

'This behaviour by Monis was typically attention-seeking and overly dramatic,' Manny says. 'It's fair to say I was furious with him. By the time the bail hearing was over, I was completely drained and exhausted, and my wife counselled me (and I agreed) that if I continued to act for Monis, it would adversely affect my health. I agreed and formed the view that I could not give my best to Monis and that in those circumstances I should cease to act for him. Additionally, I was aware that Monis could not continue to retain me on a privately funded basis, and the brief which had just been served in early January 2014 was particularly voluminous and stood about one metre high with something like thirty or so discs.'

In April 2014, Monis was charged with three counts of sexual assault relating to his time as a supposed 'spiritual healer' and bailed. In October, police charged him via a Court Attendance Notice with another 37 counts of sexual or indecent assault. Most were allegedly committed between 2002 and 2010. After many battles with Australian authorities and the legal system, the net appeared to finally be closing on Man Monis. His life appeared to be imploding. His carefully crafted public image had collapsed and he was likely to face a lengthy jail term over the criminal charges he faced. It was at this point that Monis decided to respond in the most dramatic way possible.

The siege and aftermath

Despite the seriousness of the sexual assault charges he was facing, Man Haron Monis was free in December 2014 when he terrorised central Sydney and sought international media coverage to highlight his so-called plight. At 8.33 am on 15 December, Monis walked into the Lindt café on the corner of Martin Place and Phillip Street, in the heart of Sydney's CBD, with a sawn-off pump-action shotgun. He took eighteen customers and staff hostage, ordered them to fly an Islamic State flag in the window and claimed Australia was under threat from Islamic State. After a seventeen-hour stand-off with police, the siege ended in a hail of gunfire. Just after 2 am, Monis started firing shots and killed café manager Tori Johnson, 34. Police then stormed the shop, killing Monis. Café patron and lawyer Katrina Dawson, 38, was killed in the crossfire. Several other hostages were injured.

Those present described Monis's behaviour as increasingly desperate as it became clear that things were not going to end peacefully or on his terms. He appeared to have no clear plan and made random threats to police and his hostages that made little sense. He also falsely claimed to have bombs, frustrating police who were already struggling to deal with the situation and find a solution to the stand-off.

Tori and Katrina's deaths were a tragic end to a terrifying and ultimately pointless situation. But Monis revelled in the worldwide media attention that it brought him, and knew the power of linking his actions to terrorist groups at a time when terrorism had people on edge globally. Following his death, his many secrets began to emerge, and after manipulating others for most of his life, he suffered the ultimate indignity of being disowned by almost everyone who knew him. Muslim funeral directors even refused to handle his body.

More details were revealed when the Lindt café was the subject of a high-profile inquest and a 79-page report, *The Martin Place Siege: Joint Commonwealth – New South Wales Review* (January 2015). In May 2017, the State Coroner of New South Wales's findings were published in the 472-page *Inquest into the Deaths Arising from the Lindt Café Siege: Findings and Recommendations*. It contained a frightening insight into the life of Man Monis, describing him as 'a mysterious and macabre individual who went from shunning attention to actively seeking it – from actions so secretive that not even his partners knew about them to outlandish public stunts in full view of television cameras'. The Coroner concluded that Monis was not psychotic when he took his hostages: 'Monis undertook the siege in a controlled, planned and quite methodical manner marked by deliberation and choice,' the Coroner found. 'He was not suffering from a diagnosable categorical psychiatric disorder that deprived him of the capacity to understand the nature of what he was doing. The evidence does not support a finding that Monis entered the Lindt café with the express intention of killing some or all of the hostages. However, in light of his psychopathology, I conclude that he fully understood that the death of hostages was a real possibility, and that the prospect of such an outcome was of no concern to him' (State Coroner of NSW, inquest report, 2017).

Manny Conditsis was horrified when he discovered that his former client was involved in the siege. He called police and offered to provide information to negotiators or talk to him, as he believed Monis had respected him in the past. That didn't happen. As the siege wore on, Manny believed there was no way Monis would go back to prison and that Monis knew that if he was arrested, regardless of what happened inside the Lindt café, he faced a lengthy period behind bars. Manny also perceived that Monis probably also considered the siege to be his last chance to gain the media attention he craved to draw attention to his 'supposed' cause. 'The Monis I believed I knew would not have killed anybody let alone shoot someone in cold blood,' Manny says. 'Not once did Monis speak to me about committing violence of any description. He regularly referred to himself as a peace activist and would say, "Look at my website." Based on what I knew of him, I was confident that Monis was acting alone [in the Lindt siege] and that for him to do what he did, he must have become mentally unhinged, and what may have contributed to it is his potential belief that it was inevitable that he would go back to prison. From all that I knew of Monis, other than his partner, I considered him to be, pretty much, a loner.'

Since the siege, Manny has wondered many times whether, had he been able to speak to Monis during the siege, it might have made a difference. 'I do not have delusions of grandeur,' he says. 'I simply wonder whether it was a lost opportunity.' It later become clear that Monis was irrational, narcissistic, psychopathic and paranoid. But at the time, those who had contact with him did not realise what he was capable of. Over the year during which Manny represented him, it never occurred to him that his client might be a narcissist. Monis struck him as conflicted, but by the same token he appeared sincere, passionate and committed to his causes. Upon reflection, however, following the siege, Manny changed his mind. 'Having read parts of a book on narcissism over the recent Christmas break [2014–15, after the siege], and reflecting on Monis's behaviour and conduct whilst I represented him, I believe Monis was indeed a narcissist,' Manny said in his 27-page police statement on the Lindt café siege. 'He sought, if not craved attention, particularly media attention; he always had to be right; he did not take criticism well; he had an excessive and unhealthy ego; and everyone else was wrong.'

Why did he do it?

Even before Man Monis arrived in Australia, his character was suspect and some wonder why he was allowed into the country. Monis was born Mohammad Hassan Manteghi on 19 May 1964, in Borujerd, Iran. Borujerd is in Lorestan Province, 390 kilometres south-west of Tehran. He was the youngest child of Zahra Bahmani and Mohammad Hassan Manteghi, had five older sisters and was raised as a Shiite Muslim. His father died when he was a teenager and they lived in a poor part of town.

An average student at best, Monis finished high school in Tehran and attended Imam Sadegh University, the training ground of many prominent Iranian officials. In 1983, while studying, he met and married his first wife, Zahra Mobasheri, whose father, Habibollah Mobasheri, was general secretary and deputy to the founder and president of the university. This gave Monis access to senior clerics. After graduating, he attended Abdol Azim College of Hadith Sciences, a theological academy attached to a Shiite shrine in southern Tehran. Zahra had their first daughter in 1986 and their second in 1995.

Monis later claimed that in the late 1980s he started corresponding with the leader of the Ahmadi sect of Islam in London. An offshoot of Sunni Islam, its members are regarded as heretics by both Sunnis and Shiites. Monis claimed to have secretly joined the sect, and later used this claim in his application for refugee status in Australia. In 1994, he was accepted as a hojatoleslam, or 'authority on Islam', a Shiite teacher who ranks below an ayatollah. He later dishonestly used the title 'Ayatollah' in Australia.

In 1994 and 1995, Monis founded four companies and allegedly used his connections to illicitly obtain government-owned tyres and textiles that he sold for profit, falsely claiming some of the profits would go to charity. He often name-dropped about high-ranking officials he knew, and lived in a luxury apartment near Imam Sadegh University in a gated street with other university officials. Monis did appear to have some influence. A friend later told investigators that after he dislocated his shoulder, Monis paid for him to take a taxi to and be treated in an expensive private hospital.

Monis later claimed that before migrating to Australia, he travelled to countries like Romania and Malaysia, where he was interviewed by US agents. He also claimed that he had visited CIA headquarters in the United States. In 1996, while still a director of his four companies, Monis managed the Rahelenoor Tour and Travel Agency, which was owned by influential reformist politician Rasul Montajabnia. Monis allegedly ripped off wealthy families who wanted to leave Iran to the tune of AU$550,000. He then left the country himself, leaving Mr Montajabnia to take responsibility for the scam and failing to tell his boss or his wife about his intentions.

Not only was he a fraud, Monis was a serial womaniser. In Australia he had long-term relationships with four women, two of whom he married. He met all four through his spiritual healing business, and was often seeing two or three women at once. Monis married his first Australian wife, with whom he had two sons, in 2003 while he was still married to his Iranian wife, Zahra. Zahra divorced him in absentia in 2006, around the time his Australian-born wife also dumped him. The Australian divorce papers claimed he only spent two or three nights a week at home and would not say where he spent the other nights. Monis spent very little time with his sons and did not support the family financially. He initially fought for custody, but ended up only with access every second Sunday.

Meanwhile, Monis had an ongoing relationship with yet another woman, Irene Mishra, for nine years. She knew him as Michael Hayson. While still married to his first Australian wife, Monis shared an apartment with Irene in Wentworthville and told her family he was an Egyptian who worked as a spiritualist. Irene eventually converted from Hinduism to Islam, contributed $3000 towards her partner's Laro motorbike and took out two car loans for him.

Irene died of natural causes in 2012. From January to July 2003, while Monis was preparing to marry his first Australian wife and was also seeing Irene, he had courted yet another young woman, Amanda Morsy. Amanda broke off the relationship because she felt uncomfortable around him. While with Amanda, Monis was not religious at all. He drank alcohol, did not wear religious robes and never suggested that he was a cleric.

Monis met his third and final wife, Anastasia Droudis, in 2003 and they became a couple in 2006. She was with him until he died. In 2008, the year they married, Anastasia converted from Greek Orthodox to Muslim and changed her name to Amirah. Monis had tried to reconcile with his first Australian wife not long before he convinced Amirah to murder her in 2013. Around that time, he also tried to join the Mt Druitt and Ingleburn chapters of the Rebels bikie gang. While its members refused to give evidence at the siege inquest, one reportedly said no one liked him because he was 'weird'.

While Monis saw many health professionals, including ten different GPs and mental health clinicians between May 2009 and September 2011, complaining of dizziness, weakness in his leg, shaking and pain all over his body, he had no diagnosable physical ailment. One doctor made a provisional diagnosis of delusional disorder, but this was never followed up. Another diagnosed him with schizophrenia, but noted he was high-functioning. There appears to be no reliable evidence that he suffered from schizophrenia.

Psychiatrist Jonathan Phillips told the Lindt café siege inquest that Monis was not mentally ill. He explained that a complex personality disorder caused him to behave in a deceitful, antisocial and manipulative way. As a result, Monis had adopted violent extremism as a means of self-aggrandisement. Dr Phillips concluded that he had 'a severe longstanding complex personality disorder with antisocial and narcissistic features and some paranoid features. He did not have impaired judgement and was capable of choice and deliberation in his actions.'

Dr Phillips found that Monis had for many years led 'a secretive, self-serving life', that he was 'driven at all times by his own idiosyncratic desires' and that he lacked 'any sense of understanding of the sensitivities of others'. These views were consistent with those of other health clinicians, who concluded he was a manipulative, narcissistic criminal. 'When he initiated the siege, Monis was a narcissist, a man with exaggerated ideas of his own importance and a strong sense of entitlement,' the Coroner found. 'He was antisocial, manipulative and deceitful, with little or no capacity for empathy, and had experienced episodic delusions of persecution' (State Coroner of NSW, inquest report, 2017).

The most likely explanation for Monis's behaviour is that he had an NPD. Specifically, he fitted into the subtype 'malignant narcissism', which as we have seen is a behaviour syndrome combining some of the features of an NPD and an ASPD (see pages 139–44). Someone with an NPD usually displays a pervasive pattern of grandiosity, a constant need for attention and admiration, and a lack of empathy. Monis ticked all those boxes and more. A person with malignant narcissism also displays antisocial features, dishonesty, paranoid traits and aggression. They usually lack a conscience, have little empathy for other people, crave power and attention, and have a grossly inflated sense of their own importance. As time went on, all these traits worsened in Monis to the point where he was prepared to incite and commit murder and place the lives of others at great risk. Individuals like Monis are among society's most dangerous people and should be avoided at all costs.

As a practised narcissist, Monis talked his way into Australia when he first arrived. Those with NPD can turn on the charm when it suits, making it difficult to resist their arguments. Monis told immigration authorities what he thought they wanted to hear, often embellishing the truth or making up the facts as he went along. Many of his stories were contradictory, but that would not have stopped him saying or doing what it took to promote his own interests. Once here, Monis worked the system to his advantage wherever possible. He used the court system, received Centrelink benefits, promoted himself in the media and used the internet to mislead people about his abilities and 'dog whistle' those he considered to be his followers. Nothing was off limits in his quest to paint himself as some sort of messiah (State Coroner of NSW, inquest report, 2017).

Monis was entirely opportunistic, moulding his personality to suit what he thought would elevate his standing in the community, improve his social status and secure him easy money. He changed his name and his religious status several times to suit his current situation. In fact, everything he did was designed to suit his needs, usually at the expense of others. The deception and related actions worsened, probably after Monis realised how easy it was for him to manipulate the vulnerable. He used his self-proclaimed position as a 'clairvoyant' and 'spiritual healer/counsellor' to sexually abuse women and take their money for what was clearly a phony service. To Monis, these gullible people were 'suckers' asking to be taken advantage of. He would have felt no guilt when he deceitfully took their money, despite having no qualifications in astrology, numerology, meditation, counselling or spiritual healing. At one point, Monis had managed to hook in 500 clients and was making up to $125,000 a year from them.

One advertisement he placed in local ethnic newspapers asked potential clients if they wanted to know about the future of their love and career. 'Is the time running out on you and are you still single? Are you wondering why you are unable to have successful relationship [sic]?' The ad offered 'strictly private and confidential' spiritual consultation by an 'expert of relationship', using astrology, numerology, meditation and spiritual health. It also asked, 'Do you want to know about your partner? Are you wondering if your partner loves you truly? . . . Do you need to check whether he/she is your right partner for marriage? Do you like him/her to come back? Do you want to clean the evil spirit and improve your spiritual life?' (State Coroner of NSW, inquest report, 2017).

After consulting with some of his female clients, Monis allegedly told them they needed to undress, at least partially and often completely, in order for him to treat them. He then indecently and sexually assaulted them. Experts said it was highly likely that if Monis had lived he would have been convicted and jailed over these offences.

Monis also solicited loans from people who were impressed by his so-called religious status, and he no doubt felt entitled to whatever anyone bestowed upon him. Between 1998 and 2013, acquaintances gave Monis a total of $30,000. In April 2014, he was charged with 40 indecent and sexual assault offences against poorly educated and impressionable people, particularly women and those who believed in black magic or thought they were cursed (State Coroner of NSW, inquest report, 2017).

Just as he didn't feel guilty about ripping people off, Monis felt justified when he wrote highly offensive letters to the families of deceased Australian soldiers. They were merely pawns in the games he played to draw attention to himself and make himself feel superior to others. His was the worst kind of narcissism; it knew no bounds. Some people with an NPD may have a degree of self-awareness about how their extreme actions can hurt others. In this case, even if the perpetrator was aware, he didn't care. Perhaps fuelled by his success in manipulating vulnerable people and attracting some media attention through his court protests, Monis's behaviour became even more selfish and damaging to others. He made unfair demands of his lawyers, used legal aid and did everything he could to avoid paying any other fees – even when they were warranted. To him, his lawyers were there to serve him, and he had no qualms about trying to take advantage of them too.

Things escalated when Monis manipulated his partner into killing his first Australian wife, without giving a thought to the consequences for the person he had asked to murder her or how this would hurt his two younger children, who lived with his first wife (their mother). It takes a special kind of callousness and lack of empathy to organise the murder of the mother of your children by someone you profess to care for. Monis knew that Amirah Droudis was risking life in jail to carry out his dirty work. Rather than feel guilt, he saw it as a masterstroke. Not only did he get rid of his ex-wife, but he would not be implicated because he wasn't there. Monis must have been extremely persuasive to get Droudis to do something so wrong on so many levels. Such can be the power of a malignant narcissist.

With each 'success', Monis became more emboldened. Some of his actions were laughable, such as trying to join a bikie gang, but in his mind, he believed that he could be whatever he wanted and that others would admire his inevitable prowess, importance and popularity. For once this did not work, as the bikies, who were more streetwise than his other victims, shunned him when they decided he was 'weird'. They quickly saw through his charade and knew he was nothing but a 'try-hard'. A narcissist's misplaced belief that they are on a pedestal at which others must worship can prove to be their downfall, as they don't have the empathy to realise that some more astute or experienced people are able to see through their blatant self-promotion. The bikies instinctively knew that he was a fake.

Undeterred, Monis fashioned himself as an insider on terror-related issues, telling intelligence agencies that he had important information about terror plots and making wild claims, including that the 2009 Victorian bushfires were a terrorist act. His need to feel important and admired drove him to continually reinvent himself into what he thought would gain him the most attention and admiration. At a time when people worried about potential terror attacks, Monis positioned himself as an expert and an 'insider' with access to those 'in the know'. The reality was, he made it all up. Unsurprisingly, authorities did not take him seriously, but, unfortunately, neither did they see him as the threat to public safety he actually was.

In the lead-up to the Lindt café siege, some of his worst offences started to catch up with this serial manipulator, and he faced charges over the alleged sexual assaults and being an accessory to murder of his first Australian wife. As it became clear that he could not use his so-called charm to get away with these crimes, Monis grew more desperate. He had spent time in jail and hated it. The thought of returning for a long stint horrified him, so he hatched a plan to take hostages in the name of official terrorist groups.

It was a no-win idea that would almost certainly end in the deaths of himself and others. None of this mattered to Man Haron Monis. In his mind, he would die a martyr for his supposed cause and be revered by those left behind as a brave warrior. If he had to go, he'd go in a style befitting what he saw as his status. The Lindt siege, therefore, was indeed an 'act of terror' but not directly linked to a terror organisation. It was the work of a vicious and narcissistic man who could not stand the thought of being held to account for his disgraceful and murderous conduct. Those with malignant narcissism will do anything to preserve their so-called status, and this was Monis's way of saving face.

His actions were also those of a man who could never admit he was wrong. Instead of defending the criminal charges against him, Monis chose to terrorise innocent people by holding them hostage, knowing it would be global news due to the media's fixation on terrorism, and knowing that at least some people, including him, were likely to die. In the end, Monis made sure of it, killing café manager Tori Johnson before police were able to kill him. The siege was an extension of Monis's attention-seeking behaviour of many years, and was designed to have maximum impact without regard to who was hurt. These were the actions of the worst kind of malignant narcissist, one who was prepared to murder in an attempt to inflate their own importance. In the end, Man Haron Monis failed on all counts, as police and coronial investigations revealed that he was in fact no more than a cowardly fraud who manipulated and used people for his own aggrandisement.

CHAPTER 5

MEGAN HAINES

The cast

Megan Haines: A nurse who killed two elderly nursing home residents after they complained about her nursing conduct

Haines's children: Haines had a daughter in her native South Africa and two more children in Australia

Isabella Spencer: Aged 77, died after Megan Haines injected her with insulin

Marie Darragh: Aged 82, died after Haines injected her with insulin

Wendy Turner: St Andrews Director of Care

The motive

Megan Haines killed elderly nursing home residents Isabella Spencer and Marie Darragh after they complained about her nursing conduct. Haines injected them with insulin they did not need, to try to make it look like they died of natural causes.

Introduction

Nurses are supposed to be caring and always put their patients first. Most do, and the profession has long been a bastion of honesty and dedication. A 2017 Roy Morgan survey found nurses topped the most trusted profession list for the 23rd year running, ahead of doctors, pharmacists, schoolteachers, engineers, dentists and police. Nurses were rated 'high' or 'very high' for ethics and honesty by 94 per cent of respondents.

Megan Haines was not one of them. As a nurse, she had a chequered history and had already been disciplined several times for bad behaviour on the job when working in Victoria. When Haines moved from Victoria to New South Wales and secured another nursing home position, she had a record of complaints against her for maltreating the nursing home patients she cared for. Haines cared about no one except herself and was prepared to kill to protect her own self-interest.

When her job was at risk due to her own bad behaviour, Haines chose to kill two elderly nursing home patients who had lodged complaints about her. It was the culmination of years of self-centred behaviour that saw this selfish and dangerous woman put herself before others after arriving from her native South Africa, where she grew up during the Apartheid regime. Haines's mother was white and her father of Indian background. She later claimed that her father was violent and sexually abused her mother and one of her sisters. Her parents separated when she was six, and Haines and her two sisters lived with her mother. She has had little contact with her father since.

As a person of mixed race, Haines says her mother rejected her and favoured her sisters as they were white and her skin was darker. She had trouble making friends at high school, where she claimed the other students didn't understand people of mixed race. Haines qualified and worked as a registered nurse in South

Africa, but due to its high crime rate and lack of work flexibility she migrated to Australia in December 2000. Initially she settled in Victoria with her eldest child, who turned 25 in 2016. Haines had several casual relationships and gave birth to two more children who had different fathers. They were aged sixteen and six in 2016. Their mother remained close to her eldest child, but the younger children live with a man she met in Australia and she has no contact with them.

The lead-up to the crime

In 2001, Haines began working as a registered nurse in Victoria. During her time employed in an eastern suburbs hospital, five complaints were reportedly made against her in December 2005. These included that she had pushed an elderly patient over and grabbed a phone from a doctor when the doctor told Haines that she was going to complain about her to the nursing supervisor.

Two years later, while working in a Melbourne nursing home, Haines was reportedly accused of repeatedly punching an elderly woman in the arm and was heard arguing with a senior staff member when questioned over the matter. In May 2007, she was again found guilty of professional misconduct and reprimanded. In 2008, Haines's nursing registration was suspended following allegations that she had wrongly injected two of her elderly patients with insulin on two occasions while working at a medical centre in Melbourne. She was also reportedly suspected of stealing some of their jewellery while they were affected by the insulin, but this was never proven despite some convincing evidence.

In December 2011, Haines was again found guilty of professional misconduct. This time she was reprimanded and ordered to supply 'satisfactory employer reports' every three months to the relevant health authorities. She allowed her registration to lapse for some time and then reapplied. The Australian Health Practitioners Regulation Agency (AHPRA) reinstated her licence to practice in 2012. In April 2013, her conditions were amended so that she only had to supply satisfactory employer reports every six months. Haines later claimed that the initial complaints against her were a result of her lack of sleep as a single mother. She also claimed that she was lonely and in the throes of several casual relationships and as a result she had spent much of her thirties drinking before, during and after work. She was not diagnosed with any mental health conditions.

Despite her poor work record, Haines found a job at St Andrews residential aged-care facility in Ballina, New South Wales, where she started on 13 March 2014. She was still subject to the reporting conditions imposed by the AHPRA and was initially supervised during shifts, but was soon rostered to work night shifts from 10.15 pm to 6.30 am. Five people staffed those shifts, including two care-service employees in the hostel area. The Boronia ward, which housed high-care dementia patients, had one care-service employee, as did the high-care Dianella ward. Care-service employees are not trained nurses, but they can provide support with social activities, physical support, help with bathing and assistance with meals. They are usually required to have a qualification in aged care or community care.

A registered nurse was based in the Dianella ward for most of the night, and was responsible for all the facility's residents. Care-service employees were not authorised to or responsible for administering medication in the Boronia or Dianella wards. They could administer some routine prescription medications in the hostel area. Security was relatively tight. No one could enter the facility after 5 pm unless they had a swipe card or the duty registered nurse let them in after viewing them through a video camera. Staff used personal swipe cards to access various sections depending on their role, and a security company conducted random checks of the facility overnight.

Among the Dianella ward residents was Isabella Spencer. In December 2013, soon after she turned 77, Isabella had a stroke that left her paralysed down her left side. She moved to St Andrews, where she lived in Room 4 of the Dianella 1 ward. Isabella was mentally sharp, but her physical impairment meant she was mostly confined to bed. If she wanted to move around, staff had to help. Marie Darragh had moved to St Andrews in February 2011, and lived in Room 10. Marie turned 82 in September 2013, and had complex heath issues, but like Isabella was cognitively aware. Neither Isabella nor Marie was insulin-dependent.

The murders

At about 11.15 pm on 9 May 2014, St Andrews Director of Care Wendy Turner met Haines to tell her that three residents had complained about her. Wendy told Haines that they included Marie Darragh and another woman, and gave her a letter inviting her to a meeting the following Tuesday to discuss the complaints. The letter outlined the issues raised and said the alleged behaviour breached Haines's employment terms, as well as professional practice standards. If proven, the allegations could result in disciplinary action.

Marie had complained that when she asked for cream to treat an itchy condition, Haines had refused and made rude and inappropriate comments. Another resident had reported that while Haines was helping her into bed after she used the bathroom, Haines had lifted her roughly, hurt her ankle and been rude to her. Wendy had noted, however, that the ankle did not appear injured, so this complaint was not as serious. The third complainant accused Haines of being rude and refusing to help when she needed to go to the toilet. Wendy did not name this person, but enough was implied for Haines to work out that it was Isabella Spencer.

Turner reminded Haines of the 'current reporting conditions' on her nursing registration and told her she was not to approach Marie or the second complainant to discuss the complaints. Nor was she to enter their rooms to provide treatment unless accompanied by another staff member. After the meeting, as was usual, Haines was alone in the Dianella ward for two periods of one hour, from midnight to 1 am and then again from 4 am to 5 am, while care-service staff conducted rounds in the Boronia ward. Haines was the only employee with a swipe card that could access medication rooms for both the Dianella and Boronia wards. The hostel area's medication room had a four-digit code, which was known to care-service employees.

Haines had plenty of time to stew over the meeting and was no doubt worried about the complaints. Her past record was not good, which could make it difficult to convince others of her innocence. Sometime between midnight and 1 am, Haines entered the Dianella medication room and took two syringes, filling them with Mixtard 30/70 insulin. She injected Isabella and Marie with up to 300 units each, enough to kill them. Both entered hypoglycaemic comas.

Haines actively prevented her colleagues from discovering that the elderly residents' lives were in danger, coldly guaranteeing that her victims would die. At about 1 am, after she had injected the women, Haines and a care-service colleague conducted a round in the Dianella ward. As they passed Isabella's room, she told her colleague that the elderly resident did not need any attention. Marie's room was not usually visited, so no one noticed she had been injected.

At 3.15 am, Haines disposed of the empty vials in the hostel area when she administered medication to a resident there.

During the next round in Dianella, between 4 am and 5 am, Haines again went to Isabella's room and told her colleague that the occupant was okay. This meant no one else went to the room or checked on her. When Haines knocked off at about 6.30 am, she did not report anything out of the ordinary in her handover, despite knowing that both women were almost certainly in hypoglycaemic comas, which can lead to irreversible brain damage and death if left untreated.

When morning-shift staff tried to wake Marie at about 6.50 am, she appeared to be in a deep coma. Palliative care was provided and she died at about 11.30 am. Staff tried unsuccessfully to rouse Isabella for breakfast at about 7.30 am, but she died at about 11.50 am. On 15 May, police searched Haines's home and told her they were investigating Isabella and Marie's unexpected and suspicious deaths. They didn't tell her anything else. That morning, the suspected killer called a friend to say the women had died because they were given the wrong medication.

The trials

Following her arrest in Victoria on 7 July 2014, Haines was extradited to New South Wales. She was arraigned in the NSW Supreme Court on 6 May 2016. The trial started in Lismore on Monday, 10 October 2016, but after the jury was empanelled it emerged that one of them had a grandmother living at St Andrews. Justice Peter Garling dismissed the jury. When another jury panel was summonsed on the Wednesday, fifteen panel-in-waiting members applied to be discharged and twelve were granted. Some of them knew one or more witnesses or the medical experts who would be giving evidence. Others worked for, or did business with, the family company of one of the victims. Once all five challenges had been exercised, there were not enough spare jurors-in-waiting, so Justice Garling moved the trial to Sydney.

When the trial finally started in Sydney on 17 October 2016, Haines pleaded not guilty to both counts of murder. She never admitted to her crime, but the court heard about her boast, when watching a crime show on television with her former partner, that it would be easy to kill someone with insulin. She claimed she could not remember that conversation. On 3 November 2016, the jury found Megan Haines guilty on both murder counts. In sentencing her on 16 December 2016, Justice Garling found the crimes to be 'particularly serious'. 'Each of the victims was vulnerable because of their advanced years, limited mobility, and limited capacity to detect what was happening and to take measures to defend themselves,' he said.

'Further, the offender was in a position of significant trust with respect to each victim. She was the registered nurse in charge of the whole complex whose obligation and duty it was to care for the two victims, to promote their health and well-being, and to ensure their safety. Her conduct was deliberate and calculated. It was a gross breach of trust, and a flagrant abuse of her power. The offender's motive to kill, namely that the victims had made complaints about her, was wholly insufficient and self-centred' (*R v Haines* [No. 3] [2016] NSWSC 1812).

Haines clearly thought her murder method would be undetectable, and that the deaths would appear to be from natural causes, and this was initially the case. Justice Garling noted several aggravating factors. The murders were committed in the women's homes, where they were entitled to feel safe, and Haines had authority over her victims, who had been entrusted into her care. She clearly abused this trust and exploited their physical vulnerability.

The Crown claimed that the case fell into the worst possible category of seriousness and warranted a life sentence. But Justice Garling said that while they were 'very serious' and there was some degree of deliberation and planning involved, the murders did not warrant the maximum term. Nor did either of the victims endure prolonged pain or suffering. He found Haines was unlikely to reoffend because she would be an old woman upon release. But she had not admitted to her crimes or expressed any insight into her behaviour. Nor had she shown any remorse, or tried to rehabilitate herself while in custody.

Justice Garling found that while the offences were not planned or organised, they were deliberate and calculated. He stated that the women's complaints were in no way an excuse. The only mitigating factors were that the offender's previous criminal record only involved a minor charge of possession of cannabis, and the defence team agreed on certain facts that reduced the number of witnesses that needed to be called. Haines's stepfather said in a statement tendered to the sentencing that her natural father had abused her and her two sisters when they were young, which could have had an adverse psychological effect on her later in life. But Haines did not submit a report from a psychologist or psychiatrist outlining any diagnosable mental condition.

'In my view, the offender's decision to administer insulin – a medication which is ordinarily meant to promote good health – in a way which was toxic and deadly and in the setting of a facility which provides care for older citizens, is conduct which is almost too awful to contemplate,' Justice Garling said. 'It demonstrates a complete lack of respect for human life, a failure to recognise the dignity and integrity of older citizens, and a complete abrogation of the tenets of the caring profession of nursing which underpins so much good in society. It is simply conduct which cannot be tolerated and which needs to be firmly denounced and deterred' (*R v Haines* [No. 3] [2016] NSWSC 1812).

Haines was sentenced to 30 years' jail for each murder, with a non-parole period of 22 years and six months. This was converted into an aggregate sentence with a non-parole period of 27 years starting on 7 July 2014, when she entered custody, and finishing 6 July 2041, with a balance term of nine years starting on 7 July 2041 and concluding on 6 July 2050. Haines will not be eligible for parole until 6 July 2041 (*R v Haines* [No. 3] [2016] NSWSC 1812).

Why did she do it?

Megan Haines is not a nice person. While only glimpses of her past were revealed in court, they painted a picture of a selfish, narcissistic and exploitive individual who put herself first and showed scant regard for anyone who didn't make life easy for her. When she had complaints laid against her about her nursing in Victoria, Haines blamed them on her lack of sleep as a single mother. The more likely scenario was that any excess exhaustion, which did not excuse her behaviour in any case, was due to a hedonistic lifestyle. As well as a chequered work history, Haines had a patchy record with men. Already a mother when she moved to Australia, she had two more children here to different fathers. Rather than put her children first, she spent much of her thirties in casual relationships and drinking before, during and after work.

This was a woman who, it seems, always put herself first and had no qualms about manipulating those she thought could help her, while 'paying back' anyone who dared to stand in her way at work or socially. In November 2016, Channel 7's *Sunday Night* spoke to Haines's former partner 'Richard' (not his real name), who described her as having no empathy and said she was the closest thing to evil he had come across. Richard also speculated that it might not be the first time Haines had silenced her elderly critics. He said as soon as he heard about the St Andrews murders he knew it would have been his ex-partner, as she was vindictive and knew no limits. When he was dating Haines in 2008, Richard says that she told him she knew how to commit the perfect murder. When he said that was impossible, she allegedly explained that if you inject someone with insulin, when the body dies it keeps assimilating it and leaves no trace of the drug.

When Richard asked Haines about a needle mark, she replied that if the perpetrator was any good no one would discover it and it would look like the victim had died of natural causes. *Sunday Night* reported that Haines was also accused of injecting two elderly patients with insulin at a medical centre in Melbourne in 2008. They survived, and Haines was never charged. Richard wondered how many times this had happened previously and found it difficult to understand how Haines was able to continue to work with elderly patients when she clearly saw elderly people as a complete waste and a burden on society (*Sunday Night*, 20 November 2016).

Haines was prepared to treat others as expendable because she has an NPD, and her behaviour is consistent with the malignant narcissism subtype, an extreme form of NPD with antisocial traits. As we have seen, someone with an NPD has an inflated view of their importance and wrongly thinks that they are smarter and worthier than those around them. Individuals whose behaviour fits into the malignant narcissism subtype are even more extreme and prepared to lie, steal, harm and break laws in their quest to retain their elevated view of themselves, also displaying some traits of an ASPD (see pages 336–7). Anyone who challenges their importance and superiority must be 'put in their place', and they are prepared to do whatever it takes. In Haines's case, it meant murdering two elderly women whose complaints were set to make life difficult for her.

Given her poor track record, those complaints probably would have resulted in Haines losing her job and facing further disciplinary action that may have included deregistration. Rather than fight the charges or make a genuine attempt to rehabilitate herself, she didn't think twice about what she believed was the perfect solution – eliminating the source of the complaints. If she murdered Isabella and Marie without arousing suspicion, she reasoned, their complaints might be dropped and her job would be safe. And as she had told Richard, her involvement would not be detected as the insulin would disappear from her victims' systems, making it the perfect crime indeed.

But Haines's personality disorder made her reckless and overconfident. Like most people with an NPD, especially those in the malignant narcissism subtype, Haines clearly lacks empathy and did not understand that others would be able see through her attempts to cover her tracks and act as if nothing was wrong when something clearly was. She chose to kill not one but two women who died in similar circumstances on the same morning, which was sure to arouse the suspicions of those who genuinely cared for them. Even if the insulin had disappeared from their systems, the timing of the deaths, the insulin missing from the medication room, the empty syringes and the fact that Haines had the motive, means and opportunity to use them were not going to escape the attention of astute investigators.

The victims' family members, the other professional staff who cared for the victims and the police who knew something about Haines's history quickly put two and two together and concluded that she had carried out a callous double homicide to protect herself. During the court hearings, Haines showed no emotional reaction as members of the victims' families described the grief and pain associated with losing their loved ones and their horror that someone who was supposed to care for them was the one who took their lives. She did, however, complain that she was being harassed in Silverwater jail by other prisoners who referred to her as 'The Granny Killer', and asked that something be done about it as she feared for her safety.

CHAPTER 6

ROBERT XIE

The cast

Lian Bin (Robert) Xie: The killer, who was 47 at the time of the murders
Kathy Lin: Xie's wife and sister of Min (below). Robert and Kathy had one son.
'Ms AB', name suppressed by the court: A teenage relative who was sexually abused by Xie both before and after the five murders
Yang Fei Lin and Feng Qing Zhu: Min and Kathy's parents; Robert Xie's parents-in-law

The victims

Min (Norman) Lin: Kathy's brother, who was 45 at the time of the murders
Yun Li (Lily) Lin: Min's wife, 44
Yun Bin (Irene) Lin: Lily's sister, 39
Henry Lin: Min and Lily's son, twelve
Terry Lin: Min and Lily's son, nine

Timeline

18 July 2009. Five members of the Lin family are killed in their home.
11 May 2011. Robert Xie is charged with the five murders.
9 May 2014. The first trial begins before Justice Peter Johnson, but the jury is discharged for legal reasons.
5 August 2014. The second trial begins, but is aborted when the judge falls ill.
February 2015. The third trial begins before Justice Elizabeth Fullerton.
1 December 2015. The jury in the third trial is discharged after failing to reach a verdict.
8 December 2015. Xie is released on bail.
29 June 2016. The fourth trial begins before Justice Elizabeth Fullerton.
23 December 2016. Xie's bail is revoked before the jury retires.
12 January 2017. Xie is found guilty of the five murders.
13 February 2017. Justice Fullerton sentences Xie to life in jail without parole.

The motive

Robert Xie killed five members of his family-by-marriage because he was jealous of the admiration and status that his parents-in-law bestowed upon his brother-in-law Min Lin, who was considered the number-one 'honoured son' due to his financial success and the respect he enjoyed within his local community. Xie, believing he was far more deserving of their respect and admiration, felt humiliated, resentful and embittered by the situation. Xie also put off committing his crime until a teenage relative (Ms AB) was overseas for a short time, so that when she returned she would inherit the family's wealth, over which he hoped to gain some control through having power of attorney. Xie also wanted access to this young relative so he could continue to abuse her sexually.

Introduction

What possesses a man to wipe out five members of his extended family? In some cases, the motive is as ordinary as the crime is shocking. Robert Xie killed five people – his brother-in-law Min Lin, 45; Min's wife Lily Lin, 44; their children Henry, twelve, and Terry, nine; and Lily's sister Irene Lin, 39 – because he was jealous of Min's status in the family as the favoured son and proprietor of a successful newsagency. Min was the brother of Xie's wife Kathy, and their parents, Yang Fei Lin and Feng Qing Zhu, did not appear to like or respect him. It later emerged that Xie most likely had an additional motive – his attraction to and ongoing sexual abuse of Ms AB, a young relative who was a teenager when the murders occurred.

Xie intentionally chose to kill the five family members when Ms AB was overseas on a school trip. This would give him access to her so that he could continue to sexually abuse her and gain some access to the family assets that she would inherit. Xie later reportedly used this power of attorney to evict Min and Kathy's parents from their house, which had been owned by Min and Lily Lin but specifically purchased to provide Yang and Feng with a home when they migrated to Australia. This was probably part of Xie's plan to ensure that Ms AB would not be able to live with them and would be forced to live with Xie and his immediate family. Greed also appears to have been a motive, as Xie later tried to take over Min and Lily's newsagency business.

The lead-up to the crime

Robert Xie's life was nowhere near as successful, either materially or emotionally, as Min Lin's, and it showed in the way he openly envied his brother-in-law and his successes. While Xie had claimed that he trained as an ear, nose and throat medical specialist in China, he also told people that he had been pushed into doing so by his mother and that he really wanted to be an engineer. He then supposedly quit his medical job and worked as a manager in a shoe factory before moving to Australia with his wife Kathy in 1999.

The couple ran a large buffet-style restaurant in Melbourne for several years, fighting unsuccessfully to bring three Chinese chefs to Australia and make it seem more up-market. Their son lived in Sydney with Kathy's parents during this time. After the restaurant failed and was sold in 2005, Xie and Kathy moved to Sydney, where Kathy worked in her brother Min's newsagency. Xie owned a unit and land in China, which gave him some income, but he did not work in paid employment, spending most of his time at home monitoring his small investment portfolio and stewing about what he perceived to be his humiliating situation. This resulted in his relatives seeing him as lazy and unmotivated. Xie did not appear to make any effort to gain new qualifications or employment, giving them reason to criticise him and adding to his bitterness and sense of injustice.

Xie believed he was more worthy than other family members, despite his seeming lack of motivation, hard work or success. He and Kathy lived with their son around the corner and about 300 metres away from Min, Lily and their children, including Henry and Terry. All were close to Min and Kathy's parents, Yang and Feng, and every Friday night the extended family would have dinner together at their house. Henry enjoyed playing badminton with his uncle Robert. They appeared to be a happy group, but Xie was clearly harbouring the anger and jealousy that drove him to murder. Reports later emerged that Xie was upset that Min, and not him, was considered the favoured or 'honoured' son by Yang and Feng. This wasn't surprising given that Min was their son and had been running a successful news-agency for some time. He had also been financially successful in other ways. Xie was also aware that his parents-in-law regularly told Kathy she could have done better than him for a husband when it came to both looks and money.

The murders

On 17 July 2009, the extended Lin family gathered as usual for its regular Friday-night dinner at the home of Yang and Feng. Xie's young relative (Ms AB) was on her week-long school trip to New Caledonia. In the early hours of 18 July, sometime between 2 am and 5 am, Xie sneaked out of his home and broke into Min and Lily's neat two-storey house in the Sydney suburb of North Epping. After disabling the electricity via the main meter box at the side of the house, Xie unlocked the front door with a key he had copied from the spare key Min and Lily had given Kathy for safekeeping.

Leaving the lower levels undisturbed, a sure sign that this was not a random burglary, Xie went straight upstairs and into the three bedrooms, one occupied by Min and Lily, a second by Henry and Terry, and a third by Lily's sister Irene, who was staying with them while she studied at Macquarie University. As a relative by marriage and a regular visitor to the home, Xie knew the layout of the house and how to access the meter box. He knew exactly what he was doing and where he was going.

Xie used a hammer-like weapon, which has never been found, to bludgeon his victims in the head. Crime scene analysts indicated that a rope was also used and was probably wrapped either around the handle of the weapon or hanging from the wrist of the killer to ensure that he didn't lose control of it as he used it. Xie killed the three adults in their beds, Min and Lily first and then Irene in her bedroom next door to theirs. After bashing all three to death, either while they slept or after they awoke, Xie moved them so that they were lying on their backs. He also hit Min in the face and head multiple times, before covering his body in bedclothes and leaving him under the doona near his wife. Min and Lily's two sons, Henry and Terry, were also killed with a hammer-like weapon, and were left lying on blood-soaked carpet in their shared bedroom next to Irene's. Terry must have offered some resistance, as he had been hit six times before succumbing. Police described the bedrooms as awash with blood and looking like a slaughterhouse.

Police discovered the gruesome crime at about 10 am that morning, after Kathy and Xie 'apparently' discovered the bodies and Kathy called triple 0. Initially, Xie told police he was home in bed with Kathy when the murders took place, and stuck to that story when interviewed again. On 29 July, Xie and Kathy made an emotional plea for public help in solving the crimes. When the surviving teenager returned home she lived with them for two years, oblivious to the fact that she was living with her family's killer. She later said she did not suspect Xie was capable of murder and was shocked to find out that he was. Chillingly, after his conviction, Xie's young relative revealed on Channel 7's *Sunday Night* program that he had regularly sexually abused her both before and after the murders.

While searching Xie's home in May 2010, police found a small transfer blood stain on his garage floor that matched the DNA of at least four of the victims. Blood-stained footprints at the crime scene also matched the size and brand of Xie's Asics runners. Police later secretly filmed Xie disposing of the shoebox that had contained those runners by cutting it into pieces and flushing the bits down a toilet. On 11 May 2011, after a lengthy police investigation, he was arrested and charged with five counts of murder. In December 2012, Xie was committed to stand trial.

The trials

The first trial started on 9 May 2014, before Justice Peter Johnson, but the jury was discharged for legal reasons. A second trial started on 5 August, but the jury was discharged when Justice Johnson fell ill. A third trial before Justice Elizabeth Fullerton started in February 2015, but the jury was discharged on 1 December after failing to reach a verdict. That month, Xie was released on bail, despite concerns that he could be a flight risk if he could obtain a false passport and return to China. The fourth trial started on 29 June 2016, with Xie's bail revoked in December before the jury retired. Xie did not give evidence during the 2016 trial, which heard that the crimes were meticulously planned. Prosecutors claimed that he had attached rope to a hammer-like weapon, probably to ensure that he did not lose control as he wielded it at the heads and faces of Min and Lily and their two young sons, and to ensure that he killed them quickly and efficiently.

The court heard that the murders were premeditated and Xie, who had claimed he was at home in bed with Kathy that night, had sedated her before leaving to kill their relatives without her knowledge. Kathy didn't believe that this had happened and insisted that her husband had been in their bedroom all night and did not leave her side during the hours in which the murders occurred. Prosecutors raised two possible murder motives. One was Xie's sexual interest in his young relative, which was not raised until the fourth trial. The court heard that Xie had sexually abused her both secretly before the murders and afterwards when she lived with him and his wife. The second was that Xie felt anger and resentment towards Min and his family because they were more respected and admired by his parents-in-law, and he believed that he had been relegated to what he considered an undeserved subordinate status within the extended family compared to Min (*R v Xie* [2017] NSWSC 63).

On 12 January 2017, after a six-month trial and eight days' deliberation, the twelve-person jury returned majority verdicts of guilty on each of the five murder counts. In sentencing Xie to life in jail with no parole, Justice Elizabeth Fullerton said she could not be certain about the motive but that did not detract from the gravity of the crime. 'Given that I am satisfied that the offender entered the Lin family home knowing the occupants would be asleep, that he disabled the power in order to exercise control over them and that he was armed with a weapon fashioned for the purpose of applying maximum assaultive force, the fact that I am unable to reach a point of satisfaction to the criminal standard as to what in fact motivated him to do what he did does nothing to diminish the gravity of his offending,' she said.

Justice Fullerton also said that while she considered it 'very likely' that Xie had sedated Kathy, she was unable to be satisfied beyond reasonable doubt that this had occurred. 'There remains, in my view, a possibility that Kathy Lin simply did not wake when the offender left the house sometime after 2 am on 18 July 2009, returning later that morning,' she said. 'I have taken into account Kathy Lin's evidence that she had never woken to find the offender not beside her in bed and would always wake if he left the bed for any reason. Since I accept Ms AB's evidence that the offender entered the bedroom she shared with the offender's son and sexually assaulted her on repeated occasions between August 2009, when she became a member of the offender's household, and when he was arrested in May 2011, Kathy Lin's evidence that she would always wake if the offender left the bed, and that he had never done so and gone into Ms AB's bedroom at night, cannot be accepted as reliable' (*R v Xie* [2017] NSWSC 63).

Justice Fullerton said the intentional and brutal killings of close relatives, including two children, in their family home in the early hours of the morning, in 'a single episode of brutal and calculated murderous violence', could only be described as 'heinous in the extreme'. The fact that the boys were likely to have known of Xie's presence after being wakened by the attack on their parents and aunt, was 'a further feature of the gravity of the offending'. Since Xie had not shown any remorse, the judge concluded that there was a risk of him offending further.

Justice Fullerton found that there was nothing put forward about Xie's background that mitigated the gravity of his offending. 'After full account is given to the range, spread and severity of the injuries causative of the death of all five deceased, and the multiple forms of extreme violence implicated in the infliction of those injuries, with the face and head of each of the victims being deliberately targeted, no other finding is open other than that each of the murders is within the worst case category of murder,' she said. 'The meticulous planning involved in the timing and styling of the murders, coupled with the offender's resolve to execute that plan and then to persist with the infliction of extreme violence with the intention that all occupants of the house should die, despite the active resistance offered by Terry Lin, the youngest victim, as he struggled for his life, is an ample basis upon which to make that finding' (*R v Xie* [2017] NSWSC 63).

Justice Fullerton found that the risk of Xie reoffending was amplified by the sexual violence the offender inflicted on his young relative after the murders. This had been described in a written statement. 'She described the devastating impact of the loss of her entire immediate family on every aspect of her life,'

Justice Fullerton said. 'She told me her achievements feel hollow and as she has passed various milestones from adolescence to early adulthood since the death of her family, celebrating those achievements with others is bittersweet. She described missing the support and guidance her parents had given her as their eldest child with the certain knowledge that would have continued. She has difficulty sleeping. She is dealing with an array of mental health issues and is experiencing some trouble with her tertiary studies.

'Despite Ms AB's gratitude for having been welcomed into loving families and for the support her friends have given her, she recognises, and the Court well understands, this can never be a substitute for the love, support, warmth and intimacy of her own family. I acknowledge the profound grief she has suffered and continues to suffer. I also commend her for her strength and dignity, and her courage as she faces the future without parents, siblings or a loving aunt' (*R v Xie* [2017] NSWSC 63).

Robert Xie's background

Robert Xie, who was 53 when sentenced in early 2017, was born in China. Some aspects of his background are hazy. He claimed that he had qualified as an ear, nose and throat medical specialist in China, but the *Daily Telegraph* reported on 6 May 2011 that police had been unable to find evidence of this, only that he had been a shoe salesman. Xie had also claimed that he left the medical profession because he wanted to become an engineer, instead taking a job as the manager of a shoe factory. If Xie really *had* qualified as a doctor, this would have provided him with much more status within his family than working as a factory manager, and it is likely that he would have been more respected by his in-laws. Perhaps he started a medical degree, but then either failed or dropped out. It is also possible that he fabricated the whole story to impress people.

Xie migrated to Australia in 1999, ten years after Min became the first family member to settle there in 1989. Min, then 23 and a qualified engineer, had arrived in Australia from China on a student visa and was supported by his parents, who borrowed money to fund his continuing education. As he studied, he also worked as a welder and a taxidriver, sending money home to his parents in Shenyang when he could. Min met Lily in Sydney when she was studying science. She had been divorced after a brief marriage. Min brought his parents to Australia in 1994. He later ran a newsagency in Epping, with Lily helping between school runs. The business did well, and Min and Lily were able to purchase two additional investment properties. They worked very hard and had significant debt, but that didn't stop Xie envying their life and assets.

After the murders, Min's father complained that Xie tried unsuccessfully to take over Min and Lily's newsagency. Min's parents and Xie's parents-in-law Yang and Feng had been running the business, which was worth $500,000, and refused Xie's proposal as they didn't want him interfering. Xie was shameless in his actions, which were clearly designed to improve his lifestyle and cater for his needs without a thought for the pain he put others through to achieve his goals.

Then there was Xie's obsession with his young relative, Ms AB, who spoke to Channel 7's *Sunday Night* show in February 2017. She told host Melissa Doyle that Xie had sexually abused her both before and after her other relatives died. 'That's something that . . . I'm very private about,' she said. 'And it's something that at this point in time I don't feel comfortable talking about as well. But I also don't think that something like this would warrant him to kill five people. I don't know what goes through his mind and I can't be sure and I don't think I ever will be sure about why he was motivated to do what he did.' Despite his inappropriate behaviour, the young woman never suspected he was capable of murder. 'He wasn't a murderer in my eyes,' she said. 'Realising that he might be involved was something that was life changing' (*Sunday Night*, 26 February 2017).

Why did he do it?

Robert Xie was probably reasonably intelligent, assuming he had successfully trained as an ear, nose and throat medical specialist as he claimed. But the choices he made left him bitter and unemployed. He gained some income from his investments, but still felt that he was being judged and not seen as being as successful as his brother-in-law Min. Xie was envious of and resented the attention his parents-in-law paid to Min, and Min's so-called position in the family as the 'honoured son'. This would have been torture for Xie, a narcissistic man who thought he was superior to those around him and therefore deserved to be treated as 'special'. He would have seethed as he watched other members of his family praised as hardworking and successful, while he was seen as unmotivated and lazy.

Rather than work to improve his situation, Xie, driven by his lack of empathy and selfishness, decided to flout societal norms and the law. First, he began to sexually abuse Ms AB. He then decided to kill her whole family, believing that to do so would solve two problems for him. It would remove Min from the situation, leaving him to step up and take on the role as the 'favoured son' of his in-laws, and it would give him unbridled sexual access to the young relative he was abusing (Ms AB), whom he correctly anticipated would probably have to move into his family home after the murders. Kathy did become Ms AB's guardian following strenuous efforts by her husband, and Xie obtained power of attorney over Ms AB and her family's estate. The sexual abuse also appears to have worsened as he had more opportunity. Although

Ms AB was sharing a bedroom with Xie and Kathy's son, this didn't deter Xie from entering the room at night to abuse her. Both plans were cold, callous and horrific, but to Xie they were simply a means to an end. He also thought he would get away with it all, as no one would suspect him of killing people so close to him. But this is where his narcissism led to his undoing.

Xie's thinking and behaviour clearly indicate that he has an NPD, and place him specifically in the malignant narcissism subtype (see pages 139–44). People in this subtype exhibit a combination of narcissistic and psychopathic traits, a combination that enabled Xie to act cruelly and callously and without empathy. His intense jealousy of his brother-in-law was so all-encompassing that he was determined to do whatever it took to remove him and his family from the picture so that he no longer had to feel inferior to him. Xie was prepared to use extreme violence to kill others for his own ends, without feeling any guilt, and was supremely confident he would get away with it.

But his lack of empathy also meant that he could not accurately predict how the police investigating five such horrifying murders would respond to his unconvincing claims that he was not involved. Highly trained law enforcement officers are expert at detecting liars and tripping up those who make claims that don't stack up against the evidence. They also work on the ABC principle:

- **A**ssume nothing.
- **B**elieve nobody.
- **C**hallenge and check everything.

Police were reasonably sure within six months of beginning their investigation that Xie was the most likely suspect, and they were determined to keep looking for the evidence they needed to charge and convict him with the five murders. It took time, but police and prosecutors did an amazing and strategic job of both setting up ways to obtain solid evidence against Xie and piecing the jigsaw together and tracing it back to him until they eventually had enough evidence to charge him.

Xie's arrogance led him to believe that his plan would succeed as he was clever enough to outsmart the police. But failing to 'read' how others are perceiving and reacting to what they are saying is often the undoing of malignant narcissists who commit serious crimes. They are prepared to harm others to get what they want and are so convinced of their own cleverness and superiority that they are sure others won't be able to see through them. They don't recognise the signs that others, such as police investigators, are unconvinced by their stories and are walking them into a trap. People like Xie assume that others will believe their 'clever' lies, and don't pick up the cues that this is not the case. Gerard Baden-Clay, the narcissistic real estate agent who murdered his wife Allison and then disposed of her body, stood by doing nothing to help find her as police and neighbours searched everywhere for her. Baden-Clay was unconvincing when television cameras captured him for a doorstop interview during the 2012 search, and was eventually convicted of Allison's murder (see *Why Did They Do It?* for more details of this crime).

Xie appears to have incorrectly assumed that police would conclude the murders had been a random attack or break-in by a stranger, even though it was clear from the start that whoever committed the crimes had used a key to the house to enter it and knew its layout very well. Neither was this a break-in motivated by robbery, as Min's wallet containing $1420 in cash was found near his body. Xie also fronted the media, appearing in a press conference with his wife as she struggled to explain how she felt about the murders. Xie sat stone-faced next to Kathy and held her hand as she described the pain she and others were experiencing. Wearing dark glasses, Xie appealed to members of the public who knew anything to contact police, no matter how small the clue. He asked the media not to show their faces as they were concerned for their own safety. The dark glasses and Xie's calm demeanour may not in themselves have been enough to arouse suspicion, as people react to tragedy in different ways, but as police gathered evidence it would have formed part of the big picture of his guilt. When the press conference was held, Xie may have been worried about being recognised by someone who could testify against him, such as the person who sold him the murder weapon. He may also have been concerned that his facial expressions and eye movements would give away the fact that he was lying.

At that point, Xie probably thought his plan had worked and that he would now be seen as a doting husband caring for his traumatised wife and young relative. But police and prosecutors quickly saw through his charade and worked tirelessly over several years to ensure they had enough evidence to convict him. Among the many strategies they employed, two were particularly effective because of Xie's narcissistic arrogance and his erroneous assumption that he could outsmart the police. These involved hidden audiovisual surveillance devices in Xie's home, and the collaboration of a fellow prisoner who encouraged Xie to think he might be able to help him avoid being found guilty. In return for a reduced sentence, the prisoner instigated conversations about the murders and made secret recordings and copies of letters written by Xie that could be used in evidence against him.

While Xie was still living at home, police secretly installed very small hidden audiovisual devices throughout his house that captured images of him cutting up the shoeboxes that could prove he owned and wore sports shoes that matched the size and brand of the bloody footprints found in the Lins' home. Xie was also recorded attempting to coach Kathy and Ms AB about what they should say when they were interviewed by police. He warned them that the police would try to trick them into providing information about him that they could use against him. Cameras also recorded Ms AB being subjected to 'uncomfortable touching' by Xie. After six months of audiovisual surveillance, he was arrested and charged with the five murders.

In jail, the fellow prisoner successfully encouraged Xie to tell him how he sedated his wife on the night before the murders so that she would not realise that he was absent from the bedroom. Xie also explained to him how he had purchased a hammer at a 'two-dollar shop' to use as the murder weapon because those shops didn't have functioning security cameras. He also described how to use a pressure point on the neck to incapacitate and potentially asphyxiate someone, and the best place on the head to aim for if you are trying to attack someone with a hammer. He revealed to the fellow prisoner that he planned to invent a story about doing some mechanical work with Min in his (Xie's) garage some weeks before the murders so that he could explain why Min's DNA was found in the blood stain on the floor there. Xie said that his alternative explanation would be that the blood had come from an animal while a vet had previously owned his home.

Xie then asked the fellow prisoner if he could get someone outside the jail to make a copy of the type of key that was used in the front door of the Lin family home so that it could be planted to implicate someone else in the murders. He drew a diagram that identified the technical specifications for doing this and outlined his plans to incriminate another person who knew the family. He then allegedly asked the fellow prisoner to help him contact people who could help him to do this. An undercover police officer later spoke with Xie and pretended to be the fellow prisoner's associate. These conversations were recorded and helped to convict him.

Robert Xie's malignant narcissism clearly led him to believe that he was smarter than he was, so police were able to trip him up by using their initiative and appealing to his unbridled sense of superiority. While he probably thought his fellow prisoner was admiring his exploits, he was in fact gathering evidence that would help convict him.

CONCLUSION

There are many lessons that we can learn from the actions of people with malignant narcissism such as Man Monis, Megan Haines and Robert Xie. The first and most important is that those with this extreme form of this personality disorder are arrogant, self-centred, ruthless and will stop at nothing to get their own way, particularly if they feel cornered or threatened. People with this extreme form of personality disorder should be avoided where possible, as they are quite prepared to hurt others emotionally and in some cases physically. Not everyone with malignant narcissism will become a murderer, but many will make the lives of those who question them or unwittingly get in their way a misery. They tend to be even nastier than someone with a 'regular' NPD, who may be insufferable in their bragging and criticism of anyone they perceive as a threat, but are not necessarily abusive and do not always break the law. Someone with malignant narcissism is prepared to take their need to be perceived as superior to extreme levels.

This may mean actively and sometimes publicly targeting

anyone they feel threatened by, even if that person has done nothing wrong. As discussed elsewhere in this book (see pages 144–7), US President Donald Trump has been identified by a collection of psychiatrists (Lee, 2017) as having malignant narcissism, indicated, for example, when he publicly lies about his opponents or those who dare to question him. President Trump clearly believes he is smarter and more deserving than others, and will fabricate information to suit his agenda while refusing to admit that he is wrong, even when strong evidence suggests that this is the case. These health professionals have publicly argued that Trump claims to know a lot more than he really does about politics and that he repeatedly lies, violates the rights of others and promotes bizarre and baseless conspiracy theories without regard for those hurt by such accusations. These experts cite numerous claims that Donald Trump has made that have not stood up to public scrutiny, such as Barack Obama faking his birth certificate and Trump's office being bugged by the Obama administration. One website, rightwingwatch.org, lists 58 Trump conspiracy theories it claims are not true.

In another example of how President Trump puts himself ahead of others, regardless of how sensitive the situation, he publicly chastised families whose loved ones had been killed while serving their country. When Myeshia Johnson, the wife of the late US Army soldier Sergeant La David Johnson, complained about Trump's lack of compassion during a phone call, the President denied any fault and criticised Myeshia and those with her at the time of the call, including another politician. When Myeshia complained that Trump had struggled even to remember her husband's name, he responded on Twitter, claiming that he had a respectful conversation with her and used the fallen soldier's name from the start without hesitating. Myeshia and those in the car with her strongly disputed this, yet Trump was prepared to criticise them publicly during a time of intense grief simply to prove a point, albeit a false one.

President Trump has displayed this pattern of behaviour for many years, well before he entered politics. Being elected to the most powerful office in the country did not appear to minimise this pattern, possibly because someone with malignant NPD cannot tolerate being challenged and often explodes in a narcissistic rage when someone stands up to them. The Myeshia Johnson conversation is one of many examples where Trump has attempted to 'bring down' someone who dared to dispute his version of the truth, even when his own version is dubious. His response to negative media has also been to brand it as 'fake news'. This is despite many of the claims against him being backed by multiple sources, and despite many of Trump's public claims being disputed by multiple sources. The potentially dangerous thing about this sort of narcissistic behaviour is that a person like Donald Trump will not back down, even when their claims or denials are proven wrong. In his mind, he has his version of the truth and he's sticking to it, regardless of the consequences to his own reputation or his country's.

This sort of behaviour, even when it is not in the public eye, can be very damaging. Life can be extremely challenging for the work colleagues, friends, relatives and partners of someone with malignant narcissism. They can be extremely manipulative and on the surface very charming to those they want to convince of their so-called superiority. But many are also capable of taking arrogant and/or unprincipled action to achieve their own goals. In the most serious cases, they are prepared to kill to maintain their grandiose image, to get what they want or to prevent others from exposing them.

Man Monis spent years manipulating and sexually assaulting vulnerable women and harassing the families of soldiers killed in action, as well as making vexatious claims about government authorities. He got away with all of this to a point, but when he upped the stakes by ordering the murder of his ex-wife, his world came crashing down. With charges pending over that crime and a large number of alleged sexual assaults, Monis realised that his narcissistic bubble was about to burst, and he would most likely become a long-term prisoner. The thought of being reduced to a number in jail was too much for a man who believed he was superior to others, and he could not stand the possibility of not being able to control those around him as he had for so many years.

Monis then channelled his narcissistic rage into the Lindt café siege, designing it to gain maximum attention and piggyback on the terror issue that had people on edge globally. If people believed he was linked to an organisation such as Islamic State, Monis knew he would gain worldwide attention, draw some sympathy to his cause and 'go out with a bang'. He did not spare a thought for his terrified hostages or their families, and was prepared for any number of them to die.

Megan Haines was also prepared to kill for her own narcissistic needs. In her case, a threat to her image came from two elderly nursing home residents who rightly complained about her unprofessional conduct. This sparked in Haines a murderous narcissistic rage and what she thought was the justified killing of both women, whose complaints were likely to lead to her being disciplined and humiliated.

Robert Xie had even less reason to complain. He killed five of his wife's relatives to improve his status in their family by removing the competition and to gain continued access to the teenage relative he had been sexually abusing. Xie was jealous that his brother-in-law Min Lin was more highly regarded by his parents-in-law and believed that murdering Min and his family would elevate him to the rightful position of favoured son. To do this, he was prepared to kill his brother-in-law, his brother-in-law's wife, their two sons and the wife's sister in a brutal and callous fashion. It is hard to imagine someone even contemplating, let alone carrying out such a crime, but as someone with an extreme case of malignant narcissism, Xie simply saw his actions as a means to an end.

Even if they don't resort to violence or murder, you are probably better off avoiding people with malignant narcissism where possible. Unless you always comply with their wishes and allow them to dominate your relationship, whether it be work or personal, they are likely to attempt to manipulate, use or abuse you in some way. It is true that some people with personality disorders can improve their behaviour if they genuinely attempt to do so and agree to try cognitive behaviour therapy. But in many cases, those with seriously ingrained patterns of this type of dangerous behaviour either will not or cannot change. Some will even attempt to manipulate their therapist by claiming that others are at fault and not them.

The best advice for someone living or dealing with an individual who exhibits behaviours that could mean they have malignant narcissism is to consider distancing themselves or severing ties completely. If you know someone else who is in such a situation, encourage them to do the same or at the very least seek help. Extricating yourself from the hold of such a person is not easy. They can be at their nastiest when they feel threatened, wronged or abandoned, so it is a good idea to seek professional advice first. The most dangerous time for a woman in a bad relationship is when she decides to leave, and if her partner is a malignant narcissist, she could be in physical danger. Man Monis allegedly ordered the murder of his first wife because she defied him and refused to reconcile. He later justified his actions by saying that she had betrayed him and deserved to be murdered. The horrifying part is, like others with this toxic mindset, Monis probably went to his grave believing that he was right.

*A list of support services for those experiencing relationship problems can be found on pages 403–7.

PART III

DEPENDENT PERSONALITY DISORDER

DESPERATELY NEEDY

What is a dependent personality disorder

Having some degree of mutual dependency on another person with whom you have a close and caring relationship can be adaptive (beneficial) for both people. Such relationships can provide mutual support, loyalty and encouragement, cooperation and thoughtfulness. A dependent personality disorder (DPD), however, is characterised by a pattern of behaviour across a range of different contexts that reflects a very strong need to be advised, protected and taken care of by another person. This pattern of behaviour results in clinginess, over-compliance, separation anxiety and an intense fear of abandonment. Although someone with a DPD may also display some of this 'needy' and under-confident pattern of behaviour in their workplace, it is usually most evident in their close personal relationships.

An individual with a DPD is likely to seek out someone who will compensate for what they perceive are their own inadequacies and who will support, protect and make decisions for them in most aspects of their life. They tend to be overly sensitive to criticism. They are desperate for a relationship in which they can experience acceptance and approval and where the 'right decisions' will be made for them by the other person, whom they see as more competent. These decisions are likely to be about small day-to-day issues (What should I wear?) as well as larger issues (Should I quit my job?). The 'price' for this kind of support and protection can, however, be an expectation that the person with a DPD will always be submissive and accommodating to the wishes and desires of the other person. They are often too anxious to disagree with their partner for fear that their partner will abandon them.

Michael O'Neill, Chamari Liyanage and Anthony Sherna all had a dependent personality disorder and lived with stronger partners who dominated them to some degree. All ended up killing their partners when things went wrong. O'Neill's partner, Stuart Rattle, was a well-known interior designer who had a close relationship with O'Neill but could be domineering and would often belittle him in public. Liyanage's husband Dinendra 'Din' Athukorala was a violent and sexually perverted man who forced his wife into unwanted sexual acts with him and other people. Sherna claimed his wife, Susie Wild, was controlling and cruel to him. None could muster the courage to leave their relationships and ended up brutally killing their partner after they could no longer tolerate being dominated and abused.

Recognising someone with a DPD

Bornstein et al. (2015) have identified four core key components associated with a DPD:

1. **a motivational component:** having a strong drive to seek support, acceptance and approval from others, especially a key person in one's life

2. **a cognitive component:** having a perception of oneself as powerless and ineffectual, along with a perception of the selected other person as comparatively strong, competent, confident, powerful and protective
3. **an emotional component:** feeling anxious when required to show initiative and/or act independently or when being evaluated
4. **a behavioural component:** seeking help, reassurance, support and guidance from others, especially a key person in one's life.

There are many variations both in the behaviour of individuals with a DPD and in the intimate relationships they have. Some relationships are adaptive and characterised by respect and support. Sometimes their identity becomes 'fused' with that of their partner and the relationship becomes unhealthy and manipulative. The person with the DPD may be taken advantage of in a variety of ways. For example, some people with a DPD may agree with and do things that they perceive to be morally wrong rather than risk losing the support of the other person. Some tolerate verbal, physical, psychological or sexual abuse. In particular, people with a DPD have a higher risk than others of being physically abused by their partner or spouse (Loas et al., 2011). Bornstein (2006) has also noted that several types of dependency (e.g. economic and emotional) have been linked in various research studies with an increased likelihood of being abused in some way. Liyanage and Sherna both stayed in relationships they would have known were unsuitable and abusive, but they felt powerless to escape. O'Neill's situation was not so dire, as his partner loved him and mostly treated him well, but the occasions when Stuart belittled him began to chip away at him.

People with a DPD are, however, less likely than other people to intentionally harm others (Fazel and Grann, 2004). The very small number of women with a DPD who have committed murder usually killed someone with whom they had a close relationship (Weizmann-Henelius et al., 2003), as Liyanage did. A study by Benotsch et al. (2017) found that dependent personality traits in women predicted a lack of assertiveness in sexual situations. This was linked to their engaging unwillingly in sexual health-jeopardising behaviour such as agreeing to not use a condom or participating in sexually aggressive behaviour. This was the case with Liyanage, whose husband had sex with others in front of her, and forced her to participate in sexual activities she was not comfortable with. He was also violent towards her and had inappropriate sexual material on his computer.

In another case, Cia Xia Liao didn't kill her partner Brian Mach but she did kill his wife, Mai, and his grandson, Alistair Kwong, after Brian left her to return to Mai. Liao had become extremely dependent on Mach, who unlike the other partners in our case studies did not dominate her life. Despite this, Liao was so upset with Brian for leaving her that she exacted violent revenge by taking him hostage and then brutally killing his wife and their grandson. Liao also showed signs of having a histrionic personality disorder that contributed to her murderous behaviour.

Typical behaviours of people with a DPD

According to the *Diagnostic and Statistical Manual of Mental Disorders* (DSM-5, APA, 2013), a diagnosis of DPD can be made when at least five of the following criteria are met. The individual:

- finds it difficult to make routine decisions without a great deal of input, advice and reassurance from other people
- seeks out other people who will take responsibility for many key aspects of their life

- tries to avoid criticising or disagreeing with other people wherever possible out of concern that those people might withdraw their support, acceptance or approval
- lacks confidence in their own capacity to set goals, create and implement plans or projects or act independently
- is prepared to do whatever it takes, however unpleasant, unfair or uncomfortable, to ensure that they receive protection, care and support from others
- has difficulties being alone because they feel unsafe, vulnerable and helpless; does not feel confident that they can take care of themselves
- feels desperate when a close relationship finishes, and immediately tries to find a replacement that will provide nurturance and support
- obsesses anxiously about the remote possibility that they will be abandoned and left alone and will have to take care of themselves.

Prevalence of DPDs

It has been estimated that the prevalence of DPD within the general community is somewhere between 0.4 and 10 per cent (Grant et al., 2004; Lenzenweger et al., 2007; Samuel and Widiger, 2010; Trull et al., 2010). DPD tends to be diagnosed more frequently in women than men (Bornstein, 2005).

Comorbidity (other disorders that often occur with DPDs)

Some people with a DPD also have an additional disorder such as histrionic personality disorder, NPD or borderline personality disorder (Bornstein, 2005; Millon, 2011).

Heritability of DPDs

Both genetic and environmental factors combine to create a DPD. Estimates of the heritability of DPD – the degree to which genetics plays a role in developing the disorder – range between .31 and .66 (Gjerde et al., 2012; Reichborn-Kjennerud et al., 2007; Torgersen, 2009). This means that between 31 and 66 per cent of the differences between those people in research studies who had a DPD and those who didn't were most likely due to genetic variations between them.

Other contributing factors to DPDs

Some of the environmental factors that have been identified as possibly making some contribution to the development a DPD include:

- periods of serious illness as a child
- being overly supported and/or protected by one or more older siblings
- over-anxious parents
- over-protective parenting
- separation anxiety as an infant
- school refusal as a child, which involves a child refusing, often frequently, to attend school due to an anxiety attack or temper tantrum
- very strict authoritarian parenting, where parents make most of the decisions for their child, even when they become teenagers. This can create an inability to make decisions and increases dependency.

Treatment of DPDs

The most effective treatment is likely to be cognitive behaviour therapy, which focuses on identifying current unhelpful and overly emotional ways of thinking and feeling, and then learning to substitute more rational thoughts and feelings.

Battered woman syndrome

As well as having a dependent personality disorder, Dr Chamari Liyanage, who killed her husband Din after years of serious abuse, suffered from 'battered woman syndrome', which can be very debilitating. Despite being an accomplished medical professional, Liyanage found herself unable to leave her husband, even when he physically, sexually and emotionally abused her, to the extent of forcing her to take part in degrading sexual encounters with strangers against her will. Up to 60 per cent of men who are violent towards their partner also sexually abuse them (Ewing, 1997), for example by sodomising them against their wishes, forcing them to engage in bondage activities, or forcing them to participate in sexual activities with other people or groups, as Liyanage's husband did.

It is possible to 'learn' how to become helpless in a difficult situation, such as an abusive relationship. From the outside, people often wonder why someone would stay in an obviously toxic situation. The reasons are complex, but these situations can and do develop regardless of a person's level of education or cultural background.

Seligman and Maier (1967) developed the theory of 'learned helplessness' based on their experiments. In the first part of their experiment, dogs were repeatedly subjected to a mild electric shock from which they were unable to escape. When the same dogs were then placed in similar situations where they were able to avoid the mild electric shock by jumping over a very low fence, the dogs didn't try to escape the shock. A similar experiment was conducted with human subjects, in which the aversive stimulus was a very unpleasant loud noise. The human subjects behaved in a similar way to the dogs: in a follow-up experiment, they also 'gave up' trying to avoid the unpleasant noise, even when it was possible to do so.

The term 'learned helplessness' is now used to describe the expectation that, when there have been repeated unpleasant or painful experiences in your life that you were unable to avoid or prevent no matter how hard you tried, you will be likely to assume that in the future you will probably also be unable to avoid or prevent similar negative outcomes, no matter what you try to do to prevent or manage them, and you give up trying to do so. This pattern of learned helplessness is often very apparent in abusive relationships.

The domestic violence cycle can be broken down into phases. Dr Lenore Walker (2016) developed a three-stage 'Cycle of Violence' model based on data from her interviews with 1500 women who had been victims of domestic violence. The model outlines three distinct phases that occur in each domestic violence cycle.

1. **Tension-building phase:** Verbal abuse and minor physical violence occurs. The victim attempts to placate and accommodate the abuser to prevent more serious abuse. The victim is encouraged to believe that the abuse is only temporary.
2. **Violent episode phase:** The tension that has built up in the first phase now erupts into more serious physical or sexual violence and demands on the part of the abuser. The victim feels very frightened, but is once again encouraged to believe that the violence and demands will soon stop as long as they cooperate.
3. **Remorseful/honeymoon/loving contrition phase:** The abuser becomes aware that the victim may be thinking of leaving and hence becomes loving and affectionate, encouraging the

victim to believe that the situation will soon change for the better. The victim is positively reinforced (at least temporarily) for 'staying' in the relationship.

But soon the cycle begins again and the victim thinks seriously about leaving because they recognise that nothing is going to make the abuse stop. They are, however, hampered by many factors, such as:

- threats from the abuser of what will happen (to the victim and perhaps to their children and/or pets) if they leave
- a sense of learned helplessness
- lack of access to financial resources
- fear of family disapproval for leaving the relationship and/or lack of family support
- lack of access to suitable accommodation, especially if there are children involved; many shelters are only temporary and often hard to gain access to
- feeling that the police have not been able to help enough
- not wanting to disrupt the children's schooling by changing where they live.

A small number of women who have been subjected to ongoing violence by a partner ultimately respond by killing their abuser. This occurs most commonly when the abusive partner is asleep or preoccupied, as it is safer. The legal system may not support their claim of self-defence, however, and many, if not most, are imprisoned after being found guilty of either murder or manslaughter (Ewing, 1997). Legal explanations for their being found guilty may include that the murder didn't occur when they were being abused so it isn't technically self-defence. The court may ask, 'Why did she feel it was necessary to use deadly force at a time when not being battered?' If a self-defence argument is to succeed, a good psychiatrist is needed in court to explain battered woman syndrome and why the killer endured such serious abuse for so long without leaving. According to Ewing (1997), however, these explanations don't always influence the court as much as might be expected.

Legal test for self-defence

Ewing (1997) has argued that some women *do* kill in self-defence, but not in the narrow legal sense of that term. In these cases, the woman may act after sustained abuse but not necessarily at the exact moment she is being physically or emotionally abused. Like Chamari Liyanage, they might kill when their partner is incapacitated or asleep, partly because they feel they might be killed themselves if they try to stop their partner during a violent abusive act. In Liyanage's case, she felt particularly trapped as she lacked family support and a friendship network in Australia, felt ashamed of what was happening and worried that others would be horrified if she confided in them.

It can be difficult to prove that you acted in self-defence, especially when the victim was not abusing you at the time. State laws vary, but the state of Victoria does have some provision for this type of situation. The Victorian *Crimes Amendment (Abolition of Defensive Homicide) Act 2014* outlines what it considers to be self-defence or duress in the context of family violence. Self-defence is generally defined as a situation in which the person believes that their conduct is necessary and a reasonable response to circumstances as perceived by them. It only applies in a murder case if the person believes that the conduct is necessary to defend them or another person from death or really serious injury.

In the context of family violence, the person must believe that their conduct is necessary for them to defend himself/herself and that their conduct is a reasonable response in the circumstances as the person perceives them. This applies even if they are responding to harm that is not immediate, or their response involves force in excess of the force involved in the harm or threatened harm. Evidence of family violence may be deemed relevant in determining whether the response was reasonable. When duress in the context of family violence is an issue, evidence of family violence may be relevant in determining whether a person has carried out conduct under duress.

Cobras and pit bulls

Jacobson and Gottman (2007) used their clinical research with 200 women to identify two main subtypes of men who batter their partners – the 'cobra' and the 'pit bull'. Abusive men in the two subtypes have different objectives and motives and are likely to react differently in abusive situations.

The 'pit bull'

These men tend to be jealous, dependent and very emotionally aroused when they are angered. Their heart rate increases during violent episodes They are motivated by fear of losing their partner and are emotionally dependent on them. Women appear to be less intimidated by these types of offenders.

The 'cobra'

These men tend to lash out dramatically but are also physiologically calmer when they act aggressively. Their heart rate decreases during violent episodes. They are often antisocial, demonstrate criminal traits, are more emotionally abusive and motivated by the desire for immediate gratification. Their partners are less likely to leave them. Chamari Liyanage's husband Dinendra 'Din' Athukorala was a good example of a cobra. He subjected her to degrading physical and emotional abuse and often lashed out at her physically.

Using aggression to control

Battering is a form of aggression that is intended to control, subjugate or intimidate another person. In marriage it is more likely to be the man who fits this definition. Once physical violence has had the desired effect of intimidating the female partner, it tends to occur less often but is often replaced by a never-ending stream of emotional abuse to remind them of the ever-present threat of further physical violence. The victim lives in a state of constant fear about being even more seriously injured.

The study by Jacobson and Gottman also found that repeated violent behaviour by a woman against her partner was nearly always self-defensive and in response to being battered by her partner. Contrary to the offenders' claims, their partners rarely did or said anything to provoke a vicious attack.

Jacobson and Gottman (2007) state emphatically that there is nothing a woman can do or say to stave off or abort a battering episode. In many cases during their research, when a woman tried to stop an attack by leaving, the husband pursued her and intensified the beating.

The researchers concluded that battering almost never stops on its own. Even when the physical attacks abated, emotional abuse usually continued and kept the partner intimidated and afraid. The researchers emphasised that emotional abuse can be even more damaging than physical abuse because the constant insults, harassment, humiliation and demeaning and degrading comments or demands deprive the victim of her identity and self-respect.

The researchers also found that a relatively large number (38 per cent) of women managed to escape from their abusive relationships within two years following the study. Five years later, 65 per cent had left their violent partners. Those who left demonstrated extraordinary courage and resourcefulness, because they faced the greatest likelihood of being killed when they left. But, as one woman who left said, 'Death would be preferable to continue in this living hell.'

	Pit Bull (80%)	Cobra (20%)
Motivation	Fears losing their partner. Control and check up on their partners to avoid being abandoned.	Motivated by a desire for immediate gratification. Controlled their wives to avoid being controlled themselves. Not strongly attached to their wives. Prefer to be left alone most of the time, occasionally wanting their wives for sex, money or someone to get high with.
Characteristics	Tends to be: needy insecure dependent sometimes jealous. Tends to act violently only towards their partner and often appears to be 'a good guy' and charming towards other people.	Demonstrates a pathological need to have things their way and to be the boss and ensure that their partner understands that and acts accordingly. Tends to be very emotionally abusive and lash out dramatically.

Characteristics *(continued)*		Not strongly emotionally attached to their partner, but occasionally wants them for sex or money. May have antisocial or criminal traits and is aggressive outside the home as well.
Emotional reactions	Increase in heart rate during a violent episode and therefore feels more upset.	Decrease in heart rate during a violent episode – feels calmer and more in control of partner's behaviour.
Style of abuse	Their anger and rage keeps building, and once the abuse starts it is difficult to get them to stop. May stalk their wives after they leave. Some tend to become more violent towards their partner if she leaves them.	Appears to be quiet and focused, but if they believe that their authority has been challenged they attack violently and without warning. Many tend to be sadistic. Although they do not lose control like the 'pit bulls', they are often more violent towards their wives, sometimes threatening them with weapons.
Effect of their behaviour on their partner	Partner is less likely to feel intimidated and therefore more able to consider leaving, despite the potential threat of being stalked hanging over their head.	More dangerous and violent and more likely to seriously harm their partner. Their partner is less likely to leave because it is more difficult, and they fear retaliation.

HISTRIONIC PERSONALITY DISORDER: EMOTIONAL ATTENTION-SEEKING

What is a histrionic personality disorder?

A histrionic personality disorder (HPD) is characterised by a pattern of highly emotional, overly dramatic and attention-seeking behaviour across a range of different situations. The pattern is apparent by early adulthood and indicated by the presence of at least five of the following behavioural indicators as identified in the DSM-5 (APA, 2013): The individual:

- seeks to be the focus of attention and may become anxious and resentful when this is not the case
- often interacts with other people in an inappropriate way that is intimate, seductive or provocative
- expresses very superficial emotions that are constantly changing
- tries to attract attention from others by using seductive or provocative clothing, grooming, language or behaviour
- uses an oversimplified style of verbal communication that is vague, exaggerated, theatrical and lacks specific detail (e.g. 'it was absolutely amazing!')

- expresses personal feelings in exaggerated, theatrical and overly dramatic ways
- is easily influenced by what other people do and say, and by changing circumstances
- often assumes a closer connection to other people than is justified by the actual relationship between them.

Recognising someone with an HPD

Someone with an HPD, such as Cia Xia Liao, who also had a DPD, craves attention to the extent that their behaviour is often overly egocentric, impulsive and emotionally immature. They always want to be the centre of attention, assume that, 'I am nothing unless I can charm and captivate people', and can become depressed when they are not able to do this. Someone with an HPD may have some of the same dependency needs as a person who has a DPD (see pages 218–19) and can be very demanding. They may also have some of the same traits as people with an ASPD (see page 337), such as impulsivity, behavioural disinhibition and lack of empathy.

The main female character in the classic movie *Gone with the Wind* (Scarlett O'Hara) and the play/movie *A Streetcar Named Desire* (Blanche DuBois) are typical of someone with an HPD. Scarlett O'Hara is immature, shallow, spoiled, manipulative and exploitive. She always seeks to be the centre of attention among men, continually upgrades her appearance, is overly dramatic and uses exaggerated verbal and non-verbal language. Scarlett demands that others comply with her wishes, exaggerates her emotions, is overly flirtatious and makes theatrical claims such as, 'My life is over. Nothing will ever happen to me again.'

Blanche DuBois is flirtatious and seductive, dresses provocatively and tries to manipulate people by charming them. She is obsessed with her physical appearance, overly dramatic, tries to be the centre of attention and exploits other people's vulnerabilities. Among her famous lines are, 'I know I fib a good deal. After all, a woman's charm is 50 per cent illusion,' and, 'I don't want realism. I want magic! Yes, yes, magic. I try to give that to people. I do misrepresent things. I don't tell truths. I tell what ought to be truth.'

Typical behaviours of people with an HPD

An individual with an HPD:

- is often very manipulative with others in the strategies they use to get what they feel they want from them
- often engages in emotionally and socially immature behaviour
- has a low tolerance of frustration and becomes emotional if they can't have what they want
- may act in suggestive and seductive ways that imply they are highly sexual when this is not necessarily the case
- is often very impulsive, attempts to get what they want and doesn't think things through
- tends to be very gregarious and likes to dominate conversations
- tends not to feel much empathy for others
- is often unwilling to admit their own feelings of anger or hostility and instead blames others
- may act out a role such as 'victim', 'princess', 'hero' or 'life of the party'
- often spends a great deal of time and money on their clothes, grooming and appearance to impress other people
- can become angry and upset if someone makes a comment, even jokingly, that they feel makes them look foolish or unattractive

- is usually able to turn their emotions on and off quickly
- can be overly dramatic (e.g. crying when they receive a present, having temper tantrums)
- tends to be very suggestible and is attracted to new fads and new people
- often alienates friends, family and colleagues with their constant demands for attention
- tends to crave novelty, excitement and stimulation and is easily bored with routine
- can be very impatient and intolerant
- tends to lose enthusiasm quickly and look for something new and more exciting
- will sometimes erupt with anger and physically aggressive confrontation or with threats or gestures of suicide when they feel they have been badly treated
- tends to have difficulties with 'executive functioning' – the capacity to delay gratification in order to set and pursue long-term goals (Coolidge et al., 2004).

Prevalence of HPDs

The estimated prevalence of HPD is 1.84 per cent (Grant et al., 2004). More women than men tend to be diagnosed with HPDs (Bakkevig et al., 2010).

Heritability of HPDs

Both genetic and environmental factors combine to create an HPD. The estimated heritability of HPD – the degree to which genetics plays a role in developing the disorder – is .31 (Torgersen et al., 2008). This means that 31 per cent of the differences between those people in the research study who had an HPD and those who didn't were most likely due to genetic variations between them.

Other contributing factors to HPDs

Some environmental factors that have been identified as possibly making some contribution to the development of an HPD include parents rewarding their child with attention when they throw temper tantrums or have 'emotional meltdowns' because they can't have what they want and a parent who models inappropriate behaviour and theatrical language to get attention. Cia Liao's dependent personality disorder was complicated by her also having the necessary behaviours and characteristics needed to diagnose an HPD. This combination caused her to panic at the thought of being abandoned and influenced her to act impulsively, over-dramatically, vindictively and violently, taking the lives of her former lover's wife and grandson, causing immense pain and grief to the rest of his family and, at the same time, ruining her own life.

Treatment of HPDs

The most effective treatment for someone with a DPD and/or an HPD is likely to be cognitive behaviour therapy, which focuses on identifying current unhelpful and overly emotional ways of thinking and feeling, and then learning to substitute more rational thoughts and feelings.

CHAPTER 7

MICHAEL O'NEILL

The cast

Michael O'Neill: Killed his partner Stuart Rattle
Stuart Rattle: The victim, a well-known and respected Melbourne interior designer
Jill and Ken Rattle: Stuart Rattle's parents; Ken died eight months after his son

The motive

Michael O'Neill killed his long-term partner, Stuart Rattle, after he 'lost it' when he claims Stuart belittled him once too often.

Introduction

Society couple Michael O'Neill and Stuart Rattle appeared to have it all. Together for sixteen years, they ran an interior design business popular with Melbourne's social set and enjoyed a beautiful country property that was the envy of friends and the wider community. The couple had spent years transforming a disused school building outside Daylesford into Musk Farm, a stunning rural retreat with magnificent gardens. The farm soon became a local landmark, and was feted by the interior and garden design worlds. During the week, Stuart and O'Neill lived above the office of Stuart Rattle Interior Design in Malvern Road, South Yarra. On weekends, they'd head to their picture-perfect country property. Idyllic weekends saw Stuart working hard in the garden while his partner tended to his British White cattle, before both would relax and enjoy the evening together in their lavishly decorated country home.

You could not imagine a better setting in which to enjoy your downtime. The 35-hectare Musk Farm was spectacular, as one would expect given Stuart Rattle's experience and skills in interior and exterior home design. A series of garden rooms were separated by perfectly manicured hedges. Each had its own theme and plants, such as hydrangeas, rhododendrons and gladioli. Statues were dotted throughout, and a long pond added to its classic style. Some of the property was set aside for woodland, which had a more natural feel. The vastness of the project showed just how determined Stuart Rattle was when he set his mind to something. The design, creation and maintenance had taken thousands of hours and incredible amounts of money. With O'Neill's help, Stuart had worked hard to create his own piece of paradise for them to share. It was the icing on the cake of their long and mostly happy relationship.

Stuart Rattle and Michael O'Neill, who both grew up in rural Victoria, met in 1997 when O'Neill was working as a waiter in a café. Stuart was already a well-known interior designer with a long list of wealthy clients. O'Neill later joined the South Yarra business, managing its finances, quotes and orders, and liaising with clients. The couple was popular in Melbourne's design community due to Stuart's classic, timeless style honed over many years. He had no formal training but had developed a unique approach his clients loved. Stuart had an eye for period pieces and would pick them up overseas for individual clients, making them feel special when he called to say he'd found them the ideal table or vase in France or England. People valued his opinion and knew that having the Stuart Rattle Interior Design name attached to their home would add value and social cache.

On the surface, this attractive and worldly couple was living the dream. They had many accomplished friends, wore expensive clothes, ate in top restaurants and enjoyed luxurious overseas holidays. By around 2010, however, their lavish lifestyle was catching up with them. Their financial situation had deteriorated since Stuart's parents, who had exercised some spending control, left the business in 2006. Stuart and O'Neill were spending like there was no tomorrow, taking expensive holidays and buying whatever they wanted to ensure their properties looked perfect.

O'Neill was neither trained for nor suited to his role in managing a business, and he struggled with it. He made mistakes and covered them up, upsetting some clients. When Stuart found out about his partner's mistakes, he often turned a blind eye and this made things worse. Numerous clients had to wait longer than they had expected for work to be completed, and this harmed the business's reputation. When Stuart expected their decadent lifestyle to continue regardless, O'Neill started accessing money from their joint superannuation account and delayed paying creditors. Stuart was aware of this but did not stop it.

Personally, the relationship was becoming strained. Stuart was clearly the dominant partner and, if he is to be believed, O'Neill usually let him get his way. This sometimes led to conflict, which strained things even further. O'Neill later claimed that Stuart would verbally abuse him, sometimes in front of others. He also told a psychologist that Stuart was sexually demanding.

If he refused to have sex, O'Neill said that Stuart called him a 'frigid bitch', which led to him feeling like he was being treated as a possession rather than a person. Nevertheless, they still loved each other and saw their relationship as strong. O'Neill felt that Stuart was loving and affectionate towards him much of the time, and they enjoyed their status as a popular couple in the Daylesford area, where they opened Musk Farm to the public to raise money for the Friends of Wombat Hill Botanic Gardens. In Melbourne, they were feted by society types who revelled in telling their friends that they had used Stuart Rattle as their designer.

Despite their successes, however, as business and relationship strains worsened, the veneer began to crack. O'Neill continued to struggle with his job as business manager. While some of his later claims could have been exaggerated to mitigate his crime, he also told investigators that Stuart continued to put him down and humiliate him in front of others. While he had played a significant role in developing Musk Farm, breeding cattle and helping with the renovation and gardens, the property was seen by many as Stuart's creation, which compounded O'Neill's frustration. The stress and strain of living a lie and worrying about being found out for his lack of skill only added to his precarious psychological state. For many years, O'Neill had spent time and energy creating the persona of a sophisticated 'man about town' and fudging details about his unglamorous childhood. He was often caught out embellishing or lying about his background and hiding his Catholic roots and rural upbringing. Few people knew about his family history, and Stuart never met O'Neill's relatives.

The murder

On the weekend of 23 and 24 November in 2013, Musk Farm opened to the public for a huge charity fundraiser. Stuart and

O'Neill worked tirelessly in the lead-up to the big day, which was a resounding success. Both were exhausted when the last visitors finally left and they drove back to Melbourne. On Tuesday, 3 December, 53-year-old Stuart and 47-year-old O'Neill attended their regular morning Pilates class. That afternoon, they visited clients in Sorrento. This was the last time Stuart was seen by anyone other than his partner. No one knows for sure what happened on the morning Stuart died, as O'Neill was known for embellishing stories and he was the only person who lived to tell the tale, but he later told police that on Wednesday, 4 December, the couple woke at around 6 am. O'Neill claimed that they had sex the previous night and Stuart wanted to have it again but O'Neill refused. When Stuart allegedly called his partner 'a frigid bitch', O'Neill left the bedroom to make breakfast. A few minutes later he returned with a heavy steel pan in his hand. O'Neill later told police that he had intended to apologise, but before he could do so Stuart repeated his abusive comments and called him selfish.

At that point, something in O'Neill snapped. He hit Stuart in the head with the pan, grabbed a dog lead from the floor and strangled him with it. Stuart pleaded for his life – 'Michael, don't do this' – until he eventually stopped breathing. O'Neill could not believe what he had just done and went into complete denial. After placing Stuart's lifeless body in a large plastic furniture bag, covering him up to his shoulders to avoid spoiling their precious linen, he left his dead partner on the bed, cleaned the room, had a shower and started work in the office downstairs at around 8 am, telling his assistant that Stuart was unwell and his appointments needed to be cancelled.

Later that day, O'Neill attended a client appointment on Stuart's behalf and continued to see others, telling them that his business partner was unwell. He made phone calls and sent text messages purporting to be from Stuart, and even went to the extent of preparing and laying out meals for two people. On the Friday, O'Neill left Stuart's body in bed and went to Musk Farm, where he stayed until Sunday. He visited friends in Newlyn on the way up, helping them finalise arrangements for a party they were hosting. O'Neill attended the party for a couple of hours, telling people that Stuart was not feeling well. The next day he exchanged texts with Stuart's assistant using Stuart's mobile phone, pretending to be him. Upon his return on Sunday night, O'Neill bought Indian takeaway and wine, laying out dinner for two. It was almost as if he could erase what happened by acting as if nothing *had* happened. The situation was not only tragic but bizarre.

After realising that he had to do something, O'Neill came up with a delusional plan. Just before midnight, he lit a candle next to some curtains near where Stuart's body still lay on the bed. He went to a nearby service station to buy some sweets and returned to find the apartment on fire. O'Neill and his neighbours called the fire brigade, whose members discovered Stuart's body. It had suffered 100 per cent burns and was covered in plastic. Emergency services quickly deduced that the fire was started by the candles. That night, O'Neill told police that he and Stuart had been watching DVDs, eating the Indian takeaway and drinking wine. Stuart had fallen asleep and he had gone to buy the sweets, returning to see the apartment alight.

The story quickly fell apart. A post-mortem found that Stuart had been dead for some time before the fire and had fractures to his skull and one side of his larynx. Yet O'Neill continued to insist that the fire was an accident. He played the part of the grief-stricken partner as he arranged Stuart's funeral, choosing a modest coffin that he said his partner would want. On Wednesday, 11 December, Michael O'Neill was arrested and charged with murder. He maintained the ruse for the first five hours of his police interview before breaking down and admitting that he had killed Stuart a week earlier. O'Neill never offered a motive for the murder and maintained that he did not know why he did it. There had been no trigger, but he said he had been known to do stupid things and Stuart always forgave him. Not this time. It later emerged that O'Neill had lit the fire in a warped attempt to give his partner a 'more dignified' death. If people thought that Stuart had died in a terrible accident, O'Neill had reasoned, it would afford him more dignity than having been murdered by his partner. It was hard, however, for others to see any dignity in leaving a body to rot in plastic for several days before setting it alight.

The committal and sentencing

At his committal hearing in September 2014, Michael O'Neill pleaded guilty to murder and arson. During his December sentencing hearing, prosecutors claimed that he was trying to avoid the consequences of the serious financial difficulties that his business mismanagement had caused. They argued that O'Neill had then lit the fire to conceal his crime, and this act was premeditated as he had brought candles from Musk Farm to the apartment for this purpose. Sentencing O'Neill in February 2015, Justice Elizabeth Hollingworth found that he had acted 'in the heat of the moment without aforethought'. She said there was 'some aforethought' with the arson, which was not a spontaneous act. But she was not satisfied to the necessary standard that the arson was to cover up the murder. She treated it as justifying a separate sentence rather than as an aggravating feature of the murder.

In sentencing him to a total of eighteen years' jail with a non-parole period of thirteen years, Justice Hollingworth did not accept the prosecution argument that O'Neill, then 48, was motivated by financial self-preservation. She found that he and Stuart had a complex relationship that needed to be understood against the background of O'Neill's childhood and psychological make-up. She said that O'Neill's DPD had contributed to his willingness to submit to Stuart's needs, but also led to feelings of disempowerment and resentment. 'I also accept that your personality disorder played some role in your offending, and operates so as to reduce your moral culpability, and to moderate to some extent the need for general and specific deterrence,' she said. 'I accept that you are now genuinely remorseful for what you have done. After you dropped the initial charade, you made full confessions to police including disclosing to them information that was harmful to you and not otherwise known to them' (*DPP v O'Neill* [2015] VSC 25).

Justice Hollingworth said Stuart was strong, confident and successful. 'He was also a dominant, controlling personality; everything had to be done his way, both personally and professionally. No doubt that was part of the key to his professional success. And, because of your own psychological make-up, you felt inadequate; it suited you to be with someone who took control and made all the decisions. But many of your mutual friends have described how Mr Rattle used to demean and belittle you in public. He frequently complained to them that you were not satisfying him sexually. In front of others, he would call you lazy, a parasite; he would threaten to send you back to where you came from. He was critical of your lack of business acumen. There were financial and business pressures on the relationship. In the work context, he treated you like the office boy, not his partner.

'Although each of you was aware of and tolerated each other's shortcomings, there were tensions simmering beneath the surface. Those tensions seem to have also been increasing in the lead-up to December 2013. Mr Rattle's behaviour in no way justified you killing him. But the circumstances in which you killed Mr Rattle, including the history of the relationship and your fragile psychological state, mean that the sentence to be imposed for murder must be towards the lower end of the range for that offence.'

Justice Hollingworth found that when Stuart's parents left the business in 2006, Stuart expected O'Neill to make things happen financially despite the fact that he was clearly not qualified to do so. 'You had no training for the work you were doing, were disorganised and not good at details,' she found. 'Mr Rattle, your friends and workmates were well aware of your habitual lying; it was something you'd been doing since childhood. Even though Mr Rattle was at times frustrated by your incompetence and lies, he knew he could not afford to replace you; he also did not want to trouble himself with the finances or the mundane aspects of running a business. There was no life insurance for you to benefit from if Mr Rattle died, and it was Mr Rattle who brought all the income into the business. Finally, there is no evidence that things were reaching a crisis point financially, or that the true financial position was being hidden from Mr Rattle. I accept that you killed Mr Rattle in the heat of the moment, without any forethought, for reasons which are deeper and more complicated than those suggested by the prosecution' (*DPP v O'Neill* [2015] VSC 25).

The Director of Public Prosecutions (DPP), John Champion SC, appealed against O'Neill's sentence. He claimed it was manifestly inadequate and that the sentencing judge had erred in finding that the fire was not an aggravating feature of the murder, and in categorising the offence in the 'lower end' of the murder scale and fixing a 'lower than usual' non-parole period. Among other things, the DPP argued that the seriousness of some aspects of the crime were not properly considered, including that:

- O'Neill had killed his long-term partner and left his body in their apartment for five days before setting fire to it and incinerating the body.
- It had taken one to two minutes to kill Stuart, who had pleaded for his life.
- O'Neill had admitted that the arson was designed to conceal the crime, which was a significant aggravating factor, even if he had a different motive.
- O'Neill had repeatedly lied about Stuart's whereabouts, impersonated him in phone calls and texts, and only confessed after five hours of police questioning.

On 2 December 2015, Supreme Court Chief Justice Marilyn Warren and Justices Robert Redlich and Stephen Kaye found that Justice Hollingworth was correct in concluding that 'the supervening condition in this case did not mean that general deterrence must be moderated'. 'The judge was correct in taking the respondent's disorder into account in making an assessment of the moral culpability of the respondent in committing the murder of his partner,' they found. 'It is important to note that the personality disorder suffered by the applicant was highly unusual and complex. As the evidence adduced on the plea and in particular Dr Barth's evidence made plain, the respondent's fragile psychological state and complex profile were the product of the unusual and difficult nature of his background and circumstances.

'His condition bore, in a limited way, upon the seriousness with which his conduct should be viewed, as senior counsel for the appellant conceded on the plea. That said, it is also important to recognise that the condition, whilst explaining his reaction, did not attract the level of mitigation of sentence that must be allowed where *Verdins* principles are applicable.' (In *R v Verdins* [2007] 16 VR 269, the Court of Appeal stated that mental impairment was relevant to sentencing in at least five ways.) The judges found that of the error grounds relied upon, 'none of them is an appropriate ground for a Crown appeal, as they allege no more than errors in the particular case' (*DPP v O'Neill* [2015] VSCA 325). The appeal was dismissed.

Michael O'Neill's background

Michael Anthony O'Neill migrated to Australia from Ireland with his family when he was about five. They settled in Terang, in Western Victoria, where his father worked as a dairy farmer and later a farm mechanic. The second youngest of five siblings, O'Neill identified as gay early on. He was bullied at school and at home by his siblings for his effeminate manner and dislike of sport. He found being unable to fit into such a small community extremely difficult. An older sister had autism spectrum disorder, which meant much of his mother's time was devoted to her care. Their mother later said she had no idea about the bullying and would have put a stop to it if she did.

In sentencing O'Neill, Justice Elizabeth Hollingworth found that he never fully came to terms with his sexuality: 'You are someone who was cut off emotionally from an incredibly young age, who never came to terms with your sexuality, and who was bullied as a child because of it,' she said. 'The coping mechanisms which you learned as a child were avoidance, detachment, and (ultimately) dependence on others. Even though you identified yourself at an early age as exclusively homosexual, you had great trouble coming to terms with that fact. In your teens, you had a few short-lived relationships with girls. You spent your twenties having casual encounters with men. You met Mr Rattle when you were about thirty; he was your first serious intimate relationship' (*DPP v O'Neill* [2015] VSC 25).

In all the years that they were together, O'Neill never told his family that he was gay or that he was with Stuart. Nor did Stuart meet them. Around their friends, O'Neill attempted to create an image of himself as cultured and worldly by exaggerating his history and his talents. In an attempt to boost his self-respect and engender the respect of others, he told people that he had attended an elite Melbourne private school and university, when he had done neither. He also falsely claimed that his parents were divorced and that he wasn't Catholic. When working in the business, O'Neill would tell clients white lies when his mismanagement meant something went missing or a job wasn't finished on time, insisting that he had everything under control when he clearly didn't. He eventually became known by some as 'The Talented Mr Ripley', after the fictional movie character and seasoned scammer who infiltrated a society family and murdered the adult son to assume his identity. Before he killed Stuart, however, O'Neill was not seen as dangerous – just a fantasist who embellished or lied about his achievements to impress friends, clients and society acquaintances.

The lies continued after O'Neill was arrested over Stuart's murder. He spent five hours providing police with false information about what had happened in their apartment on the morning Stuart died and in the following days, weaving an intricate but untrue tale about the events of the previous week. After realising that he could no longer sustain the charade, he cracked and admitted the truth. O'Neill had been so used to embellishing the facts to suit his narrative that attempting to deceive the police was his natural fallback position. In this case, however, he was never going to get away with it in the face of the overwhelming evidence against him.

A psychologist who treated O'Neill after his arrest, Dr Mathew Barth, found he had a DPD. He was also diagnosed with adjustment disorder (see page 408) with depressed mood, a pattern of behaviour that occurs when someone is attempting to cope with a major stressful event in their life, and used a razor blade to cut his arms while in custody. The depression had emerged since the offence, but was made worse by deep-seated feelings of inadequacy, failure and self-loathing, which he had tried to suppress for most of his life.

Why did he do it?

Michael O'Neill liked to play the role of a 'Gatsby-esque' enigma. On the outside, he was an accomplished professional with a glamorous partner and the lifestyle to match. He dressed well and provided entertaining company for his many friends and acquaintances. But underneath the façade was a flawed man who craved the approval of others more than he respected himself. When things went wrong, he was unable to cope or seek the help he needed to keep his self-respect intact and his life on track.

O'Neill's relationship with Stuart Rattle was genuine, but there was a power imbalance that made him feel belittled and abused at times. This built up over the years and caused an internal resentment that pained him. O'Neill also struggled with his role and responsibility in the business, but while Stuart was prepared to criticise him personally he did not act when he knew his partner was having difficulties. Stuart could have modified O'Neill's role to reduce his responsibility and bring in someone capable of steadying the financial ship, but he didn't. This meant O'Neill dug a bigger hole for himself, and the business side of their partnership deteriorated. O'Neill would have felt this keenly, and it added to the feelings of helplessness and inadequacy he was already experiencing.

A significant aspect of the problem was O'Neill's DPD, which amplified his inferiority complex and made it difficult for him to see a way out of an increasingly difficult situation. Someone with a DPD exhibits a pattern of behaviour characterised by clinginess, over-compliance, separation anxiety and an intense fear of abandonment. Although they may also display some of this 'needy' and under-confident pattern of behaviour in the workplace, it is usually most evident in their close personal relationships. O'Neill displayed it in both, but more obviously in his personal relationship with Stuart.

It is common for someone with a DPD to seek a partner who can compensate for their perceived inadequacies, and support, protect and make decisions for them. O'Neill felt comfortable with Stuart taking the lead, but this did not turn out well, as it led to Stuart belittling him and demeaning him in front of others for both his business mistakes and his lack of enthusiasm and prowess in the bedroom. People with a DPD are desperate for approval, so Stuart's put-downs would have been even more devastating for O'Neill than most, and probably sent him further into his shell. This amplified his submissiveness and enabled his partner to feel he could say what he wanted with impunity. It all ate away at O'Neill's confidence and self-respect, and made him resent his submissive position in the relationship, despite the fact he had allowed it to happen.

In the end, O'Neill was on a knife edge in the lead-up to Stuart's death. Both were exhausted after their charity event in the country, which meant the usual bickering may have been amplified. On the morning of the murder, it appears that Michael snapped when Stuart criticised him. If O'Neill is to be believed, that criticism was nothing he hadn't heard before. But it could have been the last straw for a man who had allowed himself to be badly treated for so long. Those with a DPD will often become so submissive to keep the peace that they end up resenting both their resultant lack of power and the person they believe has taken it from them.

It's a classic catch 22 situation and an extremely unhealthy way to live. Not only does the person with the DPD allow someone else to control their life, they end up resenting them for doing it. There can be no winners in this situation, which may lead to the submissive partner being abused when they don't offer any resistance or challenge inappropriate behaviour. If this happens, the relationship is unlikely to end well. In most cases, those with a DPD are less likely than others to intentionally harm people. This case was different, as O'Neill violently killed his partner and then tried to cover up the crime in an equally shocking way. He later acknowledged that what he did was wrong, but that offers no comfort to Stuart Rattle's family and friends, who remain deeply affected by his untimely death.

Nothing justifies taking another life like this and Stuart Rattle did not deserve to die. He wasn't perfect, but none of us is, and if O'Neill wasn't happy with the way he was treated he should have done something about it or left the relationship. He didn't. Like many people with a DPD, O'Neill sought reassurance from others and a strong partner who could take the lead on key aspects of his life. He avoided challenging Stuart to keep the peace, and lacked the confidence to set his own goals or contribute to their lives as an equal. He did have his own interests, such as caring for his cows at Musk Farm, but in most situations he deferred to Stuart's wants and needs. Even when he was unhappy and felt demeaned by Stuart, O'Neill would have feared being alone even more. His friends were Stuart's friends, which would have made it extremely difficult for him to move on if the relationship foundered.

O'Neill's family was not hostile towards him, but he had never told them he was gay or had a partner, and this would have compounded his feelings of helplessness. His life was tied up with Stuart and his glamourous interior design world. Leaving that was not an option, as he would have found it extremely difficult to survive on his own in Melbourne and would have felt that he couldn't return to life in the country if his family didn't even know he was gay. Instead, O'Neill continued to portray himself as something he was not, which became increasingly stressful and difficult over time.

Tragically, Michael O'Neill and Stuart Rattle did have a good relationship for much of their time together. But the unfortunate combination of Stuart's occasional arrogance and lack of empathy and O'Neill's DPD eventually set off a powder keg. It is difficult to know if this could have been prevented. Apart from Stuart occasionally putting Michael down in public, their relationship appeared reasonably strong, and O'Neill became adept at presenting the façade of a worldly, accomplished man to others. In fact, he was a needy and self-critical man who needed help to cope with the situation in which he found himself and the relationship difficulties that caused him distress. But no one else is to blame for what happened, as there did not appear to be any obvious outward signs that O'Neill was about to crack.

Ultimately, Michael O'Neill is responsible for his own actions. He could have confided in his close friends or demanded more respect from Stuart. He could have sought counselling support to enable him to more effectively manage his anxiety and his diminishing self-respect and to deal with the relationships issues in his partnership with Stuart. But instead he killed the man he loved because he lacked resilience and could not cope.

CHAPTER 8

CHAMARI LIYANAGE

The cast

Dr Chamari Liyanage: Killed her husband Dinendra with a mallet as he slept
Dr Dinendra Athukorala: The victim, known to most as Din
Unnamed seventeen-year-old woman: Din was grooming her for sex and wanted to have sex with her and his wife at the same time
Din's ex-girlfriend: Din continued to have sex with her, sometimes in front of Liyanage

The motive

Chamari Liyanage bludgeoned her husband Din to death with a mallet after years of physical, emotional and sexual abuse. Liyanage said she felt trapped and terrified and could see no other way out of her situation. She also feared that her husband would reveal to others a sexual relationship he forced her to start with a seventeen-year-old young woman.

Introduction

Dr Chamari Liyanage was trapped in a nightmare marriage. The young doctor lived in the West Australian town of Geraldton with her husband, fellow physician Dr Dinendra Athukorala. Both were born in Sri Lanka, where they married before moving to Australia in 2011. The couple worked at the Geraldton Regional Hospital, and on the surface appeared to be a normal happy couple. Dinendra, known as Din, knew how to turn on the charm, and his wife was clearly accomplished in her own right. But appearances were deceptive.

Behind closed doors in their Geraldton unit, Din was emotionally, physically, sexually and financially abusive. The degrading treatment that he directed towards his wife started on their honeymoon, when he allegedly told her he wanted to have casual sex and to visit prostitutes. Din then began sleeping with other women and teenagers, eventually coercing his wife, despite her reluctance, fear and resistance, into doing the same and participating in sexual threesomes with him as well. Din left Liyanage's phone number on pornography websites, forced her to perform sex acts he streamed online to strangers on sexually explicit websites, and made her watch child pornography while they had sex. It was later revealed that Din had 13 terabytes of explicit and extreme pornography featuring bestiality and child exploitation across his three computers.

While Liyanage desperately tried to keep things together at work and socially, she was constantly highly anxious and panic-stricken. She considered suicide several times as things continued to deteriorate. In her diary, Liyanage revealed that her best friends in Sri Lanka had urged her to end the relationship, but Din had insisted that she stop talking to them. She also wrote that she wanted her husband to see a psychiatrist as she thought he had bipolar disorder, and of her despair that the legal system could not help her. Some of what Liyanage was subjected to was horrendous, but she stayed in the relationship, desperately hoping the man she loved would change his ways. Din didn't, and when he forced her to start a sexual threesome relationship with a seventeen-year-old woman, Liyanage decided she could take it no more.

The lead-up to the crime

When Din first came to Australia in January 2011, Liyanage stayed in Colombo. Before leaving for Australia, he invited an old girlfriend to their house and had sex with her in front of his wife. Once in Australia, the couple spoke by Skype from about 6 pm each day until late at night. He insisted on speaking for hours each night despite Liyanage's need to study. He also questioned her sexual ability. At one point, he put her contact details on websites, saying she was a sex worker. She ended up having to field numerous phone calls and, at Din's insistence, reluctantly started a relationship with another man. In September 2011, she failed a pathology exam as she had not been able to find enough time to study for it.

In November 2011, Liyanage moved to Geraldton, where the couple lived in a rented unit. In February 2012, after three weeks of temporarily working at a supermarket, Liyanage got a job as an occupational therapy assistant at a local nursing home. When Din could not get a job as a medical officer in Geraldton, he became angry and abusive towards Liyanage. He downloaded pornography, purchased sex toys and would often insist on having sex with his wife while others watched via an online web camera. Din also became physically violent, hitting her head on a wall or bedhead and pulling her hair.

Din went to Kununurra in mid-2012 to coordinate a chronic disease management project in the Kimberley region, which was not a medical position. Liyanage stayed in Geraldton until October 2012, when she too moved to Kununurra to work for the Department of Child Protection. Liyanage stayed there from October 2012 until February 2013, when she returned to Geraldton. While they were both living in Kununurra, Din initially seemed okay. But this did not last long, and he began verbally and physically abusing his wife if she tried to interact with or be kind to others. After she helped an Aboriginal woman and her children in the street and refused his demands to stop doing so, he hit her on the back of the head, causing her to fall to the ground.

'From that day, the relationship changed a lot,' Liyanage said later in court evidence. 'I was so scared of him from that day, a lot, because he hit me so much I couldn't even breathe. I was so scared of him and I didn't want to do anything wrong, because I don't know whether he's going to hit me again. So I try my best not to do anything to make him angry and tried to stay calm and silent, not to argue or not to do anything . . . I felt I'm like a trapped animal. I just had to behave the way he want me to do. There's no free choice. If I make any of my own decisions, he would get angry' (*Liyanage v The State of Western Australia* [2017] WASCA 112).

Liyanage returned to Geraldton in February 2013 to work as a resident medical officer at Geraldton Regional Hospital. Din also found a medical position there and returned in April, sharing a unit with his wife. Liyanage later said her husband started watching pornography again, making her watch as well and controlling her actions. He was also downloading child pornography, which concerned his wife greatly. Din forced Liyanage to watch the child pornography, sometimes while having sex with him. She said that if she refused to watch, he would punish her by forcing her to have anal sex with him, which she didn't like. He also hit her on the face, chest, arms and legs. Later that year the beatings became regular, and he would make implied threats by telling her stories about people having acid thrown in their face.

After considering suicide again, at the end of July 2013 Liyanage begged Din to 'let her go'. He agreed that they could separate but only if she kept their joint bank account and passwords, so that he could access her money, and forwarded him her emails. He left their home on 1 August 2013 and moved into a unit arranged by the hospital. Concerned about his threats, Liyanage did not tell anyone about what had happened. Not long after Din moved out she visited him and found him crying on the couch. She decided to take him back.

'I was independent person and I was a doctor,' she said later. 'I am quite intelligent, but still I couldn't escape from him. He keep me almost captive and keep punishing me and keep making me doing things which I totally don't want to do. So I knew how powerful his – he is. And he has his brothers at Sri Lanka, and he might have his friends at Sri Lanka, and he has money, because – all the money I earn, plus his money. He handled them, so he has enough money to carry out anything. And I've seen [the deceased's] anger. I've seen the look in his face and I was terrified. And by that time I didn't really have any friends or anyone, and I only had my family, and they're the only people I really love in this world, and I really didn't want anything to happen to them because of me' (*Liyanage v The State of Western Australia* [2017] WASCA 112).

In late 2013 and early 2014, Din was allegedly hitting Liyanage multiple times each week with his knees, foot, fist, a wooden rolling pin or wooden spoons, and a slingshot firing small metal balls. In late February, the couple returned to Sri Lanka, where Din spent time with a former girlfriend and arranged for the three of them to have sex, despite Liyanage's reluctance. He allegedly hit his wife in front of his former girlfriend, and befriended a sixteen-year-old in the hope of having sex with her. They returned on 23 March, after which the sexual activity continued on Skype.

Din was getting more angry and irritable with Liyanage. He was downloading a great deal of child pornography, and she later said he was becoming 'more and more interested in more younger ages'. She was forced to follow him around the house at all times when he wanted her to do so. In April 2014, Liyanage tried to kill herself with a Panadol overdose, but failed when she vomited up most of the tablets she had swallowed. Around this time, the couple met a seventeen-year-old young woman whom Din tried to groom for sex. He encouraged the girl and his wife to pose for photos, including them touching each other's breasts, and made Liyanage show the girl how to stimulate herself. Sexual activity occurred but it fell short of intercourse.

On 1 June, Liyanage could take no more and told Din she was leaving him because she didn't want to be involved in what he was doing to the girl. She agreed to stay only after he begged her to do so. Liyanage considered telling police but could not muster up the courage to do it. Instead, the situation continued to worsen, and she worried about the young woman's future being ruined by her involvement with them. 'I thought about it, but then what am I going to go and tell them? If I go – if I went to police station and tell them that my husband is treating me this badly, he's keep beating me and he's verbally, physically, sexually, emotionally abuse me, how are they going to find out?' she said later. 'Because everyone who knew us outside would tell, this is a very happy couple. All the time they see us, we were hugging, kissing, holding hands, smiling. There would be no one to support what I am telling, and [the deceased] would still pretend like I'm lying.

'And if I told them he's downloading pornography and if I told them about child porn and things, they might tell these days everyone download pornography, and they might not do anything. They might not do anything about it. And, anyway, I have to go back to the home at the end of the day. So if I take a step like that, I don't know how I'm going to live rest of my life because [the deceased] has already threatened me he would really, really do something to destroy my life and my family if I do something like that. So rest of whole my life I would be so scared about the safety of myself and safety of my family' (*Liyanage v The State of Western Australia* [2017] WASCA 112).

The killing

After arriving home at 4 pm on 23 June 2014, Liyanage heated a curry on a portable gas cooker as the electricity wasn't working, and helped Din research migration information on the computer for his brother. After arguing about work, they retired to their bedroom, where Liyanage was clearly unhappy. It was a place she had grown to dread. Sometime during the night Din spoke on the phone to his brother in Sri Lanka. Before the sun rose, he was dead. At some point during the night, Liyanage took a large 1.79-kilogram mallet from a cupboard and hit her husband at least twice in the head and neck while he slept, causing extensive blunt-force trauma injuries that resulted in serious blood loss.

Not long after 6 am, Liyanage called triple 0. Ambulance officers quickly arrived, but Din was already dead. There were no signs of a struggle or physical violence, but blood had spattered on the walls, ceiling and Liyanage's clothes. Din was lying on the bed with a pillow over his head and the mallet nearby. His wife was huddled up on the couch and in a distressed state. She told police that she could not remember killing her husband and that her actions were involuntary. She could not remember anything in the five hours between going to bed and waking up the next morning.

Liyanage claimed that her actions were in response to her constant fear that Din would harm her, and that she felt that she had to do something to protect herself from him and the hopeless situation she found herself in. She felt she could take no more of the shocking physical and emotional abuse, such as him forcing her to engage in sexual acts that he recorded and in non-consensual sex with other women. She also said that Din was regularly physically violent towards her and had totally controlled her finances and social life.

The trial

At her murder trial in early 2016, Liyanage, then 35, pleaded not guilty. The court heard that the marriage was marred by the worst kind of sexual, physical and emotional abuse. Friends and colleagues revealed that Liyanage and Din appeared to be a happily married couple. But Liyanage told police that the situation was completely different behind closed doors, where Din kicked her, pulled her hair, threw dinner plates at her and beat her with furniture and a wooden rolling pin, often after making her stay home from work. He controlled their finances and forced her to participate in a range of unwanted sexual activities, including threesomes, some of which he filmed and streamed online.

The seventeen-year-old with whom Din and Liyanage had a relationship revealed that Din once gave her whisky, which saw her wake up the next morning with a headache. Din knew that she was a virgin, but at some time during the night he had moved on top of her until Liyanage told him to stop. The older couple demonstrated sex while the teenager watched, and she said Liyanage did what her husband asked, 'with a smile'. The girl, who cannot be named, also told the court that when she visited the couple she shared activities with them such as leg waxing, having a shower together and uncomfortable touching. Din bought her presents and took photos and videos of her, which she didn't like. The relationship ended when Liyanage privately told the girl that she was free to leave at any time. Until then, the girl had felt she could not say no to Din, who was always very controlling.

Liyanage's defence described her as a sleep-deprived, anxious, trapped and battered woman. She claimed she had tried to leave Din six times but he would threaten her and she felt trapped. She had attempted suicide several times and in one case tried to drown herself, making it as far as the Geraldton foreshore before thoughts of her parents stopped her from acting. Liyanage had few friends she could confide in, so continued to feel more and more isolated and trapped. The defence called two forensic psychiatrists, who said that following psychological trauma or extended abuse, people could flip into a state of automatism that saw their mind act independently of their body. They likened it to sleepwalking, during which the sleepwalker could carry out a range of tasks without remembering them.

In the end, the jury found Liyanage guilty of manslaughter. Justice Stephen Hall found that Liyanage probably knew what she was doing when she laid multiple blows on an area that, as a doctor, she knew was vulnerable. Justice Hall did accept that the accused had experienced post-traumatic amnesia and that she was acting in self-defence. But he found her response was excessive and disproportionate to the threat. He said apart from this offence Liyanage had seemed to have an exemplary character and was not at risk of reoffending. Justice Hall found, however, that while Din was a manipulative and merciless offender, his death was not justified and Liyanage had gone too far. Human life could not be taken, he said, regardless of how apparently deserving the circumstances were.

In February 2016, Justice Hall jailed Liyanage for four years. She became eligible for parole in July 2016, but did not apply because if she did so, her visa would have been revoked and she would have been deported to Sri Lanka. A community campaign backed by the likes of Australian of the Year and domestic violence survivor Rosie Batty saw authorities pledge not to deport Liyanage when she was released on parole in March 2017. At the time, Liyanage said she had felt trapped in a cycle of domestic violence, all the while clinging to the hope that her husband would change. When he didn't, being intelligent and professionally accomplished meant nothing, as she perceived that she was helpless and unable to escape. Liyanage said the emotional abuse and manipulation were especially crippling, as she did love her husband and had seen his good side.

In June 2017, Liyanage lost her appeal in the WA Appeal Court to have her manslaughter conviction overturned. The unanimous decision found that her four-year sentence was appropriate and significantly less than those usually imposed for manslaughter, even in the presence of significant mitigating factors. It was not considered to be manifestly excessive.

Chamari Liyanage's background

Chamari Rasika Denuwanthe Gunathilaka Liyanage grew up in a family that was clearly well off, as she studied medicine and her father built a home for her. She met Dinendra Athukorala in February 2009, when they both worked at Colombo North Teaching Hospital in Sri Lanka. Liyanage was 29 and on rotation in the haematology department. The couple became friends, and she lost her virginity to him. Din seemed intelligent and charming. Liyanage felt that she was in love, but became nervous when others warned her about her future husband's reputation. As the oldest daughter in her family, however, she felt obliged to go ahead with the marriage to reduce the burden on her parents. Din soon revealed his true nature as a manipulative, merciless abuser and sexual deviant.

In March 2009, Liyanage found work at Kurunegala Teaching Hospital in Sri Lanka, about two and a half hours away by car, and stayed there for six months. She and Din saw each other occasionally, and she witnessed him watching pornography on his computer, a behaviour that surprised her. In mid-2009, Din was granted a visa to visit Australia but Liyanage declined to go with him as she wanted to continue her training to become an anaesthetist. For the following year, until October 2010, she worked in anaesthetics at Mawanella Base Hospital in Sri Lanka. The couple saw each other on weekends. Din told her not to talk to others about him and she also stopped contacting her friends after he asked her to do so.

Liyanage broke up with Din in February 2010 after he cheated on her with another woman. But they reunited when he apologised and promised not to do it again. Din continued to see the other woman, distressing Liyanage so much that she planned to take her own life with a vial of muscle relaxant she found at the hospital. Din talked her out of it. Despite his apparent contrition, he then had sex with other women in front of Liyanage. Din proposed in September 2010, telling Liyanage they should marry before he changed his mind. When they did marry on 4 October 2010, Din was angry that Liyanage's family had invited about 50 guests. He hadn't wanted any friends present.

While on their honeymoon in Chennai, India, Din told his new wife that he wanted to pay someone for casual sex, which she refused to take part in. Back in Sri Lanka, Liyanage lived in the house her father built for her in Delgoda, about ten minutes away from her parents. She worked at Lady Ridgeway Hospital in Colombo, training in pathology after Din asked her to change her intended specialty from anaesthesia (which he did not like). She agreed because she 'didn't want to hurt him'. From that point on, the control Din exerted and the abuse he perpetrated continued to worsen.

Why did she do it?

Chamari Liyanage's experience shows that domestic violence does not discriminate. Women of all backgrounds, levels of education and social status can find themselves in violent situations they cannot see a way out of. Liyanage was a highly educated doctor and responsible for the health of her patients, yet she felt unable to leave an abusive husband who forced her to perform degrading sexual acts. He also allegedly hit her with his fists and household appliances. When women stay with an abusive partner like this, those on the outside often ask why she didn't leave. It is true that Liyanage could have left her husband, approached the police or domestic violence services and returned to her family in Sri Lanka. But, like many women in similar situations, she felt powerless and unable to act. It also must be emphasised that for many women, the most dangerous time in a volatile relationship is when they do decide to leave. Some are killed when they signal their intention to leave or physically attempt to.

In Liyanage's case, a number of factors conspired to keep her in this most unsuitable and dangerous situation. Living in Geraldton, in regional Western Australia and more than 400 kilometres north of Perth, made it difficult for her to flee. With few family and friends in Australia, it would have been logistically challenging to walk out, particularly if she wanted to stay in Australia. By this stage she knew what Din was like and how violent he could be, so she would have worried about what he was capable of should she break up with him for good. She also loved her husband and hoped he would see the error of his ways and return to being the caring man she believed she had married. That was highly unlikely, and inevitably his behaviour worsened and became more brazen over time. This meant Liyanage became more desperate.

Another contributing factor was the high likelihood that Liyanage had a DPD (see pages 217–30). People with a DPD have a very strong need to be protected and cared for by another person. They become clingy, over-compliant, have separation anxiety and an intense fear of abandonment. As we have seen, they can be like this at work but are usually most needy in their personal relationships. Since the killing, Liyanage has spoken about her compulsion to stay with her husband, despite the disrespectful way he treated her and other women. Even after everything, she said she still loved him, a fact many people would find hard to believe. Liyanage was clearly dependent on her charismatic partner, who appears to have worked hard at denting her confidence further to make her feel even more reliant on him.

Those with a DPD are statistically more likely to be abused in some way than those who don't have the disorder. A study by Benotsch et al. (2017) found that dependent personality traits in women predicted a lack of assertiveness in sexual situations. This was linked to behaviour that could jeopardise sexual health, such as agreeing not to use a condom or participating in sexually aggressive behaviour. Liyanage's husband coerced her into a range of sexual acts she found degrading, painful and abhorrent. Despite this, she did not know how she could stop him or refuse to participate. His physical violence convinced her that it was not safe to leave the marriage.

Din physically, emotionally and sexually abused his wife for years, and his behaviour completely sapped her confidence and enjoyment of life. Living with someone who not only physically abuses you but openly cheats with other women and forces you to participate in unwanted sexual activities would be difficult to cope with for even the strongest woman. For someone who lacked confidence in their personal relationships, and who lived thousands of kilometres from her family, it would have been completely crippling.

Eventually, Liyanage felt that there was no way out. Physically she could have left, but mentally she did not feel it was possible. Her self-respect would have been at rock bottom, and even if she had found the courage to leave, how would she tell others about what had happened? And what violence would he inflict on her if he found out that she was trying to escape from him?

When Liyanage snapped and killed her husband, it was a terrible situation for all involved. Din was cruel, but he did not deserve to die. No one has the right to kill another person, even if that person is abusive. Unfortunately for Liyanage, she did not feel that there was anything she could do to protect herself by seeking help or leaving. Nor did anyone realise the depth of her distress. Some women in abusive relationships are very good at hiding it, and she was no exception. Liyanage later admitted that from the outside they appeared to be a happy couple, so it was unlikely that anyone would have tried to counsel or help her. This shows how difficult it can be to pinpoint abuse by a manipulative abuser.

Liyanage and battered woman syndrome

As well as having a DPD, Chamari Liyanage suffered from battered woman syndrome, which can be debilitating. Liyanage killed her husband after years of horrific abuse. Up to 60 per cent of men who are violent towards their partner also sexually abuse them (Ewing, 1997), for example by sodomising them against their wishes, forcing them to engage in bondage activities, or forcing them to participate in sexual activities with other people or groups.

As we have seen, the term 'learned helplessness' (see pages 223–4) is now used to describe the expectation that, when someone has had repeated unpleasant or painful experiences in their life that they were unable to avoid or prevent no matter how hard they tried, they will be likely to assume that in the future they won't be able to avoid or prevent similar negative outcomes, no matter what they try to do to prevent or manage them, and they give up trying to do so. This pattern of learned helplessness is often apparent in abusive relationships such as Liyanage's.

She also found herself caught in a cycle of domestic violence that mirrored Dr Lenore Walker's (2016) 'three-stage Cycle of Violence' model (see page 224). When the verbal and minor physical abuse started, Liyanage attempted to placate and accommodate Din to prevent more serious abuse. He showed some contrition, but then progressed to more serious physical and sexual violence. Liyanage felt very afraid, but Din insisted that things would improve. Din then became aware that his wife wanted to leave and tried to make her stay by promising to change. But the cycle soon began again and Liyanage again contemplated leaving because she had realised nothing was going to stop the abuse. By then, she felt trapped by Din's threats, a sense of learned helplessness, a lack of financial resources, not having family close by and a lack of access to suitable accommodation. Feeling scared, helpless and frustrated, Liyanage decided the only way out was to kill her husband.

CHAPTER 9

ANTHONY SHERNA

The cast

Anthony Sherna: The killer. Born Anatoli Chernishoff, he was 41 at the time of the killing.
Susanne (Susie) Wild: The victim and Sherna's partner of eighteen years. She was 53 when she died.
Lorna Brazendale: Susie's mother

The motive

In 2008, Anthony Sherna fatally strangled his partner of eighteen years, Susie Wild, after what he claimed were years of torment, abuse and humiliation at her hands. He said he could not take it any more.

Introduction

According to Anthony Sherna, his partner Susie Wild was a 'control freak' who tormented him for years and would not even allow him to defecate in his own toilet at home because of the potential 'mess' and 'smell', forcing him to 'hang on' until he could go at work or use the toilets at a nearby shopping centre. As a result, Sherna claims he tried to control his bowel movements so he could use toilets outside the home, but found long weekends 'a problem'. He also says his partner of eighteen years would not allow him to choose his own work clothes and banned him from Friday-night drinks with his mates. Wild allegedly controlled their finances 'down to the last five cents' and threw beer cans at him when she was not happy. She also reportedly forced him to change his surname by deed poll from Chernishoff to Sherna to prove his love to her.

Other claims that emerged about their relationship included that Susie gave Sherna no spending or lunch money, despite him being the breadwinner, made him three sandwiches each day, one for morning tea and two for lunch, rationed his cigarettes to twelve per day, limited his TAB phone account bets to $1.50, never allowed a Christmas tree in their home and made him give up playing cricket, which he had loved. She also reportedly spent time with her ex-boyfriend, called Sherna a weak bastard for tolerating it and wrongly accused him of infidelity. At night, the couple ate prepared meals heated in the microwave, and Susie would tell her partner what time to retire – in their separate bedrooms.

Eventually, Anthony Sherna snapped and killed his partner. But nothing excuses his actions, even if Susie Wild did everything he said she did.

The crime

On Friday, 1 February 2008, Sherna left work at around 5.30 pm. A friend had asked him to an Australia versus India Twenty20 cricket match at the Melbourne Cricket Ground that night, but he declined. Instead, Sherna and his diminutive partner, who was just 152 cm tall, spent the evening at their home in Tarneit, 25 kilometres west of the Melbourne CBD. He drank six to eight beers and she had several glasses of red wine. As the night wore on, they argued over a mobile phone bill before Susie rang her mother, Lorna Brazendale, in Tasmania just before 10 pm. They spoke for almost two hours.

As midnight approached, Sherna was rocking his pet Maltese terrier, Hubble, to sleep in the laundry as he usually did each night. He later claimed that Susie stormed in yelling, screaming and distressing the dog. Upset, he followed Susie into the kitchen after grabbing the cord from his dressing gown, then strangled her with it until she could no longer breathe, despite her pleas for him to stop. 'I was real angry,' Sherna later told police. 'What happened was I had left the laundry, my dressing gown hangs on the door, I grabbed the cord off the dressing gown – I was just so angry I just – because I was drunk – that's, I grabbed the cord to kill her. I was so angry' (*DPP v Sherna* [2009] VSC 526).

Sherna admitted that while his initial intention was to kill Susie, he had tried to calm himself down but then changed his mind when she again taunted him about the mobile phone bill. 'And at that inexplicable moment I had a surge of emotion,' he said. 'It's impossible to explain. And I lost all rationality. I didn't decide anything. There was nothing in my head. It was a complete surge of emotion. I had no rationality about it. The next thing I knew she was dead' (*DPP v Sherna* [2009] VSC 526).

After killing his partner, Sherna went to a poker machine venue at the nearby Werribee Plaza, where he drank more alcohol and played the pokies for up to four hours. He then visited a brothel and returned home at around 5 am. He later dragged Susie's body into her bedroom and put it on the bed, where he left it for several days in the summer heat. On the Monday, he called his employer to say he needed the week off because his wife had left him. The next day, he dug a hole in the backyard and buried her body, planting several plants nearby. Sherna also reportedly took Hubble to a pet resort, not wanting him to be traumatised by Susie's decomposing body. It may also have been to prevent the dog from trying to dig it up. Eight days later, on 9 February, police arrived to check on Susie's welfare and Sherna confessed that he had killed her. In his few days of freedom before his arrest, he had drunk beer, played with Hubble and placed numerous bets on horse races via his phone account.

The sentencing

Sherna's first murder trial ended with a hung jury. At the second, which saw him convicted of the lesser crime of manslaughter, Sherna's counsel argued that the prosecution could not prove beyond reasonable doubt that he intended to kill Susie or cause her really serious injury. The jury accepted this. In sentencing Sherna in November 2009, Justice David Beach said that whatever view one might take of Susie and their relationship, 'she was a person who was obviously loved, and is now deeply missed, by her mother'. In her victim impact statement, Lorna Brazendale said she found it very difficult to come to terms with her daughter's sudden death. She was having trouble sleeping and felt overtired and stressed all the time. 'I would say the emotional trauma and ongoing anxiety is probably the worst aspect,' she said (*DPP v Sherna* [2009] VSC 526).

Justice Beach accepted that the partnership between Sherna and Susie was 'one of considerable unhappiness over a prolonged period of years. Further, I accept that the deceased was both controlling and domineering of you and that from time to time this involved significant episodes of unpleasantness on her behalf. Nonetheless, even if everything you said in evidence concerning the deceased and your relationship with her was true, it would not justify or excuse killing her. The account you gave in evidence was an exaggerated one which over-emphasised some of the negative aspects of the relationship.

'I accept that you and the deceased had a very abnormal relationship, with each of you being dependent on the other to an extent considerably greater than would be regarded by others as usual or normal. Mr Cummins, a consulting clinical and forensic psychologist, gave evidence that yours was "an extremely symbiotic relationship with each of you being inappropriately dependent on the other". I accept Mr Cummins' evidence in that regard. However, again, it does not provide any justification for placing a cord around the neck of the deceased' (*DPP v Sherna* [2009] VSC 526).

Justice Beach accepted Mr Cummins' view that when he killed Susie, Sherna had a chronic adjustment disorder (see page 408) and a dysthymic disorder, a specific depressive disorder one level below a major depressive disorder. 'However, I do not accept that the seriousness of these conditions warrants more than a limited moderation of deterrence considerations,' he said (*DPP v Sherna* [2009] VSC 526).

Justice Beach said that until the killing, Sherna had been a man of good character who had not been in trouble with the law. He had successfully held down responsible jobs and there was nothing to suggest that he was 'other than a law abiding and self-supporting member of the community'. Justice Beach also accepted that Sherna had good prospects for rehabilitation and considered his plea of guilty to manslaughter. But he said the crime was a brutal attack on someone much smaller and weaker, and sentenced Sherna to fourteen years' jail with a non-parole period of ten years.

Anthony Sherna's background

Anthony Sherna was born Anatoli Chernishoff. His Russian Orthodox mother, Fatima Chernishoff, came to Australia in 1962. The second youngest of eight siblings, Sherna was born in July 1966. Fatima divorced his alcoholic father when he was young. Claims later emerged that Sherna's vision was affected when his father punched his mother while she was pregnant with him. His father also reportedly put a noose around an older brother's neck during one of his rages.

Sherna was working with the Department of Consumer Affairs when he met Susie Wild on a train in 1989. He was 23 and she was 35. Susie was from Tasmania and had a son from a previous relationship, whom she never saw. She was largely estranged from her family. Sherna quickly became infatuated with Susie and they soon moved in together. But the union was not a happy one. Sherna's family found Susie to be dominating and extreme in her behaviour. She did not work, was agoraphobic and rarely left the house apart from shopping trips. Both drank heavily – he up to eight cans of beer a day and she up to eight bottles of wine a week.

In 2002, they moved into the house in Tarneit. Sherna later told police that they had no children, family or friends. He said they never had a holiday and slept in separate bedrooms for most of their time together. 'The last time we had sex was three years ago,' he said. 'We never kissed open mouthed. It would just be a peck on the cheek. We argued like all couples do, except other couples can go and talk to someone, a friend, family, et cetera, but because we had no friends or family that we could confide in, it just built up – built up years of abuse. Her favourite term was "low-life". Used to call me low-life' (*DPP v Sherna* [2009] VSC 526).

Sherna claimed that Susie was 'a mouth' and the neighbours did not like them. Susie did not have a driver's licence, so Sherna did all the shopping and drove her around. At his trial, Sherna described his partner as an aggressive, difficult and controlling person who completely dominated him. Among other things, she allegedly grazed his chest with a knife, forced him to sleep on a camp bed in a spare room while she had the main bedroom, threw full beer cans at his head, abused him and made various threats (*DPP v Sherna* [2009] VSC 526). But none of this excuses Sherna taking his partner's life.

Why did he do it?

The relationship between Anthony Sherna and Susie Wild was toxic, and even a well-adjusted adult would have struggled to make it work. Given Sherna's life challenges, it was doomed to fail. The court heard that he had a chronic adjustment disorder and a dysthymic disorder, a type of depression. Neither excuse his actions, but they do form part of the picture. It's not surprising that he wasn't coping with the stress of their dysfunctional relationship. Sherna also has a DPD, which made him overly dependent on a dominant partner. As we have seen, DPD is characterised by clinginess, over-compliance, separation anxiety and an intense fear of abandonment. However bad things got, Sherna probably saw the alternative – leaving his partner – as worse.

Most people with a DPD find it difficult to make decisions without help, which means they often seek a partner who will do this. They become submissive for fear of the wrath of others, and lack confidence in their ability to set or achieve goals independently. Many stay with an inappropriate partner as they fear the alternative more. They don't like being alone or having to look after themselves. Sherna was a classic case of DPD and would have worried and stressed about the prospect of being abandoned, even though the situation he found himself in was often degrading and dysfunctional.

Sherna was desperate for a relationship where he could find acceptance and approval. If this meant allowing a dominant partner to make decisions on day-to-day issues, in his mind that was the price he had to pay. He was prepared to be submissive to avoid being abandoned. Sherna was probably too scared to challenge Susie, and this enabled Susie to bully him without fear of him challenging her. She may not have realised how unusual and unfair her behaviour could be, as she had no one alerting her to its inappropriateness. It also appeared that due to her apparent agoraphobia – fear of leaving an environment you are familiar with and of being in a crowded place or in wide open spaces – Susie was also dependent on Sherna to an unhealthy degree, but in a different way. She most likely needed him to protect her from her agoraphobic anxieties by helping to minimise the amount of time she had to spend alone outside their residence.

They both persisted with a disastrous relationship that probably should have ended years earlier. Neither partner demonstrated much capacity for resilience. It probably suited Sherna to have a dominant partner and for Susie to have someone she felt she could mould and control as well as rely on when she felt unable to leave the house by herself because of her agoraphobia. They each played their role, in Susie's case mostly a dominant one where she made most of the decisions and he accepted them. This suited them both up to a point. But as her behaviour became more extreme and Sherna did not have the courage or resilience to challenge it, the situation became untenable. At some point, things were almost certainly going to come to a head as, according to Sherna, Susie became even more controlling and emotionally abusive, and on occasions was also physically violent. While others would have left, Sherna did not see leaving as an option. The thought of having to rebuild his life alone would have terrified him.

Instead, he continued to put up with an unhealthy environment and failed to tell Susie what needed to change for things to work. Nor did he seek help that could have given him strategies to deal with the power imbalance and give Susie a chance to modify her behaviour. This meant that Sherna's anger at his treatment grew and festered to the point where he could take it no longer. When Susie upset his dog that night, he snapped and strangled her.

Nothing excuses Anthony Sherna's behaviour, but we can hopefully learn from it. If those who have a loved one with a DPD can recognise that they have the disorder and are in a dysfunctional relationship, they may be able to gently suggest that they seek help, while pointing out the benefits of leaving a toxic partner. If the person is offered counselling and support in establishing a new life, then they may be able to move on. In Sherna's case, he either did not confide in anyone or those around him did not realise how hopeless his situation had become until it was too late.

CHAPTER 10

CIA XIA LIAO

The cast

Cia Xia Liao: Killed her lover's wife and his young grandson. She was aged 45 when she committed the crime. Many media reports named her 'Cai', but the official sentencing document and Supreme Court of Victoria officials spelled it 'Cia'.
Giangwa 'Brian' Mach: Husband and grandfather of the victims and Liao's former lover. He was aged 61 at the time.
Mai Mach: Brian's wife and murder victim, who was aged 60 when she died
Alistair Kwong: Brian and Mai's four-year-old grandson and murder victim

The motive

Cia Xia Liao killed the wife and grandson of her former lover Brian Mach after taking all three prisoner and assaulting Brian, to exact revenge on him after he decided not to leave his wife and move in with her.

Introduction

Born in 1970, Cia Xia Liao grew up poor in a mountain village in China's Guangdong Province. Formerly known in English as Canton, Guangdong borders Hong Kong in the south-east and has more than 4300 kilometres of coastline. After Liao's father died when she was nine, she was raised by her mother, whom she was close to. Liao had an older brother and a sister-in-law, whom she later claimed emotionally and physically abused her when she went to live with the family.

At fourteen, Liao left school, learned to make Chinese food and returned to her home town to start a business with her cousin selling bread and cakes. At twenty, she married her first husband and had a daughter soon after. They were happy until her husband died in a car accident when Liao was 30. Grief-stricken, she considered suicide, but taking care of her nine-year-old daughter kept her going. Two years after her husband's death, Liao married an older cousin. The union lasted for several years but broke up when her second husband was unfaithful. The couple divorced in 2004, but they continued to live together in the same house until 2007. Liao ended up having to pay her ex-husband a significant amount of money to get him to leave.

While this was playing out, the newly single mother ran a successful business. In 2008 she sold some property, which enabled her daughter to enrol in Year 10 at a school in Australia. Liao visited her daughter occasionally but continued to live in China and run her business ventures there. In March 2011, she met Melbourne-based Brian Mach, a friend of her uncle's, when Brian was in China. At the time, he was separated from his wife, Mai. Liao's relationship with Brian developed in 2012, largely over WeChat, and she later claimed that he had promised to marry her both privately and in the presence of her family. During 2013, however, Brian decided that he wanted to continue his marriage, despite also allowing his relationship with Liao to continue. He and Liao lived together for a while during 2014, but by early 2015 it was increasingly clear that Brian did not want to commit to Liao.

The crime

On 29 March 2015, 45-year-old Liao, who was in Australia on a tourist visa and living in Albion, asked Brian to come to her place to discuss the relationship. This conversation occurred. On 30 March, she went to Brian's house in Albanvale, near Caroline Springs in Melbourne's western suburbs, unannounced. She demanded that he accompany her to Sunshine Police Station to sign a statutory declaration that she thought would in some way nullify his marriage. He went, but once at the police station he refused to sign anything and wrote a letter, which was signed by a justice of the peace, affirming his marriage to his wife.

On 31 March, Liao left her home at about 5.44 am and drove to Brian's house. At 6 am she watched his wife, Mai, leave to go to work. She then let herself in the front door. Brian, who was minding his four-year-old grandson, Alistair Kwong, asked Liao to leave but she refused. They again argued about her wanting him to leave his wife. Alistair woke several times and Brian settled him back to sleep.

Brian's memory of the rest of the day is virtually non-existent. At some point, Liao slipped a drug into his drink and he lost consciousness. When he woke, he was tied up on the lounge-room floor, his arms and legs secured with masking tape and his mouth stuffed with a rag. He had been that way for several hours. While Brian was unconscious, Liao went to the bedroom where Alistair slept and used a pair of garden shears to viciously attack him around the face, head and throat, killing him where he lay. The tiny boy had no chance. After he had died, Liao covered him with a doona and left him.

When Brian finally woke up, Liao asked when his wife was expected home and kicked him in the head, face and chest as he lay bound on the ground. As she terrorised her petrified former lover, she told him she was going to kill Mai when she got home. When Brian asked how Alistair was, Liao did not respond. She also threatened him with the garden shears and said she would push the pointed ends into his eye if he called out or made any noise. Mai, 60, returned home at around 5 pm, driving her car into the backyard and closing the gates. Before she even made it inside, Liao raced at her with the shears, chopping and cutting at her head, face and neck. Mai died at the scene after screaming for help several times. While this was happening, Brian lay helplessly inside, listening to his wife's dying screams. He still did not know that his grandson was also dead.

Children from neighbouring homes heard Mai's desperate call for help and alerted their parents, who called police. Liao then returned to the lounge room, brandishing the shears and boasting to Brian, 'I used these. I cut the bitch's throat.' She then threatened to kill Alistair's mother when she arrived to pick him up. 'I've killed everyone to make you suffer and if I'm happy I'll let you go with them,' she told him. Police arrived soon after to find Liao sitting on a couch next to where Brian lay on the floor. She was immediately arrested. Brian was taken to hospital and treated for a cut to his leg and bruising to his hand, head and abdomen. When police interviewed Cia Xia Liao on 1 April, she declined to answer questions, as was her right. But she eventually pleaded guilty to the murder of Mai Mach and Alistair Kwong, and to injuring and forcibly imprisoning Brian Mach.

The sentencing

Liao wept during her plea hearing in the Melbourne Magistrates' Court in August 2015, and sobbed, rocked and leaned against her translator during her November sentencing hearing. The court heard that she had had a strong desire for Brian to divorce so that they could be married. The Crown had suggested that this desire was primarily motivated by her ambition to obtain Australian citizenship, but the defence team denied this. The court was told that Liao had offered Brian money to marry her, so she could live with her daughter in Melbourne. When he did not want this, she turned to using illicit drugs to cope. It was claimed, however, that the drug ice played no role in the killings. Liao's counsel, David Gibson, said his client had invested great faith in her relationship with Brian and that the relationship was strong. When it failed, she became desperately unhappy and had threatened to kill Mai as early as November 2014. In his victim impact statement, Brian said that as a result of the murder of his wife and grandson, his daughters and their families no longer spoke to him and his whole family had fallen apart.

In sentencing Liao in December 2015, Justice Lex Lasry found that her relationship with Brian extended beyond just being for potential convenience 'and was characterised by a strong emotional commitment, at least on your part'. Consultant psychiatrist Associate Professor Andrew Carroll prepared a report on Liao's mental state and gave evidence. He found that she showed evidence of personality disorders, predominantly DPD but with some histrionic features (see pages 231–2 for details of the core features of histrionic personality disorder). The disorder was primarily connected with her intimate relationships and had not obstructed her progress in other areas of her life.

'Among other things, you are apparently prone to becoming intensely preoccupied with fears of abandonment within relationships and will behave in any way you think is necessary to maintain the relationship,' Justice Lasry said. 'In Associate Professor Carroll's opinion, you were severely distressed at the time of committing these offences and your behaviour is, according to him, only understandable in the context of your personality structure and your turbulent and dysfunctional relationship with Brian Mach. In his opinion, your personality disorder and related distress were part of a matrix of factors that contributed to the offending behaviour. You have no issues involving drugs or alcohol. In his report, he also referred to what he described as a "diagnosable" adjustment disorder (see page 408). That condition worsened with a depressive episode after you went into custody but that has resolved as has the adjustment disorder' (*R v Liao* [2015] VSC 730).

In giving evidence, Associate Professor Carroll described how active and passive aggressive behaviour can be triggered in people with a DPD when the relationship that person values so strongly is threatened. He said that Liao's plan to kill Mai was consistent with the behavioural tendencies of someone with a personality disorder, given that she perceived Mai as a threat to her relationship with Brian. In summing up, Justice Lasry said that when Carroll was asked whether Liao's personality disorder contributed to her offending, he said, 'in the absence of your disordered personality you would not have lost perspective in the way that [you] did over the months, hours and moments prior to the offence, but that it was not a sufficient explanation for your offending'.

Justice Lasry said the correlational rather than causative type of relationship between Liao's mental state and offending made it problematic in considering whether, and to what extent, it reduced her moral culpability. Liao's counsel, David Gibson, submitted that her condition did reduce her moral culpability and that denunciation was less likely to be a relevant sentencing objective. He also claimed that due to her personality disorder there should be some moderation of the significance of the principle of general deterrence. Justice Lasry said that Associate Professor Carroll had provided a further report that added a separate adjustment disorder, arising from the distress caused by the ending of her relationship with Brian, which was also a factor in Liao's offending.

'Your counsel submitted that your severe distress which was indicative of your adjustment disorder, should because of its effect, reduce the moral culpability of your offending and result in the significance of general and specific deterrence being moderated as sentencing considerations,' Justice Lasry said. 'As becomes obvious, I do not consider there is a significant role for specific deterrence in any event. I respectfully agree with the prosecutor that it is not feasible to "disentangle" the links between an adjustment disorder and the overlying personality disorder. The diagnostic labels are starting to achieve an inflated importance in this matter. In my opinion, it is appropriate to take your personality and adjustment disorders into account in considering your personal circumstances and endeavouring to understand why you committed these terrible offences.

'The adjustment disorder to which Associate Professor Carroll refers is linked to the personality disorder he also identified and explained in his first report. I am willing to accept Associate Professor Carroll's opinion that at the time of committing these offences you were severely distressed in the context of your failed relationship with Brian Mach and that was a consequence of your vulnerable personality. There was therefore some effect on your judgment. It is appropriate for me to conclude that to some degree only, your moral culpability is lessened. However, I agree with the prosecution's submissions that there is nothing about your mental state that requires me to moderate the effect of general deterrence in the sentence I will impose on you' (*R v Liao* [2015] VSC 730).

Justice Lasry found Liao's actions were premeditated. 'In my opinion you went there with an existing intention to kill Mai Mach,' he found. 'There was nothing spontaneous about what you did. You waited for a number of hours before you acted to kill her, having already killed once. In relation to the child that was more spontaneous, but nonetheless a product of your existing agitation about the failure of your relationship with Brian Mach. Your actions in relation to the child were extreme, grave and callous. Given that this killing occurred in circumstances where your object was to do whatever you could to harm Brian Mach no matter how extreme, this murder falls into the worst category. Having committed this crime, you waited with Brian Mach imprisoned so you could kill again, and you did so apparently unperturbed by what you had already done' (*R v Liao* [2015] VSC 730).

Liao's counsel submitted that she displayed profound remorse, and Justice Lasry acknowledged that she had pleaded guilty at the earliest possible opportunity. 'The question is whether your plea of guilty and your attitude generally is one which includes a deep regret for the wrongs you committed,' he said. 'While I do believe you show some genuine remorse in relation to your offending against Alistair Kwong, I am not persuaded that you have the same degree of remorse in relation to you offending against Mai Mach or Brian Mach' (*R v Liao* [2015] VSC 730).

Justice Lasry found that Liao had until the crime been without conviction and of good character. She was also in contact with her daughter, by then a Monash University student, who visited and called her. 'By the time of your release you will be very much older and, as the prosecutor accepts, there is little chance of you re-offending and specific deterrence is of less importance,' he said. 'That may not be properly described as rehabilitation because I am not sure that you yet have a proper insight into the gravity of what you have done but I am willing to accept that, in time, that may occur. There are, I think, some prospects for your rehabilitation but the life ahead of you is very difficult.'

In sentencing Liao to life imprisonment with a 32-year minimum, Justice Lasry said she would be deported upon release. 'Your conduct in committing these offences was horrendous,' he said. 'As occasionally occurs in cases such as this, to me your conduct is almost unbelievable. That you would kill a defenceless four-year-old child as he slept in his bed and then wait a number of hours, apparently without regret or second thought, for the purpose of killing the child's mother and Mai Mach is extremely serious, as I suspect you may be now starting to appreciate' (*R v Liao* [2015] VSC 730).

Why did she do it?

How and why does someone without any prior criminal conviction lash out and brutally kill two innocent people, slashing them with a sharp blade? Before she killed Brian Mach's wife Mai and their grandson Alistair, Cia Xia Liao had presented as an accomplished businesswoman and mother who wanted the best for her child. She had done well to build a business following the early death of her husband, and worked hard to ensure that her daughter had the best possible education. This was a woman determined to do well in life and give her daughter every opportunity to do the same.

Yet there was another side to this apparently unassuming businesswoman. Whether Brian Mach saw it emerge or not when he decided to return to his wife, we will probably never know. But once he told Liao that he did not want to continue their relationship, possibly due to her dependency and neediness, the worst began to emerge in her. It is possible that Liao saw Brian as her ticket into Australia and once that plan was foiled she panicked and thought she would be forced to return to China while her daughter remained in Melbourne. But she could have found another partner if that was her goal. Rather than move on, she became obsessed with revenge.

Liao's actions were largely driven by the combination of her DPD and histrionic personality disorder (HPD). Hers was an unusual case in this sense. Many people with a DPD and/or HPD show symptoms in several aspects of their lives, such as their personal relationships and at work. But Liao was a successful businesswoman and her personality disorders did not appear to hamper her progress in business. She was extremely dysfunctional, however, when it came to relationships. The fact that she lost her husband at a young age would not have helped, and could have compounded the crippling anxiety that gripped her when a relationship was not working.

Someone with a DPD seeks out a strong partner on whom they become overly dependent. They feel the need to be taken care of, and Liao had the added motive of wanting to become an Australian citizen. Once they are in a relationship, a person who has a DPD exhibits a pattern of behaviour that results in clinginess, over-compliance, separation anxiety and an intense fear of abandonment. They want their partner to compensate for what they perceive to be their own inadequacies, protect them and make decisions for them. They are also desperate to experience the acceptance and approval of the dominant partner, which may not happen if they are too submissive, as the partner may lose respect for them and treat them badly. In some cases, the more they submit to keep the peace, the less respect their partner is likely to have for them. It can become a vicious circle.

We don't know all the facts about her relationship with Brian, but Liao demonstrates some of the behaviours that are consistent with a diagnosis of a DPD. She lacked the confidence to move forward independently, felt unsafe and vulnerable when she was alone, became desperate when the relationship ended, and was obsessed with being abandoned and having to care for herself. Liao was prepared to do whatever it took to ensure that she received Brian's protection. Making matters worse, she also exhibited characteristics of HPD. Someone with an HPD craves attention to the extent that their behaviour is overly egocentric, impulsive, overly dramatic and emotionally immature. They want to be the centre of attention and believe their self-worth revolves around charming and captivating people. They can be very demanding, attention-seeking, inappropriately seductive, provocative, theatrical, disinhibited, easily influenced and lacking in empathy. If they are not the centre of attention, they can become anxious and resentful.

When Brian Mach said he no longer wanted to be with her, Liao became desperate and vengeful. She could not accept the fact that he wanted to be with his wife and not with her, and made her displeasure known in no uncertain terms. Revenge became more important than behaving in a mature, rational way that could have seen her rebuild her life alone or with someone else. She became desperate, but few people would have contemplated what she did next.

Determined to make Brian 'pay' for his 'betrayal', Liao hatched her gruesome plot. After failing to get him to sign a statutory declaration committing to her, she set in motion a chain of events that will haunt the Mach family forever. It is unclear exactly whom Liao wanted to hurt or kill, but at the very least she planned to inflict serious physical damage on Brian and/or his loved ones when she arrived at his home, drugged him and tied him up. After brutally stabbing Alistair with the garden shears, she taunted and tortured Brian until Mai returned from work. Having no second thoughts, she viciously attacked and killed Mai before she could make it into her own house.

The murder was so brazen that neighbours were immediately alerted to Mai's piercing screams and Liao was quickly arrested. She was so focused on inflicting as much pain as possible that she did not seem to care that she would almost certainly be caught. To Liao, all that mattered was exacting revenge on someone that, in her mind, deserved what he got. An objective observer reading details of this brutal crime would be horrified by what Liao was prepared to do. But Liao's relatively low level of empathy due to her personality disorders means she was less able than others to feel and be deterred by the distress and pain of Alistair and Mai. While most people were shocked by her actions, she believed they were completely justified.

Liao's unconscionable crimes do not mean that everyone with a DPD is dangerous. They are not. Liao's dependent and histrionic traits combined with her desperation over the failure of her relationship with Brian to drive her to seek revenge above all reason. Her low levels of empathy also enabled her to kill in such a callous way, causing untold heartache for an innocent family.

CONCLUSION

Is it a problem if someone is too dependent on their partner? Not necessarily, but it can be. In many relationships, one partner is more outgoing than the other, or may dominate their conversation or even day-to-day decisions. But this is not necessarily a problem if the quieter partner likes it that way. The old saying 'opposites attract' can work, but only if both partners feel comfortable in their roles and neither feels dominated to the point where they feel unhappy or emotionally abused. In the cases discussed in this book, one partner felt aggrieved to the point where they could take it no longer and responded with the ultimate act of violence. Unfortunately, the killers also had a DPD, which contributed to their neediness and lack of confidence, and allowed them to stay in a relationship that was clearly not good for them. It also meant that they seethed quietly rather than acted to improve their situation through counselling or reporting inappropriate behaviour to others or, in Chamari Liyanage's case, the police. Nor could they bring themselves to leave and go it alone, especially when they had no one to support them in doing so. To them, that option was just not possible.

Michael O'Neill had created a public image he could never live up to. While he wanted his society friends to think he was worldly, educated and well connected, he was in fact a needy man who built his self-image around his partner, Stuart Rattle, an accomplished interior designer. They did love each other but Stuart was dominant. O'Neill claims that his partner often belittled him, but O'Neill did not have the courage to stand up for himself and demand that he be treated with more respect. Rather than rock the boat and threaten to destroy the life he had built, O'Neill allowed his hurt to bubble below the surface and failed to deal with it adequately. In the end, he snapped and killed Stuart after his partner allegedly questioned his sexual stamina as he had done in the past.

Chamari Liyanage's situation was much worse, as her husband Din physically and sexually abused her while openly cheating and forcing her to engage in unwanted and degrading sexual activities. But like O'Neill, Liyanage felt trapped and unable to find a way to leave what was for her an abusive situation. She could not see a way out, which is not uncommon when women or men are subjected to extreme physical and/or emotional abuse. Her situation was made worse by having a DPD and being so far from family and friends who were overseas in Sri Lanka. Anthony Sherna, who killed his partner Susie Wild after what he claimed was years of abuse, was similarly unable to find a way out of what was clearly a toxic relationship that left him feeling abused, threatened and belittled.

Cia Xia Liao was desperate for her lover Brian Mach to marry her, in part so that she could become an Australian citizen and live in Melbourne with her daughter. Instead, he decided to stay with his wife. Liao's case was further complicated by her also having an HPD. She felt so aggrieved and agitated that she tied Brian up and tortured him while killing his wife and grandson in separate frenzied attacks. Rather than find another partner or return to China, Liao decided to commit two brutal murders, knowing that she would almost certainly be caught and would probably spend more than 25 years in jail.

These are all extreme examples of what can happen when relationships become toxic and one of the partners has a personality disorder that impairs their ability to deal with a difficult situation. Working on or walking away from a relationship that is failing is never easy, especially if, as in Liyanage's case, the partner is physically and emotionally abusive. When you have a DPD, which may predispose you to being introverted, having low self-confidence and feeling inadequate, it can be very difficult to leave an abusive situation over which you feel you have very little control.

Michael O'Neill's friends probably did not understand just how upsetting it was for him when his partner put him down in public and let him flounder in a job he was clearly unable to handle. They may have assumed that if things became too difficult, O'Neill would tell Rattle and they would hire someone else to manage the business and maybe attend relationship counselling. But that didn't happen, and O'Neill slowly dug himself into a bigger hole by trying to cope when he clearly could not. On the outside he appeared socially confident and comfortable with his relationship, but inside he felt like a failure and would have had very low self-confidence.

In Liyanage's case, few if any people would have realised that she was in such a toxic and abusive relationship, as she did not feel that she could confide in anyone. No one could have predicted what she was going to do, as those who knew them in

Western Australia most likely perceived them to be successful professionals who were also a happy couple.

While Anthony Sherna's friends and family knew his relationship with Susie Wild was not a very good one, he did not reveal the true extent of his feelings and tolerated her alleged emotional abuse to the point where he felt his only option was to kill her. Sherna's friends and family may have been able to dig deeper when it was clear he was not happy, for example when he was prevented from going to the cricket or office drinks. If a friend or loved one is in this type of situation, it might help to ask them why they are unable to socialise and whether they are happy with that arrangement. You could also suggest relationship counselling or even individual counselling to identify why this situation has arisen and how it could possibly be improved. If Sherna had sought help, health professionals would probably have recommended that he seek relationship counselling or leave, and then would have helped him with strategies to achieve those goals.

This is extremely difficult for anyone who has suffered battered woman syndrome, as they can be literally beaten into submission and may refuse help even if it is offered. People in this situation, and it can be men as well as women, may feel that their position is hopeless and there is no point trying to change it. They may even wrongly believe that they are to blame for not standing up to their partner, as a particularly manipulative abuser can make the victim feel responsible by constantly putting them down, emphasising their faults or weaknesses and telling them that they are to blame. Even well-educated, competent professionals such as Chamari Liyanage can find themselves in this situation, which may seem unbelievable to those who know them outside the relationship. Someone like Liyanage can also be good at hiding the problem and continuing at work as if nothing is wrong. But they may show some signs, such as avoiding social situations, having physical injuries or becoming more negative in their general talk about relationships and life.

When someone is trapped in a relationship that is toxic, it can sometimes help if a colleague, friend or family member provides support, offers a sympathetic ear and possibly organises outside help. The person may resist, but it may at least plant a seed, and if things do not improve they may consider doing something before the situation becomes potentially serious.

*A list of support services for those experiencing relationship problems can be found on pages 403–7.

Responding to partner violence/abuse

Partner violence/abuse comes in many forms, both physical and emotional. It can also be financial, such as withdrawing access to money needed to buy food for your children. An abusive partner may make threats to hurt you, your children, people close to you or your pets. They may put you down and mock you when you are with other people, or try to control what you can and can't do. They may also check up on you when you are not at home, forbid you to do certain things, such as seeing friends or dressing in a certain way, or become angry and aggressive when you don't do what they want. Partner violence/abuse may also involve insults, such as 'Nobody else would ever want you', forcing you to do something that is unacceptable to you, hitting you or throwing things at you. Such behaviour, which can be perpetrated by men and women, is both insidious and debilitating. It may be subtle and designed so that the victim slowly loses confidence in themselves and ends up believing that they are to blame because the abuser has continually told them that they are worthless. In other cases, partner violence/abuse may be more blatant and involve potentially life-threatening violence.

Such abuse affects all genders. Australian Bureau of Statistics figures (ABS, *Personal Safety Survey*, 2016) revealed that one in six (17 per cent) women and one in seventeen (6 per cent) men had experienced violence by a partner since the age of fifteen. This included physical and sexual violence. Women were eight times more likely to experience sexual violence from a partner. Almost one in four (23 per cent) women had experienced emotional abuse from a partner, compared to one in six (16 per cent) men.

Early signs that your partner may be abusive include:

- controlling or possessive behaviour
- taking over control of the family finances without negotiating with you
- threats to harm you or your children (or your pets)
- attempts to coerce you into sexual activities you don't like
- ongoing put-downs.

Responding to partner violence/abuse can be extremely difficult. Many victims are too scared or embarrassed to admit that they are being controlled, manipulated or abused by the person who is meant to be closest to them. A surprising number of educated, outwardly confident professional people have found themselves in this position. Their distress can be difficult to detect, as they may become expert at hiding their emotional pain and physical injuries. But it is extremely important that those in abusive relationships either seek help or leave before things become more serious or even life-threatening.

How to respond to partner violence/abuse

- Be aware that there are many types of abuse within abusive relationships. It may be physical, sexual, emotional, financial or verbal, or a combination of several of these. It may also be social abuse, in which the other person humiliates you or puts you down in front of others.

- Remind yourself that you have choices and you have the right to feel safe and be safe.
- Put your safety and the safety of any children who live with you first.
- Identify warning signs and patterns, and try to remove yourself from the potentially abusive situation when you can.
- Remind yourself that it is never your fault if you are being abused.
- Try not to retaliate as it usually makes things worse.
- Don't be taken in. They may say they love you, but their actions communicate their real feelings. You don't try to harm someone you love.
- Don't minimise what they say or do to you or assume that it is a one-off behaviour on their part and won't happen again. Be on your guard. Things might be okay for a short while after one of their abusive behaviours but they will most likely do it again.
- Don't accept what they say as the truth. Their words are intended to cause you harm.
- Once a pattern of abuse has been established, recognise that things won't get better unless you take action to get support, and/or leave the situation.
- Reach out to people you trust for support, and confide in them.
- Have a back-up if you are worried about what they might do to you or your children if you try to leave them. Ask people you know and trust if they would be available if you needed them.
- Investigate key professional people (e.g. social workers or counsellors) and/or organisations (and their locations) that could provide you with support and shelter if needed.

- If you feel physically unsafe, consider talking about what is happening to a police officer.
- Always keep your phone with you in case you need to call for help. Don't leave it lying around where it might be taken and hidden from you.
- Call one of the many helplines that can offer support and advice (see the list of partner violence/abuse and other help services on pages 403–7).

PART IV

PARANOID PERSONALITY DISORDER

YOU CAN'T TRUST ANYONE

What is a paranoid personality disorder?

A paranoid personality disorder (PPD) is characterised by a longstanding, ongoing pattern of thinking and behaviour across many situations and contexts in which the individual is chronically suspicious and distrustful of other people. They assume, without justification, that others are trying to harm, deceive, exploit or humiliate them, or are plotting against them in some way.

Although it is adaptive (beneficial) for people to be cautious and mildly alert for signs of potential harm or mistreatment, most people recognise that it is also important to assess the quality of evidence on which they are basing these 'safety checks', to ensure that they are not jumping to unwarranted conclusions. A loud noise that sounds like gunshots may cause alarm, but when the person who hears it checks outside and sees that it is a fireworks display, they know that they need not worry.

In some situations, a paranoid approach may be useful and appropriate. Hampton and Burnham (2003) have highlighted how a certain amount of paranoid thinking might, for example, aid the work of a military spy. They also mention the approaches taken by World War II UK Prime Minister Winston Churchill, and 1920s FBI head J. Edgar Hoover as examples of how a degree of paranoia helped the United Kingdom and the United States to manage what were seen at the time as significant threats to national security.

But ordinary people who have a PPD worry excessively about the motives of others and become paranoid that friends, family or acquaintances are 'out to get them'. Ian Jamieson, who murdered three of his country Victorian neighbours in 2014, had an extreme PPD. In Jamieson's mind, his neighbours were deliberately making his life difficult by driving along a shared dirt track and spraying dust onto his belongings. In reality, the problem, if anything, was minor and caused no harm to anyone. Yet he used it as an excuse to kill Peter and Mary Lockhart and Mary's son Greg Holmes.

Recognising someone with a PPD

Someone with a PPD takes paranoid thinking to the extreme and becomes suspicious when there is no genuine reason to be. The *Diagnostic and Statistical Manual of Mental Disorders* (DSM-5) suggests that a diagnosis of PPD can be made when at least four of the following criteria are met. The individual:

- suspects, without justification, that other people are deceiving them, taking advantage of them or plotting to cause them harm of some kind
- obsessively worries, without good reason, about whether their friends, family or associates are loyal to them and can be trusted

- rarely confides in other people because they unnecessarily worry that such information could be used to harm them in some way
- wrongly perceives hidden malicious or insulting intent in the innocent comments and behaviours of other people
- won't forgive other people for what they perceive (rightly or wrongly) to be insulting or malicious comments or behaviour directed towards them; they hold grudges against people they believe have behaved towards them in this way
- becomes angry and returns fire when they conclude, despite others disagreeing with their perceptions, that their character or reputation is being attacked
- frequently suspects, without justification, that their partner is unfaithful.

Typical behaviours of people with a PPD

The thinking and reasoning of individuals with a PPD is characterised by several cognitive distortions:

- **a hostile attributional style:** They blame negative outcomes that they experience on the behaviour of other people, even though there is no evidence to back up their beliefs (Freeman, 2007).
- **an intentionality bias:** They assume that the behaviour of others is *intended* to deceive or harm them in some way, rather than being incidental or accidental. For example, when someone is walking near them they might conclude that 'this person is following me'. When they observe a neighbour looking at them, they might interpret that behaviour as 'my neighbour is spying on me'. When, without good reason, they conclude that another person is spying on them, trying to

take advantage of them or harming them, they often become very obsessed and preoccupied with these irrational thoughts (Blakemore et al., 2003).

- **self-righteousness:** They believe that they are always right and certain of their own 'virtue' in most situations. They take the 'high moral ground' and overly focus on what they see as their own personal rights.
- **self-justification:** They perceive their own negative or vengeful behaviour to be a 'defensive necessity' rather than a choice.

People with a PPD tend to be cold, aloof, argumentative and frequently complain about the behaviour of others. They often act as if everyone is a potential enemy (Millon, 2004). Generally, they find it difficult to get along with people and don't cope well with group activities. Although they tend to be highly critical of others, they respond to criticism of themselves with hostility and/or defensiveness. They tend to be humourless, guarded and socially withdrawn. They don't make friends easily, which isn't surprising given that trust and respect are key ingredients for mutually satisfying relationships. They often quarrel with, or become estranged from associates, neighbours and family members due to a combination of some of the following behaviours:

- a lack of insight into their own thinking and behaviour
- suspiciousness and hypersensitivity to the comments, behaviours and body language of others. For example, they often read what they believe are hidden meanings in the innocuous remarks or casual looks of other people.
- a tendency to misinterpret what is said or done by others
- constant complaints about others

- defensive ways of responding and being quick to retaliate
- an aggressive, angry manner and stubbornness
- difficulty with responding appropriately to justified criticism or accepting well-intended advice
- a tendency to be unforgiving about what they perceive to be previous insults, injustices or slights; they hold grudges and are often vengeful
- difficulties with cooperation.

Many people with a PPD do better living on their own or with a partner who is tirelessly loyal and who can help to insulate them by acting as their 'eyes and ears' (Millon, 2004). Most have difficulties participating in collaborative work projects. These difficulties may be part of the reason why their unemployment rates are higher than those of other people and their satisfactory and continued rates of employment are lower. They are also more likely to leave the workforce at a younger age and be employed in more menial work positions than the general population (McGurk et al., 2013).

Some people with a PPD can become quite litigious and take legal action against people whom they perceive, usually incorrectly, want to harm or exploit them in some way. Such litigation is often vexatious (i.e. legally unjustified) and primarily undertaken to inconvenience, harass, harm or exact revenge. People with PPD are rarely psychotic (i.e. out of touch with reality), but some may display brief episodes of psychosis-like symptoms under conditions of extreme stress (Miller et al., 2001).

Ian Jamieson is a classic case of someone with a serious PPD who takes his paranoid behaviour to the extreme. Jamieson has spent his adult life being suspicious of others, exaggerating their intent in his mind and justifying his anger with a warped belief that his neighbours were deliberately taunting him when they clearly were not. Through no fault of anyone else but Jamieson, the situation ended in tragedy and severe distress for the families and loved ones involved.

Prevalence of PPDs

The prevalence of PPD has been estimated at between 2.3 and 4.4 per cent of the general US population (Grant et al., 2004; Lenzenweger et al., 2007). PPD is diagnosed more frequently in women than in men (Grant et al., 2004).

Comorbidity (other disorders that often occur with a PPD)

Paranoid personality disorder may be comorbid with NPD, avoidant personality disorder, borderline personality disorder, one or more of the several anxiety disorders or major depressive disorder (DSM-5, APA, 2013).

Heritability of and risk factors for PPDs

Heritability estimates for PPDs are somewhere between 28 per cent (Torgersen et al., 2000) and 66 per cent (Kendler et al., 2007). This means that up to 66 per cent of the differences between those in research studies who had a PPD and those who didn't were most likely due to genetic variations between them.

Individuals who have relatives with a family history of schizophrenia have a higher likelihood of developing a PPD than those who don't (see, for example, Asarnow et al., 2001; Baron et al., 1985; Nicolson et al., 2003). Individuals who have experienced significant trauma or have had one or more of the following experiences as a child or adolescent are also more likely than others to develop a PPD:

- periods in institutionalised care (see Yang et al., 2007)
- parental neglect (see Johnson et al., 1999)
- physical or sexual abuse as a young person (see Ashcroft et al., 2012; Lobbestael et al., 2010; Fisher et al., 2012)
- emotional abuse or being humiliated when younger (see Lobbestael et al., 2010)
- harsh and degrading punishment as a young person (see Benjamin, 1996)
- migrating from another country (see Bentall et al., 2001; Selten et al., 2007).

Treatment for PPDs

The most effective treatment for individuals with a PPD is cognitive behaviour therapy, which challenges maladaptive and paranoid beliefs, and encourages more rational interpretations of situations and events.

Individuals with a PPD in prison

A study by Arroyo and Ortega (2009) identified that 3 per cent of a prison population had been diagnosed with PPD. Any personality disorder can be linked to violent crime, but a PPD is one of the three most commonly identified personality disorders linked to criminal behaviour (Stone, 2007). Adolescents who have been diagnosed with a PPD are more likely than others to engage in a relatively high degree of violence and crime in adulthood (Johnson et al., 2000 [both entries]).

CHAPTER 11

IAN JAMIESON

The cast

Ian Jamieson: Killed his neighbours, Peter and Mary Lockhart, and Mary's son Greg Holmes

Janice Jamieson: Ian Jamieson's wife. They had three adult children.

Peter and Mary Lockhart: Popular local couple murdered by Ian Jamieson. They were 78 and 75 when they died.

Greg Holmes: Mary's son from a previous marriage, who was also killed. He was 48 and had four siblings.

Lynette Mordue: Greg's de facto partner

The motive

Ian Jamieson claimed that he killed three of his neighbours because they continually antagonised him by spraying dirt onto his property when they drove along a track next to it. There was no evidence that they had done anything untoward.

Introduction

How does a neighbourhood dispute over dirt and dust escalate into a triple murder?

It is hard to comprehend that a relatively petty complaint by Ian Jamieson against his neighbours in rural Victoria could lead to a major falling out, let alone their brutal deaths by his hand. The worst they were guilty of, if anything, was driving vehicles down a dirt track on Jamieson's immediate neighbour's property and spraying dust into his. Yet he later claimed that these actions were so infuriating he was justified in killing all three of them.

Jamieson, who worked on the local railways, and his wife Janice lived for many years on a farm on the Logan–Wedderburn Road outside Wedderburn, an old gold rush and farming town established in the 1850s about 75 kilometres north-west of Bendigo in regional Victoria. Gold fossickers still like to visit the area and try their luck in the old diggings on public land surrounding the town. Others enjoy bushwalking among the local box and ironbark trees, spotting native flora and fauna including kangaroos, wallabies, native birds and the odd echidna. Wedderburn is close to many rustic country pubs, boutique wineries and historic buildings dating back to the gold rush era. With an older than average population, the town is perfect for those seeking a relaxed, quiet lifestyle.

In 2006, Peter and Mary Lockhart moved into a farm across the road and down a bit from Ian Jamieson and his wife. A popular local couple, the Lockharts had moved to be closer to town. Peter was a fourth-generation local farmer and Mary, his second wife, hailed from Bendigo. A past president of the Wedderburn Historical Engine and Machinery Society, Peter had also been involved in the local footy and tennis clubs.

Mary's son Greg Holmes was a former fitter and turner in the Australian Army and served in Iraq, East Timor and

Afghanistan. In early 2014, two years after he was discharged for medical reasons, Greg moved to a property on nearby Mulga Ridge Road to be closer to Peter, Mary and his siblings. It also allowed him to help on Peter's farm. Ian Jamieson's property adjoined Greg's, separated by a typical wire fence. One of the access points to Greg's farm was a tree-lined dirt track that was owned by the government and ran along Jamieson's boundary fence, on Greg's side. The occupiers of Greg's farm had permission to use the track under the terms of a licence from the Department of Environment and Primary Industries. Once Greg moved in, he, Peter and Mary used it. Peter would sometimes take water from Greg's dam and graze his sheep on the property. Peter moved the sheep from his place to Greg's through the gate where the government road began, as it was the quickest and easiest route.

Before Greg moved in, Jamieson and the Lockharts got along well. When Jamieson's house caught fire, Mary and Peter did all they could to help. But things deteriorated after Peter, who was semi-retired but still active on his farm, started using the track to visit Greg.

The lead-up to the crime

When Greg arrived, Ian Jamieson became extremely hostile. Greg was a gentle person and treated women with respect. He opened car doors for his de facto partner, Lynette Mordue, and would hand her the seatbelt to ensure she was safely strapped in. Greg avoided criticising others, but Jamieson's behaviour frustrated him to the point where he referred to him as 'the dickhead next door'. When Lynette visited her partner and both their dogs were around – a labrador and a Staffordshire terrier – he'd tell her not to let the dogs onto the neighbour's property or Jamieson would shoot them. He had obviously worked out that his neighbour could be dangerous, and had called police several times in the past to report Jamieson's behaviour.

All Greg wanted was a quiet life. He had been deployed overseas three times and been through some tough times, so it was recommended that he move close to family members who could support him. Despite what he'd been through, Greg remained composed and tried not to let minor irritations get to him. He was coping quite well in his new life and doing jobs around the house, but wasn't working in paid employment. Greg was gifted with practical tasks and enjoyed helping some of his neighbours, who paid him with a few beers and sometimes cash. He fixed a water pump for one, and helped start a tractor for another. After a few rough years, it felt good to be contributing and having his thoughtfulness appreciated. Greg also entered the Bendigo Inventor Awards with attachments he made for ride-on mowers, such as rakes and graders.

Jamieson was obsessive about keeping his property clean, and had laid crushed bluestone in front of his house and garage, running down to the driveway, presumably to make it look neat and prevent weeds growing. Some who passed by thought it looked out of place on a rural property, but Jamieson obviously disagreed. To him, it was a way to keep everything in order. He'd also close the big front gates whenever he left his property, obviously paranoid that someone might come inside when he wasn't there. Jamieson had CCTV cameras installed on his shed to enable him to watch the shared road reserve. Despite having no livestock, he owned up to six high-powered rifles, which he felt he needed to protect himself from threats, real or imagined. He also carried a hunting knife with him most of the time.

Jamieson's neighbours posed no threat to him or anyone else, but in his mind they were making his life a misery and he needed protection from them. To Peter, who was 78, Mary, 75, and Greg, 48, Jamieson was a cranky pest from whom they tried to keep their distance. Mary never said anything to Greg's partner about worrying about her safety. Nor did Mary write anything in her personal diary, which indicates that Jamieson's behaviour was not enough of a concern for her to raise it when she made notes about what was happening in her life. Given the lack of concern expressed by either Mary or Peter, they probably thought they would be fine if they stayed out of Jamieson's way. Peter was typical of his generation and reasonably opinionated, but did not knowingly do anything to antagonise his neighbour.

Despite this, Jamieson often complained that when people used the road reserve it blew dust into his farm, dirtying his house and polluting his drinking water. The situation deteriorated further when Peter began to use the road reserve more often to visit his stepson. Over time, Jamieson became 'utterly obsessed' with their use of the track. He told friends and later the police that he had felt aggrieved by Peter's behaviour for years, and he believed that Peter had been deliberately baiting or provoking him. He also became angry with Mary and Greg, due to their relationship with Peter.

In reality, it was Jamieson who behaved in an annoying fashion. While complaining about non-existent grievances he did things like spot burning on his property, which is standard practice in the country to prepare for the bushfire season but created large clouds of smoke that hung above Greg's washing. Unlike Jamieson, Greg didn't protest. He told others not to worry about it; he'd just leave the washing out for a few days to air it. To him, small issues like that weren't worth worrying about. As a war veteran who had seen some horrific things overseas, he tried to keep life in perspective.

The murders

On Wednesday, 22 October 2014, Greg's farm was a hive of activity as he prepared for a huge bonfire to be held on his property as part of a social event on the coming Saturday. He was building a huge pile of unwanted flammable goods to burn, and used the attachments he invented for his ride-on mower to clear space for guests who wanted to stay in their caravans or camp in their tents overnight. Many guests had been invited, and Greg was really looking forward to it. That morning, Jamieson drove Janice to Bendigo Hospital for a medical procedure. They returned at around 2.30 pm. A couple of hours later, Peter drove his tractor, which was towing a small water-tanker trailer, along the road reserve. CCTV footage shot from Jamieson's property showed him driving slowly, not creating any dust. Jamieson went outside, walked towards the boundary fence, then went back inside. A few minutes later, he called Wedderburn Police Station, which was unmanned so he left no message. Jamieson later told police that Peter had yelled abuse at him as he drove along the road reserve.

At around 7.45 pm, Peter spoke on the phone with a friend for more than ten minutes. Greg also spoke on the phone and exchanged text messages with Lynette. Their last contact was at 7.55 pm. None of those conversations mentioned Jamieson or any issues with him. Sometime between 7.55 pm and 8.14 pm that night, Jamieson walked towards Greg's house, climbed through the wire fence and onto the road reserve on Greg's side of the fence to confront him. At 8.14 pm, Greg called the local Wedderburn Police Station, which was unmanned so he did not leave a message. At 8.15 pm, Greg called triple 0, asking police to attend an emergency. He said Jamieson was on his property and 'annoying the hell' out of him. He said there had been no threats of violence and no weapons involved, so he was told to keep calm until police arrived.

Sometime after this call, and before the police arrived at 8.30 pm, Jamieson hit Greg in the head with a blunt object, which was likely to have been a rock he grabbed while on Greg's property, which, like many in the goldfields area, was scattered with numerous rocks that surfaced after rain. Jamieson then attacked Greg with a hunting knife that he was wearing in a leather scabbard on his belt, stabbing him to death.

Greg sustained at least 25 sharp-force injuries, including multiple stab wounds to his upper back and neck regions, the back of his head, and his chest. There was also evidence of blunt-force trauma to his head, and defensive-type injuries to his hands. Despite the frenzied attack, Greg did not die instantly; nearby campers heard him cry out for help three or four times. They drove over to investigate, arriving at around the same time as the police, just after 8.30 pm.

By then, Jamieson had left Greg critically injured on the road. The killer later told police that when he left he thought, 'He's buggered,' and then decided to 'sort this out for good' and 'clean the other ones up' too, meaning Peter and Mary. Jamieson walked home, loaded two shotguns, grabbed a pocketful of ammunition and walked to the Lockhart farm, where he shot Peter on a stone path at the back of the house twice in the head and twice to the body from point-blank range, before Peter even had a chance to speak. Peter and Mary had been watching television and Peter had come outside to investigate after the dog started barking. Two shots came from a double-barrelled 12-gauge shotgun and two from a single-barrelled 20-gauge shotgun.

Jamieson then reloaded the 12-gauge shotgun and shot Mary once in the head and twice in her body, which was found on the floor of the meals area inside the back door. At 8.38 pm, while police were speaking to the campers at Greg's farm, they heard shotgun blasts coming from the Lockhart farm. When police called Greg's phone, they heard it ringing nearby and found him lying on the ground. He was already dead. After shooting Peter and Mary Lockhart, Jamieson went home. When Janice asked why he was covered in blood, he said he had shot the Lockharts and stabbed Greg. He removed his bloodied clothes and she put them in the laundry basket. At 8.48 pm, Jamieson called triple 0 and asked police to attend. He said he had killed his neighbours because they had taken him on and 'pushed, pushed, pushed and that's it'.

While waiting for police to arrive, Jamieson told Janice he was sorry that what he had done would have an impact on her, but his neighbours had pushed him too far. He also called several friends to tell them what he had done and asked them to look after his wife. He continued to blame his victims for the situation. After his arrest, Jamieson told police that his neighbours had pushed him for years and he'd had enough: 'After they stirred me up, I went there . . . had a go at him, and then he got into me so I finished him off, I think. And then . . . I thought, well bugger it, I'm gone, I might as well go and clean the other ones up and that's what I did.' Asked what had started things that day, he said Peter had created dust with his tractor as he drove up the road reserve that afternoon. He claimed that Peter only drove on the road reserve to annoy him (*DPP v Jamieson* [2016] VSC 407).

The crime was horrific, but others later wondered what might have happened if the bonfire had gone ahead as planned and Jamieson had decided to act when Greg's property was teeming with adults, children, motorbikes and music. Greg had been expecting quite a crowd on the weekend, and those close to him now shudder at the thought of what could have been, given the killer's obvious paranoia and anger. After the murders Jamieson, then 63, told police that he was not sorry for what he had done. 'They didn't give me any choice,' he said. He claimed that Greg had previously pulled a gun on him, which was why he'd armed himself with a knife when he went to confront him on the night of the murder. This would have been highly unlikely, as on the day in question Greg was preparing to go to Melbourne and left in the early afternoon. Jamieson also claimed that on the night he killed him, Greg had attacked him and grabbed his knife, and that while wrestling, 'I must have stabbed him' (*DPP v Jamieson* [2016] VSC 407).

The court appearances

On 1 July 2015, Ian Jamieson was committed to stand trial for the murders of his neighbours, Gregory Holmes, Peter Lockhart and Mary Lockhart. Not long before the jury was empanelled on 5 April 2016, he pleaded guilty to all three charges. At that point, Jamieson sacked his lawyers and through his new lawyers applied to change his plea for Greg Holmes's murder to not guilty. On 11 July 2016, Supreme Court Justice Elizabeth Hollingworth dismissed his application following an almost farcical set of events over the previous year that saw Jamieson change both his lawyers and his pleas several times.

Over time, Jamieson also gave inconsistent accounts to police about who started the fatal confrontation. Early on, he said he had started it when he 'fronted' Greg. He later claimed that Greg had started things by 'roaring out' of his house at him. During his second formal police interview, Jamieson said he was not even at Greg's farm when things started – he only climbed the fence in response to his neighbour's actions and words. Jamieson told police he had gone to the Lockharts' home only intending to shoot Peter, but shot Mary as well when she came out of the house and 'had a go' at him. He tried to downplay his culpability throughout, accusing his neighbours of pushing him too far and tipping him over the edge. He expressed no regret or remorse.

Jamieson claimed he had some memory loss and an early form of dementia, which may have contributed to his decision to change his plea. It was also reported that he had claimed Greg Holmes injected him with a syringe filled with the drug ice during the altercation in which he killed his neighbour. There was no evidence to support this claim. Those who know Greg insist he was 'very anti-drugs', did not take hard drugs and never had syringes in or around his home.

All of this was extremely distressing for the loved ones of Peter, Mary and Greg, who had to watch helplessly as proceedings dragged on due to Jamieson continually changing his claims and legal teams. Some believe this was a deliberate ploy to further antagonise the victims' families and that Jamieson enjoyed the attention and notoriety it gained him. 'These claims were all excuses for attention and gave him the ability/control to further distress all victims,' one of them says. 'This was very calculated we believe. He exhausted every avenue within the judicial system intentionally.' It is highly likely that Jamieson learned some of those tactics while in jail, and the victims' loved ones are still infuriated that he was allowed so many avenues to challenge the charges. For example, despite admitting to killing his victims, Jamieson later claimed that he acted in self-defence in killing Greg Holmes, when those close to the case believe the evidence clearly shows that it wasn't an act of self-defence.

In sentencing Jamieson on 22 July 2016, Justice Elizabeth Hollingworth dismissed the ice allegation and detailed the shocking reality of the crime. 'You killed Mr Holmes and the Lockharts for no reason other than your longstanding and powerful animosity towards them,' she said. 'The first murder was preceded by your entering the Holmes farm at night, uninvited, armed with a hunting knife and, at the very least, intending to confront Mr Holmes. He was concerned enough about your presence and behaviour to call the police. Mr Holmes was unarmed when you confronted him. You told police that Mr Holmes had initiated the physical attack, somehow managing to take your knife off you. That seems highly improbable, in all the circumstances. But, even if that version of events was accepted, by the time you came to stab Mr Holmes, the tables had turned completely. On your own admission, you stabbed him when he was pinned underneath you, and unarmed (*DPP v Jamieson* [2016] VSC 407).

'You inflicted a large number of the more than two dozen stab wounds to the back of his head, neck and body, when he could have posed no conceivable threat to you. You admitted to police that you wanted to kill Mr Holmes. The number, location and severity of the stab wounds inflicted by you clearly demonstrate a murderous intent. When you stabbed Mr Holmes, you were not acting in self-defence, but out of longstanding and utterly misplaced animosity' (*DPP v Jamieson* [2016] VSC 407).

Justice Hollingworth found there was 'simply no evidence' to support Jamieson's relatively recent assertion that during his struggle with Greg, Greg had stabbed him with a syringe 'containing some sort of illegal drug (probably ice)'. 'No syringe was found at the crime scene,' she said. 'You were treated after your arrest for injuries to your hands, yet you did not report to medical staff that you had been stabbed with a syringe, and no puncture wounds were noted on examination. At no stage during your many hours of interviews and discussions with the police did you make such an allegation.

'None of the witness statements described you as appearing or sounding drug-affected. Your actions that night after you killed Mr Holmes were calm, purposeful and goal-directed. The assertion seems to have been made by you for the first time in the month before the trial. Given the state of the evidence, I agree with the prosecutor's description of the assertion as "a complete fabrication".

'You readily admitted that your intention at the time of walking to the Lockhart farm was to kill Mr Lockhart, the person towards whom you felt the greatest animosity. As soon as you got there, you immediately sought out Mr Lockhart, and shot him four times. You must have reloaded the twenty-gauge shotgun once in order to do that. After killing Mr Lockhart, you must have reloaded the twelve-gauge shotgun twice, in order to shoot Mrs Lockhart three times with it.

'These are all very serious examples of the most serious crime known to our legal system and our community. You intentionally took the lives of three other human beings, fuelled by your anger and hatred for them. You sought out each of your unarmed victims at night, on their own properties (where they should have felt safe). You took dangerous weapons with you. You inflicted appalling injuries on all of them. The murders of the Lockharts are particularly serious: not only were they premeditated, you callously shot your elderly victims multiple times, from close or relatively close range, without warning, and without any conceivable provocation' (*DPP v Jamieson* [2016] VSC 407).

Justice Hollingworth said Jamieson's actions had had a profound effect on many people. Thirteen victim impact statements by members of the Lockhart and Holmes families talked about how their lives had been shattered by the violent, senseless deaths. She described his actions as 'cowardly and despicable', and said they had caused disbelief, anxiety, depression, nightmares and loss of sleep in the relatives of his victims and to Greg's de facto partner. 'It has been almost impossible for them to celebrate what should be happy family occasions – events like birthdays, weddings, anniversaries, Christmas, the birth of a new grandchild – when so many loved ones are gone,' she said.

'Music was a shared passion and pleasure, with Mary's singing and Greg's guitar playing being an integral part of so many family gatherings. Some family members have become socially withdrawn – partly because they no longer feel any joy in their lives, and partly because it can be difficult to avoid being drawn into discussion about a case which has attracted such a degree of publicity. Many complained that the enormous media attention has caused them additional grief, because they have been robbed of their privacy, and their right to mourn in peace. For that reason, half of them asked that their victim impact statements not be read out in open court' (*DPP v Jamieson* [2016] VSC 407).

Some of Peter, Mary and Greg's loved ones attended court hearings, as it helped them to process what was happening. They had found that some of the media coverage was not accurate, which added to their distress. Attending the court hearings gave them more certainty about what had happened and the consequences for Jamieson. Some, including Greg's partner, socialised less following the murders as they found it easier to be alone. It also meant less exposure to painful triggers that would see the awful memories flood back. In a way, doing so was an act of self-preservation; the alternative was just too painful.

Justice Hollingworth said that while Jamieson had pleaded guilty, the extended process in reaching that point had added to the distress of the victims' families, many of whom attended court hearings. 'Apart from any remorse which is taken to be implicit in your guilty pleas, you have not shown the slightest remorse for your appalling crimes,' she said. 'On the contrary, even now you continue to blame your victims. Although you had several heart attacks while visiting New Zealand in 2000, there is no evidence that you currently suffer from any medical problems that would be relevant to sentencing.

'You have no history of psychiatric problems. However, your counsel suggested that your sentence should be reduced having regard to the evidence of a neuropsychologist, Associate Professor Warrick Brewer. In his report dated 26 March 2016, he described you as: "a man of average intelligence who suffers significant verbal new learning and higher level memory function [loss] on objective assessment. Moreover, he suffers significant reduction in his speed of processing. In addition, Mr Jamieson is demonstrating a constellation of subtle executive (higher level reasoning and organisation) inefficiencies"' (*DPP v Jamieson* [2016] VSC 407).

Justice Hollingworth said Associate Professor Brewer attributed this to a gradual cognitive and behavioural decline over a period of at least ten years, probably beginning around the time of Jamieson's heart attacks. He still understood, however, that his actions were wrong, and was able to think clearly and make calm, reasoned decisions and appropriate judgements. 'His opinion was that the overall constellation of cognitive and behavioural vulnerabilities that was present at the time of the offending, reflected a "mild-moderate impact" on your ability to inhibit your impulses, and a "mild impact" on your ability to regulate your behaviour,' Justice Hollingworth found.

'While his report is not entirely clear in this regard, it appears that Associate Professor Brewer's remarks were primarily directed to the impact of your cognitive deficits on the murder of Mr Holmes. He noted that your cognitive abilities at the time of the deaths of the Lockharts reflected "apparent recomposure following the assault on Mr Holmes"; I accept that assessment.

'Although impulsivity may have played a role in your confrontation with Mr Holmes, your subsequent actions (in walking home, collecting and loading two shotguns, walking over to the Lockhart property, and searching for your targets) were deliberate and considered, not impulsive. In fact, Associate Professor Brewer's conclusion that you suffer from cognitive defects is not supported by a psychiatric report obtained from Dr Lester Walton by one of your previous solicitors. Dr Walton examined you on 30 March 2015. He could identify no mental state defences. He described you as "cognitively intact", and of normal intelligence.

'Even if Associate Professor Brewer's assessment of your compromised cognitive abilities is taken at its highest, it would only result in a very modest moderation of your sentence, given that he describes the impact of the impairment on your behaviour as only "mild" or "mild-moderate" ' (*DPP v Jamieson* [2016] VSC 407).

Justice Hollingworth found the primary driver of the crime was Jamieson's animosity towards Peter Lockhart and his family. She sentenced him to life imprisonment for each of the murders of Peter and Mary, and 25 years for the murder of Greg. The sentences were to be served concurrently. 'I fix a period of thirty years before you become eligible for parole,' she said. 'But for your age, I would have fixed a longer non-parole period. But for your pleas of guilty, I would have sentenced you to life imprisonment without parole' (*DPP v Jamieson* [2016] VSC 407).

It was a sad end to a tragic case that left locals and those who read about it shaking their heads in disbelief. How could such a situation arise over something so trivial? Why would a man murder three of his neighbours, simply because they were using a dirt track with full permission from the relevant authorities? In May 2017, Ian Jamieson signalled that he would appeal his murder conviction for killing Greg Holmes, claiming he acted in self-defence. The following month his application to appeal was refused on the grounds that it lacked any merit.

Why did he do it?

To understand why this happened it is important to look at the thoughts and motives of the man responsible, which from the outside look inexplicable. Ian Francis Jamieson was born in New Zealand in December 1950. His father was a violent alcoholic. After his parents separated when he was twelve, Jamieson and his eight siblings were put into various types of care. He initially lived in a boys' home, before being fostered out. He completed Year 9 at school before working as a labourer.

This cannot have been easy. Not only did his parents put him into care, but on the cusp of his teen years Jamieson was separated from his parents and some or all of his siblings. Given that his parents were still alive, this may have instilled in him feelings of abandonment and rejection, regardless of how tough it had been living with his violent alcoholic father, and it most likely would have made it very difficult for him to trust others. Jamieson's lack of education would not have helped. He entered adulthood with limited knowledge of the world around him, a chip on his shoulder and ill-equipped to handle some of life's challenges. His employment prospects were not great, and he would have had to work in unskilled jobs.

Jamieson's childhood no doubt contributed to the extreme level of paranoia he displayed as an adult. But not everyone who has a tough time as a child develops a PPD. The way we handle adversity depends on a combination of our personality traits, experiences and life circumstances. Ian Jamieson most likely had a PPD that developed around the time he was living in care and worsened as he entered adulthood. He lived in various types of foster care at a time when it was not as well regulated as it is now, and that may mean that he had some very negative experiences such as being abused. Even if he didn't, the many changes and moves he experienced would have been disruptive and difficult to cope with for someone going through their teenage years, which can be tricky at the best of times.

As a result, the adult Ian Jamieson was extremely paranoid and possibly chose to live in rural settings to avoid having to deal with too many people. He migrated from New Zealand to Australia in the mid-1960s and married Janice in 1973. They had three children. In 2014, the couple was planning to move to a Tasmanian property they had owned for about seven years. They put their Wedderburn home on the market in the spring and were due to holiday in Tasmania when Jamieson killed his neighbours (*DPP v Jamieson* [2016] VSC 407).

When Peter and Mary first moved in, the situation with their neighbour was not too bad. Jamieson seemed a bit strange, with his crushed rock and closed gate, but he did not appear to be dangerous. As time went on, however, his paranoid view of the world led him to believe that his neighbours were deliberately stirring up dust to 'get at' him. When Greg moved in, because he lived next door, the access road was used more often. Greg used it and Peter and Mary used it more than they had before to visit him. Jamieson became even more paranoid and used his CCTV camera to 'catch them in the act'.

It is difficult to understand why he went to such extremes when he and Janice were planning to leave their current situation anyway. Even if his neighbours were hard to get along with, which by all accounts they weren't, if and when Jamieson sold his house he wouldn't have to live near them for much longer. Most people in such a situation would have cut their losses and looked forward to moving on. But Jamieson's paranoia had reached new heights. He just couldn't help himself and became angrier and angrier at what he incorrectly perceived were intentional injustices against him.

Ian Jamieson's PPD is clearly extreme. Those who have one

display a longstanding, ongoing pattern of thinking and behaviour in which they are almost always suspicious and distrustful of others. They assume, without justification, that people are trying to harm, deceive, exploit or humiliate them or are plotting against them. Jamieson thought his neighbours were deliberately stirring up dirt to ruin his property, pollute his water tanks and antagonise him. In reality, the situation was nowhere near as bad as he thought, and if there was dust it was probably carried by natural wind and occasional dust storms. Nor did Peter, Mary and Greg think about Jamieson anywhere near as often as he stewed over their actions. To them, he was an annoying neighbour that they tried to avoid lest he have a go at them verbally.

Greg did worry that if his dogs got into Jamieson's property he might shoot them, which shows that he was wary of what his neighbour was capable of with animals. But he did not think Jamieson was a physical threat to him, his de facto partner or his family. If someone had looked closely and had known what to look for, they may have seen that Jamieson's behaviour fitted the classic cognitive distortions of someone with a PPD. But even then, they may not have predicted his extremely violent behaviour in response to what he thought were the wrongs of others. A personality disorder does not necessarily make someone violent. Jamieson demonstrated all the cognitive distortions typical of someone with a PPD:

- a hostile attributional style, which leads someone with a PPD to blame negative outcomes in their life on the intentional behaviour of others but without foundation. Jamieson blamed Mary, Peter and then Greg for making him stress and worry about his property, when they actually did very little to annoy him intentionally. They were simply carrying on with everyday life.

- an intentionality bias, which sees them assume that others want to deliberately deceive or harm them. Jamieson believed his neighbours were deliberately trying to damage his property with dirt from the track. This was not true, but he could not be convinced otherwise and became obsessed with thoughts about Peter, Mary and Greg's perceived negative intentions against him.
- a self-righteousness that sees them take the moral high ground and overly focus on what they see as their rights. Jamieson believed that his interpretation of Peter, Mary and Greg's actions as intentional aggression and disrespect directed towards him was correct when it wasn't. He was actually the annoying person who behaved without justification, but in his eyes, they were.
- a self-justification bias in which they believe that their own actions, however drastic, are always justified. To the end, Jamieson claimed that even though he killed his neighbours, they drove him to do it with their 'terrible' behaviour. This was ludicrous. Murder is never justified, even if the victim is a nasty person. In this case, Jamieson believed people would understand that he killed his neighbours because they had stirred up dirt that blew onto his property and didn't, in his eyes, treat him with respect.

Ian Jamieson became a multiple murderer when his PPD led him to misinterpret the circumstances in which he found himself, and created an unwillingness and inability to evaluate his own contribution to the situation and challenge his own distorted and irrational thinking. Hindsight is a wonderful thing, but even if his own family had noticed his extreme paranoia, there was probably not a lot they could have done to prevent what happened. Janice probably thought she was simply stuck with a grumpy old man for a husband. She may have coped by ignoring his rants or busying herself with other things. Whatever he said to her, she could not have predicted the shocking crime he would commit for the flimsiest of reasons.

CONCLUSION

Someone with a PPD is often easier to identify than people with another type of personality disorder who may be may be manipulative and cunning. Someone with a PPD is more likely to directly and loudly communicate their views about what they see as the persecutory behaviours of others. They are likely to believe that most people they deal with have a hidden agenda or are out to get them, and communicate these views to those who are close to them. For example, they may believe that a neighbour who waters their front lawn every night is spying on them or accessing their water supply. They may tell others at work that the colleague whose role it is to supervise them is really a stalker. They may also act in overtly paranoid ways, such as having excessive security around their homes. Taken separately, these actions do not mean that someone has a PPD. It is not overly paranoid to wonder about the motives of a neighbour who is constantly out walking in the street, but when someone is overly suspicious about most people they deal with in their day-to-day life, they may have a significant problem with trust, and inaccurate and distorted perceptions.

Those with a PPD may also grossly exaggerate any potential threat to them. Ian Jamieson's thought processes turned the possible incidental spraying of some dust into his property into a major feud that he believed that his neighbours had started in order to 'get at him'. Jamieson also shut his farm gates whenever he left his property, which most people in rural areas do not bother to do, in a clear sign that he didn't trust his neighbours or others to keep out of his property when he was away. In fact, Greg Holmes, his mother Mary and her husband Peter had done nothing wrong towards Jamieson and posed no threat. They knew Jamieson's thoughts were irrational, and Greg had told people not to let their dogs wander onto Jamieson's property because he thought his neighbour would shoot them. Although Greg knew his neighbour's attitude and behaviour were not normal, neither he nor anyone else realised how dangerous Jamieson was.

Whereas people with conditions such as NPD can be cunning and blend into a home, friendship or office situation without people realising their way of behaving and thinking is disordered, people like Ian Jamieson can be easier to diagnose, as their words and actions usually give them away. They will complain unreasonably about people others know are upstanding and reputable, or refuse to entrust those close to them with sensitive information even when it is clear that they can be trusted. Jamieson's neighbours were well respected in the community and had done nothing to harm him, but he clearly thought they were out to get him and that he was justified in using CCTV to spy on them and keeping guns to protect himself from the perceived threat.

Unlike Jamieson, most people with a PPD are often annoying and irrational but relatively harmless. They do not enjoy life as much as they could because they cannot trust other people and tend to look for and highlight the worst in them. They may also lose friendships and alienate themselves from relatives. For example, if a neighbour tries to help them or innocently leaves a Christmas card in their letterbox, rather than feel grateful, they may believe that this person only acted so that they can use them to borrow their garden tools. They may also question the motives of relatives and accuse those who visit often of interfering or wanting their money, even if that person is genuinely looking out for them. At work, they might be suspicious of colleagues who invite them onto team projects, thinking that they are only doing so to take credit for their work. To them, other people either have a selfish agenda or are out to get them. Instead of seeing the best in people, they will almost always see the worst.

The situation can escalate if, like Ian Jamieson, the person's thoughts start to become more and more extreme. Jamieson believed that his neighbours were a physical threat to him when they clearly were not. In cases such as this, the person with a PPD can become very dangerous. They feel that they need to defend themselves against a perceived threat at all costs. In the end, Jamieson's paranoia became so acute that he felt he had to kill not only Greg, but also Peter and Mary. His actions were in no way justified and he knew what he was doing was criminal. Jamieson then lied to police when he told them that he had acted in self-defence with Greg, whom he accused of attacking him with a syringe. His actions before and after the murders were cold, calculated and designed to convince people that they were justified. While most of those who knew and interacted with Jamieson knew that his thinking was irrational and his behaviour far from justified, in his view he was right and everyone else was wrong.

Most people with a PPD will not resort to such extremes

of behaviour but a few do and can be difficult to have in your life. Many find themselves with few friends, as their constant 'paranoid perceptions' wear thin. They may become isolated in their workplace as others avoid working with them if they can. Only the most patient of partners will stay with someone who has a PPD, as their attitude and behaviour can be difficult to live with. If things are to improve, they must admit to themselves that they have a problem. Unfortunately, this may not happen, as someone with a PPD is likely to be suspicious of the motives of anyone who tries to help them, or may blame others for their predicament. They feel that their thoughts are keeping them safe and believe that they are protecting themselves by being cautious about anyone they perceive as a threat – which in the case of someone with a PPD may be many of the people they know or meet.

If you know someone who appears to have a PPD, approaching them about it can be tricky, as they are likely to question your motives in doing so. They may think that you are trying to undermine them or make yourself look better in the eyes of your family or friendship group. If the person with the PPD is older, they may incorrectly think you want to move them into a nursing home. If their paranoia is not too extreme, it is probably best to gently disagree with them when they wrongly accuse others of attempting to exploit or undermine them. Quietly point out that the people they are criticising are extremely unlikely to have ulterior motives, and reassure your friend or loved one about why that person acted the way they did: 'Norma gave you those lemons because she has a tree full of them and knows you like lemon slice; she doesn't want anything in return.'

When a PPD is extreme, such as Ian Jamieson's, it can be potentially dangerous. If you know someone whose paranoid thoughts extend to making physical threats about others, you may need to seek professional help for them. In some cases, you may want to consider warning anyone that they have a grudge against to be very careful in their interactions with them. Be wary of challenging them directly, as they may then target you as well. In Jamieson's case, his neighbours did not do anything to directly challenge, hurt or threaten him. His paranoia was so extreme that all it took was for them to drive down a dirt track next to his property for him to believe incorrectly that they were threatening him. It is likely that in the lead-up to his crimes, Jamieson commented about the situation to his wife and family. But how could they have known that their husband and father was capable of murder? They had probably decided he was simply a cranky man and ignored his more outlandish outbursts. If they had challenged him, he may have directed his anger at them as well.

Anyone who is worried about the actions of someone close to them who appears to be overly paranoid should seek professional advice about what to do next. As well as indicating that they might have a PPD, severe paranoia can also be caused by a serious mental illness such as schizophrenia. Some people with schizophrenia might believe that people they have never met are conspiring against them, or that someone they had a brief encounter with many years before and who has not seen them since is now stalking them. They may also accuse their own friends and family of conspiring against them. If these thoughts, whether they are caused by a PPD, schizophrenia or another mental illness, begin to impact negatively on a person's life or relationships, they probably need professional help. They may resist, and they cannot be forced to seek help unless they become a physical danger to others, but it is worth trying. Otherwise, that person is less likely to enjoy life and the situation may deteriorate further. In some cases, like Jamieson's, people's safety and even lives may be threatened.

*A list of support services for those dealing with someone who displays extreme paranoia and other psychological issues can be found on pages 403–7.

PART V

ANTISOCIAL PERSONALITY DISORDER

LIFE OUTSIDE THE RULES

Imagine someone who deceives, manipulates and belittles you – and enjoys doing it. Someone with an antisocial personality disorder (ASPD) preys upon others for their own benefit, to take advantage of them personally, rip them off financially, or cause them physical or emotional pain. A partner with an ASPD will not think twice about cheating on their partner or stealing money from their joint back account, while a businessperson with the disorder has no qualms about breaking tax laws, selling inferior products for a huge profit or talking customers into spending money they don't have. A work colleague with an ASPD might lie about a workmate to have them sacked, or sleep with the boss to secure a promotion and then stab that boss in the back as well. These people can be cunning and often have very little shame.

For this reason, people with an ASPD can be dangerous and difficult to detect. They lurk in homes and workplaces, playing the role of the perfect partner or colleague until they decide to use and abuse those around them for their own ends. Some are more obvious because their actions are so predatory – the serial workplace cheat that aggrieved women know to steer clear of, or the con artist who has been repeatedly declared bankrupt. But many are difficult to spot because they have the capacity to blend in with their environment to avoid detection. When someone suspects them of having an ulterior motive, they can be capable of turning on the charm, arguing that it was all a misunderstanding or that they were just about to repay that loan they'd ignored for six months.

Michael Cardamone, who viciously murdered his neighbour Karen Chetcuti in rural Victoria, has an ASPD. In a sexually motivated crime, Cardamone tortured Karen and then murdered her by burning her alive to prevent her from giving evidence against him. He had previously sexually assaulted a young woman, who later gave evidence against him that sent him to jail, so he didn't want that to happen again. To save himself from more jail time, Cardamone committed a brutal murder and then lied about it and tried to implicate an acquaintance. He most likely did all of this without feeling an ounce of guilt.

Convicted murderers Angelika Gavare, Simon Gittany and Adrian Bayley, who appeared in our first book, *Why Did They Do It?*, also have an ASPD. Gavare killed an elderly Adelaide pensioner, Vonne McGlynn, in an attempt to steal her home and other assets. Gittany threw his fiancée, Lisa Harnum, to her death from a fifteenth-floor Sydney balcony when he found out that she was trying to leave him. Adrian Bayley murdered Jill Meagher in Melbourne because she fought back after he sexually assaulted her. Like Michael Cardamone, they showed no mercy to their victims.

What is an ASPD?

People with an ASPD exhibit a repetitive and sustained pattern of behaviour characterised by a lack of concern for, and a preparedness to violate, the rights of other people in order to achieve their own desired outcomes (DSM-5, APA, 2013). The DSM-5 states that this disorder can be diagnosed when there is evidence of three or more of the following behavioural indicators in a person who is over the age of eighteen and who displayed some of the symptoms of a conduct disorder before they were fifteen. The individual:

- repeatedly behaves in ways that reflect an indifference to community expectations and a disregard of criminal laws
- acts in ways that are intended to deceive others for their own gain, such as by lying, conning, stealing and manipulating
- acts impulsively without first thinking things through or engaging in forward planning
- displays frequent episodes of irritability and verbal and/or physical aggression towards others
- disregards their own safety and the safety and wellbeing of others
- fails to act in a responsible way and to honour work commitments and/or financial obligations
- shows little remorse for their behaviour after they have harmed or mistreated someone.

Recognising someone with an ASPD

Diagnosing someone with a personality disorder is difficult and requires some professional knowledge, but it is possible to recognise some of the more common behaviours that might indicate someone you know has such a disorder. As with other personality disorders, the severity of ASPD can range from mild to extreme. Two people with an ASPD may behave differently in some ways, depending on which specific criteria they meet, other factors in their lives, and whether they fit into the 'psychopathy' subtype, a single variant of ASPD outlined in the DSM-5. In addition to the ASPD behaviours, the psychopathy subtype is characterised by psychopathic features such as low levels of anxiety (relative 'fearlessness'), interpersonal exploitation, assertiveness and 'boldness', callous unemotional behaviour and a lack of inhibition. This subtype corresponds with Hare's conception of psychopathy (1996).

The DSM-5 notes that the ASPD pattern has also been referred to by some researchers as both 'psychopathy' and 'sociopathy'. The first version of the DSM in 1952 used the term 'sociopathic personality disorder', which was replaced in later editions by the term 'antisocial personality disorder'. The terms 'psychopath' and 'sociopath', which have been used to name individuals with many of the behaviours that are also characteristic of an ASPD, have since been used interchangeably by many writers, clinicians and researchers and within popular culture.

There has also been considerable unresolved debate over the years about whether these are identical, similar or quite different disorders. It has been argued that they are identical, but that the term sociopath is more useful as it focuses on the fact that the suffering ('path') is caused to other people ('socio') rather than to the wellbeing ('psycho') of the person with an ASPD. Others have argued that although 'psychopaths' and 'sociopaths' share some of the core features of someone with an ASPD, psychopaths are more extreme and dangerous, as they are likely to be more callous, violent and physically cruel. They are also more likely to be imprisoned and to reoffend when released.

Some argue that sociopaths are more 'high functioning' than psychopaths because they tend to be more socially competent, have a more developed conscience, have some (but still limited) capacity for empathy, are less likely to be cruel or violent, are less likely to be imprisoned, and tend to be more 'successful' than psychopaths in terms of their positions in society and in their career. This is the assumption made by the authors of books such as *The Sociopath Next Door* (Stout, 2006), *Confessions of a Sociopath* (Thomas, 2013) and *Difficult Personalities* (McGrath and Edwards, 2009).

A conduct disorder (DSM-5, APA, 2013) is characterised by a violation of age-appropriate societal norms before the age of fifteen, as indicated by a range of behaviours such as:

- aggression towards others (including bullying)
- cruelty to animals
- damage to the property of others
- lying
- stealing
- staying out at night and/or running away from home
- truanting from school
- sexual assault
- fire setting.

Typical behaviours of people with an ASPD

Those with an ASPD display a wide range of behaviours. They tend to do whatever it takes to get what they want, even if they have to deceive, cheat, steal or hurt people to do so. They have low levels of empathy, and their deceitful and manipulative behaviour is often callous, unemotional and indifferent to the rights, feelings or suffering of their partners, family, work colleagues or friends. They rarely feel guilty or remorseful, and are focused on what they perceive to be 'survival'. When confronted, they will usually try to lie their way out of it and often become aggressive, as Michael Cardamone did when cornered by police. Many are superficially charming when they are trying to con someone, and some can blend in and act like 'chameleons', making them difficult to identify.

Those with an ASPD are often sexually promiscuous, unfaithful to their partners and behave in other manipulative or deceitful ways in their intimate relationships. They usually make poor parents, as they neither notice nor respond very well to their children's feelings and needs. They tend to have poor impulse control and are often sensation-seeking, as they struggle to cope with boredom. This can make them reckless and indifferent to their own safety as well as the safety of people around them. In Cardamone's case, rather than respect Karen Chetcuti's wishes when it became clear that she was not sexually interested in him, he kidnapped, tortured and mutilated her, leaving her body in a place where it would certainly be found by authorities. He knew his actions were completely reckless and he was likely to be caught, but he did it anyway.

Someone with an ASPD can become very frustrated when they don't get their way, as Cardamone did when his sexual interest was not reciprocated. They are easily irritated and may respond with aggression when annoyed, often ending up in fights or hurting people, including relatives. Some behave irresponsibly and experience significant periods of unemployment, often due to absenteeism. They may abandon or neglect their family, default on loans or fail to pay child support. Those at the more extreme end of an ASPD, who fit into the 'psychopathy' subtype, as Cardamone does, may use aggression and violence to get their way. They may break into homes, rape and sexually abuse others, or attack or kill those who stand in their way. A few will kill simply for the excitement.

Prevalence of ASPDs

An estimated 0.2 to 3.3 per cent of the general population has an ASPD, and it is more frequently diagnosed in men (up to

5.8 per cent) than women (up to 1.2 per cent) (Lenzenweger et al., 2007; Torgersen et al., 2001). An estimated 47 per cent of male prisoners and 21 per cent of female prisoners has an ASPD (Fazel and Danesh, 2002).

Comorbidity (other disorders that often occur with ASPDs)

In some people, an ASPD has been shown to occur with depression and anxiety disorders (Rotgers and Maniacci, 2006).

Heritability of ASPDs

The heritability of ASPD is estimated to be .69 (Torgersen et al., 2012). This means that 69 per cent of the differences between those in research studies who had an ASPD and those who didn't were most likely due to genetic differences between them. In particular, people with an ASPD appear to be genetically more at risk of developing lower levels of empathy and higher rates of behaviour such as irritability, impulsivity, aggression and irresponsibility (e.g. Baker et al., 2006).

Other contributing factors to ASPDs

Like other personality disorders, an ASPD results from the interaction of genetic and environmental factors. Despite many research studies, the picture is complex and still unclear. This may reflect the different combinations of behaviours that individuals with an ASPD display. Some people with an ASPD have highly dysfunctional backgrounds. This may involve parental rejection, abandonment, neglect or abuse, weak parental supervision and/or inconsistent discipline, family alcohol or substance abuse, antisocial role models and associating with people living a lifestyle with antisocial elements. This picture is complicated by the fact that some parents who create such dysfunctional family environments are also likely to have some degree of ASPD themselves and may have passed the genetic predisposition to their children as well.

Some people who develop an ASPD come from homes where no parent modelled or stressed the importance of empathy or encouraged moral thinking such as compassion, respect, guilt and shame, sociocultural norms and the ability to be 'morally motivated' to care about the needs of other people. Research into the factors that contribute to an ASPD has tended to focus more on genetic and neurological factors than environmental factors. The disorder is more common among the first-degree biological relatives of those with the disorder – parents, children and siblings who share 50 per cent of their DNA – than in the general population.

Several recent studies have used neuroimaging and neurochemical measures to identify a range of possible neurological and biological factors that help pinpoint some of the ways the brains of many people with ASPD might function differently from those of other people, and what the impact of those differences might be in terms of their behaviour. Some of the outcomes from these studies are:

- People with an ASPD are more likely to engage in sensation-seeking behaviour, possibly because they tend to have a lower than average resting heart rate. This can contribute to a sense of feeling calm but can also result in often feeling under-aroused and bored (Ortiz and Raine, 2004; Raine et al., 2014).
- Some people who have an ASPD and are also violent tend to have a smaller volume of grey matter in the anterior rostral prefrontal cortex and temporal poles of their brain (Gregory et al., 2012). This results in difficulties with learning and

experiencing 'moral' emotions, such as guilt or shame, which help to develop prosocial behaviour and encourage moral learning.

- Some people who have an ASPD and are also impulsively aggressive are more likely to have lower than normal levels of the brain neurotransmitter serotonin (Moeller et al., 1996).
- Many people with an ASPD have significant abnormalities in parts of their brain, some of which have been found in sections of the orbital frontal cortex that controls impulses, behavioural inhibition, attention, reasoning, decision-making, planning and consequential thinking (Blair, 2007).

Some people with an ASPD appear to be relatively 'fearless' in some ways. Some have structural and functional impairments in the amygdala region of their brain. The amygdala is at the centre of our 'emotional brain' and is part of the 'empathy circuit' (Baron-Cohen, 2011). It alerts us to potential danger, helps us to learn to feel fear in response to certain situations, and contributes to us acting empathically towards those in distress. Such impairments can lead to these people being less able than others to 'feel fear' and therefore less likely to respond defensively to potential threats such as punishment.

In studies where people have been taught to anticipate a mild electric shock when a loud buzzer goes off, those with an ASPD were also less likely to act in a way that suggested they anticipated fear, such as having a higher heart rate or flinching. Their vital signs stayed the same even when there was a possibility that they would receive such a shock (Hare, 1978). In other studies, compared to people who didn't have an ASPD, those who did were more likely to have a diminished or non-existent 'startle reflex', such as an automatic 'jump' or 'blink', in response to a sudden loud sound, an object suddenly coming towards them or being shown graphic, violent or unpleasant photos (see, for example, Baskin-Sommers et al., 2013).

Such relative 'fearlessness' is also found in many individuals without an ASPD and who also have a normal capacity for empathy, self-control and moral behaviour. These people are often engaged in work or hobbies that most of us wouldn't be brave enough to do and which, to some extent, require not only well-developed skills but also 'nerves of steel', such as being an astronaut or deep-sea diver, aerobatic flying, sky diving, bomb-disposal work, military leadership or public performance. Being a 'daredevil' does not automatically mean you have an ASPD.

Two or more of the factors listed above may combine to produce in someone with an ASPD the capacity to stay calm under threat, and make other people feel apprehensive in the face of such calm. With little fear of the potential consequences of their actions, they can develop 'punishment insensitivity', making it less likely that they will learn from their mistakes. Such fearlessness can make some people with an ASPD seem confident and genuine, as they easily make and maintain eye contact with others. That makes it easier for them to persuade people or con them. Others will maintain eye contact in a threatening or unnerving way that warns you not to challenge or oppose them because they could be dangerous.

People with an ASPD are less accurate than other people when asked to recognise fearful or sad facial expressions in photographs (Marsh and Blair, 2008). Not recognising such emotional reactions may make it easier for them to harm or use people or to ignore their distress. One study, however, in which researchers used neuroimaging techniques to monitor the brains of people with an ASPD as they watched videos of people in pain or distress, obtained some interesting results. They found that the subjects initially didn't show a 'brain response' to the distress of others in the video as measured by activation of their mirror neuron system, but if they were asked to try harder to empathise with how the people in the video were feeling, they were more likely to activate those mirror neurons (Meffert et al., 2013; see pages 413–14). This suggests that people with an ASPD *can* empathise, but choose not to do so unless it suits them. They can switch into 'non-empathy mode' while working towards a desired goal, such as conning or hurting someone, when empathy would get in the way of them achieving what they want.

Treatment of ASPDs

Few people with an ASPD seek treatment, but many of their work colleagues, family members or partners do. Some psychologists and psychiatrists are reluctant to treat people with an ASPD, as their own experience and many studies suggest that insight-oriented psychological treatment is ineffective (see, for example, Harris and Rice, 2006). Some people with an ASPD are encouraged or pressured by partners or relatives to seek treatment for related issues, such as the damage they cause to those close to them. Others are ordered to have counselling after breaking the law, but their goal in joining a treatment program is usually self-serving.

One study found that prisoners with an ASPD who participated in a treatment program based on teaching anger management and interpersonal skills were more likely to reoffend after being released than those who did not participate in the program (Hare et al., 2000). It seems that, through the program, they may have learned how to exploit other people more effectively. Before killing Jill Meagher, for example, Adrian Bayley underwent counselling following an earlier sex crime. But he later admitted to simply telling the counsellor what he thought they wanted to hear (see *Why Did They Do It?* for more details of this case).

It is also unlikely that Michael Cardamone would respond to treatment. As someone with an ASPD characterised by extreme violence, he would have very poor insight into the damage he has caused to his victims and their families, and very little concern about their reactions and feelings. His complete disregard for the safety and wellbeing of his victims, the legal system and the acquaintance he tried to blame for the murder he committed, clearly indicate that his actions are completely motivated by self-gratification and self-preservation – whatever the cost. He knows he has done the wrong thing according to society's rules and expectations, but feels no empathy for his victims and is solely motivated by what works for him. That is why someone with an ASPD can be so dangerous. They may not go to the extremes of a Michael Cardamone, but their actions are designed to provide them with what they want, without a thought for the rights or safety of anyone else.

CHAPTER 12

MICHAEL CARDAMONE

The cast

Michael Cardamone: A career criminal who lied to cover his tracks after killing his neighbour
Karen Chetcuti: A divorced mother of two who lived next door to Michael Cardamone and was murdered by him
Tony Chetcuti: Karen's ex-husband
Maria Cardamone: Michael Cardamone's mother, who pleaded guilty to one count of attempting to pervert the course of justice after giving $9000 to someone she thought was a hit man to help her son avoid being convicted of murder

The motive

In a sexually motivated murder, Michael Cardamone tortured Karen Chetcuti and then murdered her by burning her alive to prevent her from giving evidence against him as a young woman had done previously after he sexually assaulted her.

Introduction

A popular member of the wider Wangaratta community, Karen Chetcuti was about to celebrate her 50th birthday. Karen was divorced from her husband, Tony, and their two children regularly stayed with her on the four-hectare property she lived on at Whorouly, a small town about 30 kilometres south-east of Wangaratta. Karen lived alone but worked in the City of Wangaratta's records department, where she was well liked and respected.

Life was good, but Karen had become unsettled by the unwelcome attention of her neighbour, Michael Cardamone, who occasionally offered to help around her farm. Those feelings proved to be well founded when she disappeared on the night of Tuesday, 12 January 2016, three months before she was due to turn 50 on 24 April. Karen was last seen at picturesque country pub the Whorouly Hotel, about 200 metres from the entrance to her property, between about 6 pm and 7.45 pm. It had been a hot day – 37 degrees Celsius – so Karen enjoyed a beer with neighbour Brian Gambold and publican Graham Wood, before going home and having a meal and a glass of wine. After attending to several tasks around the house, she disappeared. Karen's last known communication was several messages she posted on Facebook, the last of them at 9.18 pm.

At the time, Michael Cardamone was on parole after serving time in prison for the rape of a fifteen-year-old girl and for making threats to kill and inflict serious injury. Cardamone had committed the offences in 2005 and moved back to Whorouly in January 2016, after his release from jail in July 2015. He had nine months left of his parole period.

The murder

On the morning of 12 January, Cardamone contacted Eddie George, a Myrtleford man, to obtain methylamphetamine to feed his longstanding drug habit. What happened later that night will never be fully clear, as Cardamone has constantly lied about it and changed his story, but phone records show that when he rang Karen at 9.09 pm, she did not answer. He later falsely claimed that she was at his place at 9.15 pm to collect some cherry tomatoes.

At 9.40 pm, Cardamone again rang Karen's phone. A call of 66 seconds was recorded. He phoned her again at around 9.55 pm, but it is unclear whether she spoke to him. It is most likely that between 9.18 pm and 10.30 pm, Cardamone physically attacked Karen, then bound and possibly gagged her with cable ties, duct tape and rope. He probably left her, terrified, in his shed while he worked out what to do next. Cardamone again contacted Eddie George, and at about 10.30 pm drove Karen's Citroën to Myrtleford, where he obtained some drugs, returning home close to midnight.

At some point, Cardamone decided to kill his petrified neighbour. In the early hours of Wednesday, 13 January, he drove her Citroën to Myrtleford, left it in town and caught a taxi home about 3.30 am. He then drove his Nissan Patrol four-wheel drive to the Lake Buffalo area, 20 kilometres south of Myrtleford, where phone records indicate he stayed for two and a half hours. During that time, Cardamone brutally and callously murdered Karen. While she was bound, he administered a strong veterinary sedative, xylazine, as well as methylamphetamine. He also injected battery acid into her. Cardamone then inflicted serious head and torso injuries, fracturing Karen's skull and six ribs. But she did not die until Cardamone doused her with petrol and set her alight. He then used his large SUV to drive over the body, causing more injuries, and pushed it to the side of the track, where it was later found.

The sentencing judge later found that there was not enough evidence to conclude whether Cardamone had sexually assaulted his victim. The nature of her injuries was so serious that investigators were unable to determine one way or the other. But given his previous history, it is highly probable that Cardamone sexually assaulted Karen at some point. He then returned to Myrtleford and purchased two cigarette lighters at a Caltex service station in bare feet, having disposed of his shoes. He later attended a car wash with his Nissan Patrol, returning a few hours later to wash it again. In the afternoon he returned a third time, this time vacuuming near the driver's door. That day Cardamone was also seen driving Karen's car.

By Wednesday night, police were investigating her disappearance. Cardamone lied to police when they interviewed him and tried to send them on a wild goose chase after telling them they should search the Ovens River area, knowing that nothing would be found there. He told police Karen left his place after popping over for some cherry tomatoes, knowing that he had already placed some in her fridge to back up his story. But the container in the fridge had only his fingerprints, not hers. Later that night, as police and Karen's family and friends searched desperately for her, Cardamone visited Eddie George for more drugs and asked him to help dispose of Karen's car, telling Eddie that it was an insurance job for drug dealers. They took the car to a remote location and incinerated it.

The investigation

When Cardamone spoke to police at length on Friday, 15 January, he denied any involvement in Karen's disappearance. He even complained that people unfairly suspected him because of his history of offending. Cardamone spoke to a newspaper journalist and claimed that whoever was responsible must have been lying in wait when she returned from his house on the Tuesday night. He claimed that he had heard cars leaving that night and that he had seen Karen's car in Myrtleford. On 16 January, Cardamone falsely told his solicitor he'd been kidnapped by two Lebanese men and held in the boot of a car. The solicitor rang police and a description of the so-called vehicle was circulated Victoria-wide. At the time, Cardamone was actually in Melbourne withdrawing cash from automatic teller machines.

After he was arrested in Melbourne on Sunday, 17 January, Cardamone changed his story again, claiming that the two 'mythical' Lebanese men must have killed Karen and that he was limited in what he could say about them as they were threatening his family. He told police that these men had told him how they had killed Karen and where her body was, and he claimed to have seen her restrained by these men in her car. Later, after Cardamone became aware that police had spoken to Eddie, he abandoned the Lebanese story and claimed that he was there when Karen died but that Eddie had killed her. His lies became so bold that Cardamone had the gall to pretend that Eddie, having murdered his neighbour, was now trying to blame him.

Five days after she disappeared, police found Karen's body 35 kilometres from Myrtleford in an area called Dandongadale. Cardamone independently directed them to the crime scene, still claiming that Eddie was responsible. Police already knew this was not the case, and due to overwhelming evidence against him, Cardamone was charged with murder on 19 January.

While on remand, the alleged killer told another prisoner that he needed Eddie George silenced and was prepared to pay someone to do it. The prisoner contacted police and they came up with a plan for him to give Cardamone what he thought would be the phone number of a hit man. The plan worked when Cardamone called an undercover officer who was masquerading as a hit man and said he needed Eddie killed in a way that made his death look like a suicide by drug overdose. Cardamone even asked the 'hit man' to force the victim to write a suicide letter confessing to killing Karen. He promised to pay $25,000 for the hit and got his mother, Maria, to hand over $9000 as an advance on 23 March 2017. This drew her into his evil plot and she ended up being charged with, and later pleading guilty to, one count of attempting to pervert the course of justice. Maria Cardamone was jailed for 140 days, the exact time she had already served on remand.

The sentencing

In June 2017, Michael Cardamone pleaded guilty to the murder of Karen Maria Chetcuti and to incitement to murder prosecution witness Edward George. The guilty plea came more than seventeen months after the crime. Sentencing Cardamone in August 2017, Justice Lex Lasry was appalled by his actions and the web of lies he wove to avoid responsibility. 'I believed I had ceased to be amazed at the level of violence that some men are capable of inflicting on defenceless women, but what you did to Karen Chetcuti over a number of hours and for no apparent or logical reason, does indeed amaze me,' Justice Lasry said. 'You have declined to subsequently explain your conduct in any worthwhile or logical sense. What you have said about Ms Chetcuti's death on the eighteen occasions you said anything, was designed to mislead police and incriminate others, though some aspects of your later accounts may carry an element of truth concerning what was actually done to Ms Chetcuti. Your conduct in relation to the murder of Ms Chetcuti was extraordinarily vicious, callous and thoroughly unprovoked. The crime you committed was, quite simply, horrifying, depraved and disgusting' (*R v Cardamone* [2017] VSC 493).

Justice Lasry also expressed his disgust at Cardamone's blatant attempts to cover his tracks. 'Having done what you did, and without any apparent regret, you took every conceivable action to avoid responsibility for Ms Chetcuti's murder,' Justice Lasry said. 'On the afternoon of 14 January 2016, after police came to your house and requested it, you made a sworn statement about your contact with Ms Chetcuti at the time of her disappearance. In that statement you told a series of elaborate lies. You described how you had had a conversation with her on the night of 12 January and had invited her to come and obtain some tomatoes. You said she gave you her mobile phone number. You claimed she had come to your house to obtain that produce and that you and she had a "big chat" about "farm stuff". She finally left your house, you said, and when you looked at the time it was 9.15 pm. That, you claimed, was the last contact you had with her. After the written statement was completed you approached police and told yet more lies about why they might find your cigarette lighter in Ms Chetcuti's car, telling them you were in the car "the other day" and left it there' (*R v Cardamone* [2017] VSC 493).

Justice Lasry said the murder had several aggravating features. 'From the time you first attacked her until her death, in her conscious moments, she must have been terrified,' he said. 'The method by which you killed her, as I have already described, was grossly violent with her apparently dying from being burnt by fire whilst alive. In addition, you viciously attacked her with heavy blows to the head and body. After she had died you drove a vehicle over her body. You then dumped her body and clothing. Once the murder of Karen Chetcuti had been committed you engaged in an elaborate concealment of what you had done designed to divert the police investigation away from you. These measures included the various lies you told to police and others over a number of days, together with your later efforts to arrange for the killing of Eddie George. Your conduct after murdering Karen Chetcuti demonstrates a complete lack of regret or remorse for what you had done. It is now claimed that you are remorseful for this crime. Based in part on your conduct to this point, I find that very difficult to accept. Your conduct over the entire period commencing on 12 January 2016 and concluding with your plea of guilty on 30 June 2017 was extraordinary and, in my opinion, devoid of any regret or remorse' (*R v Cardamone* [2017] VSC 493).

Cardamone's actions were not mitigated by any mental health issues. When psychiatrist Dr Lester Walton assessed Cardamone in July 2017, he found him unwilling to explain why he killed Karen or discuss what he did in any detail. 'Dr Walton's report indicates that you have no mental health problems of any consequence and there was no psychiatric or psychological condition that played any part in your offending,' Justice Lasry found. 'You are not psychotic. You have a history of polysubstance abuse, more recently heroin and methylamphetamine. Similar observations were made in 2006. Clearly you had no insight into your offending then or now and need to deal with your drug issues. I acknowledge that the mixed anxiety/depressive disorder from which you now suffer will make your sentence more onerous' (*R v Cardamone* [2017] VSC 493).

Through his counsel, Cardamone tried to use Dr Walton's report to demonstrate his remorse, but Justice Lasry noted that while the report talked about Cardamone expressing sorrow and empathy for Karen's family, it did not comment on how genuine this was. 'I am not persuaded that you are genuinely remorseful although I do not doubt you regret the situation you now find yourself in,' Justice Lasry said (*R v Cardamone* [2017] VSC 493).

Justice Lasry sentenced Cardamone to life in prison for the murder of Karen Chetcuti, eight years' jail for the charge of incitement to murder Eddie George, and the maximum three months' in prison for breaching his parole. He did not set a non-parole period, making Cardamone the first person in Victoria not previously convicted of murder to be sentenced to life without parole. In September 2017, Cardamone launched an appeal against the sentence, claiming it was too harsh.

Michael Cardamone's background

Michael Cardamone was born in 1967 to Italian immigrant parents. He has a younger sister and was raised outside Wangaratta on the family's tobacco farm. Cardamone completed Year 12 and took over his family's two farms when his father died in 2014. Socially his life was difficult, and he ended up reliant on illegal drugs, which he started taking in his teenage years. As an adult he used significant amounts of amphetamines and methylamphetamine. Due to a circulation condition, he had also taken anticoagulant medication for about fifteen years.

A seasoned criminal, Cardamone was first in trouble with the law when he was eighteen, with an unlawful assault conviction in the Myrtleford Magistrates' Court. He was placed on an adjourned bond and three years later committed the same offence with almost the same result. In 1991, he was convicted of multiple thefts in Wangaratta and Melbourne, which resulted in non-custodial sentences. By 2003, he had added convictions for trafficking and using amphetamines, as well as dishonesty. He again escaped jail with non-custodial sentences.

In December 2006, Cardamone was found guilty of threats to inflict serious injury and to kill, sexual penetration, committing an indecent act with a child under sixteen and rape. He was sentenced to ten years and three months with a non-parole period of seven years, which was reduced on appeal to nine years with a non-parole period of six years. He was sentenced as a serious sexual offender and registered as such for life.

Those offences were committed against a fifteen-year-old girl who lived with her boyfriend in a caravan while he worked on a tobacco farm. Cardamone threatened the girl with a large wrench while directing her to undress, then threatened to kill her if she did not comply with his demands. He sexually assaulted her several times, forced her to perform a sex act on him and said if she told anyone he would kill her and have her family killed.

Cardamone was released on parole on 1 November 2012. On 20 May 2013, the parole was cancelled but he was released again on 17 March 2014. On 9 February 2015, the parole was again cancelled when charges believed to involve child pornography were laid against him after he took a photo of a six-year-old girl baring her bottom. They were later dismissed, and he was released on 14 July 2015. On 21 September 2015, the new parole conditions were added. When Cardamone was arrested for the murder of Karen Chetcuti, he had 274 days owing on his parole period. While on remand for Karen's murder, he tested positive for methylamphetamine.

Why did he do it?

Michael Cardamone has a severe ASPD. Throughout his adult life, he has had no qualms about committing serious crimes, without a thought to his traumatised victims and their families. Those crimes also appear to have become more serious over time. While he clearly has an ASPD, there are few outward clues as to why Cardamone is so violent and uncaring. When his father Tony died in September 2014, he was remembered as an upstanding local citizen. Tony and Maria had moved to Whorouly in 1964 and become tobacco farmers. Tony was described as a gentle, hardworking man who loved his family and life's simple pleasures, such as growing fruit, producing award-winning extra virgin olive oil and sharing his produce with family and friends. The *Whorouly Newsletter* reported that Tony and Maria operated the Ovens Valley Café in Myrtleford for eleven years and ran a catering business for 35 years. Tony also operated the local school bus for 28 years (*Whorouly Newsletter*, October 2014).

Tributes for Tony Cardamone revealed that his son had a sister and a wife, but it is unclear if his wife was still in his life at that point. In total, there were four grandchildren. In a death notice published in the *Myrtleford Times/Alpine Observer* on 24 September 2014, Michael and his sister paid tribute to their father. They noted that he taught them how to appreciate hard work and perseverance, and to value love, kindness and family. They promised to live their lives knowing that he had left them a legacy that would be remembered forever and for which they would be eternally grateful. It was signed, 'Your loving children'.

It appears that Michael Cardamone did not heed his father's advice at any stage during his adult life. His criminal record demonstrates a complete disregard for the safety, feelings and rights of others. He has no excuse for the path he chose to take as an adult, which involved extensive drug abuse, related criminal activity, criminal assault and sexual abuse, torture and murder. When he was caught, Cardamone had no qualms about lying to cover his tracks, or threatening those who could prove his guilt. Given his previous criminal record and the result of his first rape case, in which the victim testified against him, Cardamone may have killed Karen Chetcuti simply to prevent her from putting him in jail for a long time. As it turned out, he has ended up in prison for the rest of his life.

Cardamone also conspired to have a key witness in his murder trial killed, embroiling his elderly mother, Maria, in a doomed plan that unravelled when an astute fellow remand prisoner informed police and helped them set Cardamone up. The fact that he was prepared to kill someone for giving evidence in a criminal trial, which witnesses are obliged to do once called by police, shows how callous his thought process is. Rather than mount a defence case, he planned to rid the defence of a key witness. To him, this was nothing more than a solution to a problem.

Michael Cardamone's behaviour over many years fits with a diagnosis of an ASPD, which is characterised by a pervasive pattern of disregard for, and violation of, the rights of others. As we have seen, the typical antisocial behaviours of someone with an ASPD include ignoring community laws, lying to and deceiving people, acting impulsively, using violence and aggression to get what they want, recklessly disregarding the personal safety of others, and a lack of remorse when their actions harm other people. Those with ASPD also display characteristics of conduct disorder when they are younger. We don't know if Cardamone physically or emotionally hurt people as a child, but he certainly did as an adult.

His preparedness to kill Karen Chetcuti, at least in part to prevent her testifying against him as his earlier teenage victim had done, showed a complete disregard for the law and for Karen's life. This man was prepared to kill someone he knew was a loving mother and a productive and valued member of the community to satisfy his depraved sexual desires and to protect himself from prosecution and serious jail time. His willingness to kill and then lie and implicate innocent people in his brutal crime showed that he had no regard for anyone but himself, and was prepared to hurt and kill others for his own ends.

People like Michael Cardamone will stop at nothing to protect their own interests and, if identified, should be avoided at all costs. Not all of them are potentially physically violent, but many are. Like Cardamone, some will kill without an ounce of guilt if they think it is necessary to protect themselves. His efforts to deceive the police failed dismally when they quickly saw through his lies and were able to corner him. He then pleaded guilty to murder to protect himself. Cardamone knew that the evidence against him was very strong, so pleading guilty would have been driven by a desire to reduce his sentence, and not by any empathy for the loved ones of Karen Chetcuti.

CONCLUSION

Living or working with someone who has an ASPD can be challenging. Even someone with a mild ASPD can make your life difficult. Someone with this type of personality disorder has no qualms about violating social norms or breaking the law, and often enjoys doing so. Depending on the severity, someone with an ASPD will develop an ingrained pattern of antisocial behaviour designed to get them what they want and make their life easier without regard to how it might hurt or exploit others.

As adults, those with ASPD may manipulate and cheat on their partners if it suits them, fiddle their tax returns and run shonky businesses that rip off unsuspecting customers, such as the fake tradespeople who prey on elderly pensioners, promising to fix their roof and then disappearing after securing a deposit of thousands of dollars. Serial con man Peter Foster is a good example of someone with an ASPD. Foster has been involved in countless 'get rich quick' scams involving entertainment promotion, money laundering, slimming products and betting scams since he was a teenager. He has been jailed in several countries. Like others with a personality disorder, Foster has not learned from his mistakes, and over the years has continued to surface in various countries with yet another 'sure thing', convincing people to invest in business deals that usually end badly.

Losing money to a scammer is distressing enough, but some people with ASPD are prepared to go even further in their quest to put themselves and their desire ahead of the welfare of others. To some, it's a game, while to others, like Foster, it's a way of making them rich. Michael Cardamone was prepared to do whatever it took to have his way with his neighbour, Karen Chetcuti. When she refused to reciprocate his sexual advances, Cardamone 'punished' her by torturing and murdering her. Investigators could not be sure, but he probably sexually assaulted her as well. The remorseless killer then tried to blame someone else for his murderous actions. Not only was he prepared to kill, but he was quite happy to see an innocent man jailed for his crimes, and wasn't the least bit concerned about dragging his mother into the situation.

How do you recognise someone like this who has an ASPD, and if you do, how should you respond? Most are dishonest and deceptive, but some are also potentially dangerous to have in your life, emotionally, financially or physically. They may not target everyone they know, but will have no qualms about lying to you, cheating on you, ripping you off and/or physically hurting you if it suits their agenda. Watch out for behaviours that might signal that you need to be on your guard, such as:

- repeatedly borrowing money without paying it back or paying it back very slowly
- starting or repeating untrue rumours about colleagues, friends and/or loved ones

- borrowing expensive items and not taking care of them properly or not returning them
- knowingly selling dodgy products for an inflated price
- stealing from family members, colleagues, strangers or in shops
- defrauding the government via welfare fraud or through their tax return (and often boasting about it)
- repeatedly telling lies in the workplace or to a partner, friends or relatives
- cheating on you, often with more than one person at the same time
- inflicting physical or emotional violence on you and/or children
- threatening to hurt people
- sexually harassing or assaulting people
- starting physical fights.

If you know someone who regularly does some or all these things to you or others, be very wary of them. If the incident or incidents are isolated, and the perpetrator has shown genuine remorse after they are caught and does not repeat the behaviour, it may have been a genuine mistake. But if they continue to repeat similar behaviours that clearly hurt others, are morally wrong, and ignore rules or break the law, that person may have an ASPD. If you are unsure, seek advice from a health professional who is qualified to diagnose such disorders. If it is established that the person probably does have an ASPD, you may need to distance yourself from them. This is not always immediately possible if it is a close relative or your partner, but it may become necessary to protect you and/or your children from potential harm.

A person with a serious ASPD is unlikely to change, as their behaviour is usually deeply ingrained. Once exposed, serial scammers will simply find another scam and another target, while serial cheats and abusers will find another partner. If you or someone you know is dealing with someone like this, try to minimise your contact with them. In the case of a partner, you may need to leave if it is you who is being lied to and cheated on. If it is a friend or family member who is being mistreated by a partner with an ASPD, try to support them where you can. Don't be surprised, however, if their partner manages to win them over and convince them that they're not guilty of what they have been accused of and that you are just trying to break them up. Statistically, the most dangerous time for someone in an emotionally and/or physically abusive relationship is when they decide or attempt to leave, so ensure that you or your relative does so safely.

Someone like Michael Cardamone, who had been jailed for sexually assaulting a fifteen-year-old girl before he killed Karen Chetcuti, would not hesitate to hurt or kill someone they believe stands in their way or could put them in jail. Cardamone displayed a pattern of sadistic criminal behaviour that only stopped when he was incarcerated, and perhaps not even then. Someone like him is extremely dangerous and doesn't learn from their mistakes. They are only concerned about their own needs, desires and urges, and should be avoided wherever possible.

*A list of support services for those dealing with someone who has a serious personality disorder can be found on pages 403–7.

PART VI

CRIMINAL AUTISTIC PSYCHOPATHY AND SEXUAL SADISM DISORDER

A DANGEROUS COMBINATION

What is an autism spectrum disorder?

Most individuals with an autism spectrum disorder (ASD) do not act violently or commit crimes. An ASD is characterised by difficulties in socialising and communicating with others and with understanding others. Many people with an ASD can attend regular schools and can do well in the workforce. Others may need additional support within the context of a special school or special services within a regular school. Some well-known and very successful people have been diagnosed or have diagnosed themselves with an ASD, such as scientists Albert Einstein and Professor Temple Grandin, actors Dan Aykroyd and Daryl Hannah, author John Elder Robison and singer Susan Boyle. John Elder Robison has written two very interesting, useful and optimistic books on his personal journey with an ASD: *Look Me in the Eye: My Life with Asperger's* (2007) and *Switched On: A Memoir of Brain Change and Emotional Awakening* (2016).

The most recent *Diagnostic and Statistical Manual of Mental Disorders* (DSM-5, APA, 2013) merged three previously separate diagnostic categories from the earlier DSM IV (APA, 2000), listed below, into a single disorder:

1. autistic disorder
2. Asperger's syndrome
3. pervasive developmental disorder (not otherwise specified).

The newer single DSM-5 diagnostic category is autism spectrum disorder (ASD). A simple summary appears below, and more specific and elaborated details can be found in the DSM-5 (APA, 2013). Those who are diagnosed early can improve their social and intellectual potential when they have opportunities to access a range of appropriate support services. In most cases, they can live happy and fulfilling lives.

Using the DSM-5 criteria (see references for specific details), a diagnosis of ASD can be made when there is evidence of behaviours such as those listed in the following two categories:

1. behaviours that indicate deficits in social communication and interaction
2. restricted and repetitive patterns of behaviour, interests or activities.

Deficits in social communication and interaction include:

- persistent difficulties in social communication and reciprocity, such as using atypical ways to approach others, difficulties with normal conversation, limited sharing of interests or feelings with others, rarely initiating social interactions or responding to the social overtures of others

- inadequate non-verbal communicative behaviours when interacting socially, such as lack of eye contact and atypical body language during communication
- difficulties with developing, maintaining and understanding relationships, difficulty making friends and a lack of interest in communicating with others or engaging in shared social activities.

Restricted and repetitive patterns of interests, activities and behaviours include:

- stereotyped or repetitive motor movements, use of objects or idiosyncratic speech (e.g. humming), formal 'lecture-style' speech, unusual repetitive hand movements (e.g. flapping), unusual ways of walking
- insistence on sameness and adoption of inflexible and repetitive routines/rituals, resistance and overreaction to even small changes in routines
- narrow and fixated interests of abnormal intensity or focus, such as strong attachment to, or preoccupation with, unusual symbols or objects, perfectionistic behaviour, a narrow range of interests, unusual phobias or fears
- excessive reactions or sensitivity to sensory input and sensory aspects of the environment, such as preoccupation with the touch, taste, smell and texture of items, visual fascination with light and movement of objects.

Prevalence and gender issues with an ASD

The US Centers for Disease Control (2015) estimated that in 2015, one in 68 school children in the United States had an ASD. The Global Burden of Disease Study (Baxter et al., 2015) concluded that ASD is three times more common in males than females.

Heritability of an ASD

Tick et al. (2015) estimated that the heritability of ASD (i.e. the degree to which genetics plays a role in the development of the disorder) is somewhere between .64 and .91. This means that up to 91 per cent of the differences between those in research studies who had an ASD and those who didn't were most likely due to genetic variations between them. In other words the genetic component is very strong.

Comorbidity (other disorders that often occur with an ASD)

Numerous studies have reported an increased prevalence of psychiatric comorbidities (additional disorders) in people with an ASD (e.g. Ghaziuddin et al., 1992). Simonoff et al. (2008) found that 70 per cent of individuals with an ASD had at least one other psychiatric disorder, and 41 per cent had two or more additional disorders. Joshi et al. (2010) found that 95 per cent of young people aged three to seventeen who had been diagnosed with an ASD, and who had been referred for psychiatric treatment, had at least three or more additional disorders. These additional psychiatric disorders have been identified as significant risk factors for increased criminal offending by some individuals with an ASD (Mouridsen, 2012).

Specific deficits

Lerner et al. (2012) suggested that high-functioning people with an ASD are more likely to experience three specific 'deficits' that can, in a small number of cases, potentially lead to criminal behaviour.

1. **deficits in 'theory of mind':** This is the ability to understand how others are thinking and feeling, and to correctly interpret social information. Many people with an ASD have more difficulty understanding and predicting the behaviours, beliefs and intentions of others. This often leads to deficits in the ability to understand and respond appropriately to the feelings of others, in other words difficulties with empathy.
2. **deficits in emotional regulation:** This is the ability to resist expressing their own strong emotions. A deficit can lead to poor impulse control, aggression and negative social interactions.
3. **deficits in moral reasoning:** This is a social-cognitive process by which we judge an action to be morally right or wrong.

Vincent Stanford, who raped and killed schoolteacher Stephanie Scott when she was at her school on Easter Sunday in 2015 to prepare lesson plans for her honeymoon replacement, is a high-functioning individual with an ASD who demonstrated by his behaviour that he has major deficits in 'theory of mind', empathy, emotional regulation and moral reasoning. But that is only part of the picture.

Is there a link between ASD and criminal behaviour?

There is strong evidence that having an ASD does *not* automatically predispose a person to being violent, or increase the likelihood of their committing violent sexual offences any more than the general population (Bjørkly, 2009; Ghaziuddin, 2013; Gómez de la Cuesta, 2010; Im, 2016; King and Murphy, 2014; Mouridsen, 2012; Woodbury-Smith et al., 2006). Most people who have an ASD are law-abiding (Murrie et al., 2002; Woodbury-Smith et al., 2006).

Several recent studies have, however, suggested that people with an ASD may be more likely than the general population to enter the criminal justice system (e.g. Browning and Caulfield, 2011; Freckelton, 2013; Haskins and Silva, 2006; Kroncke et al., 2016). For example, in a sample of Netherlands juvenile sex offenders, those who had committed offences had more ASD symptoms than their non-offending peers (Hart-Kerkhoffs et al., 2009).

Some people with an ASD *do* break the law and/or behave aggressively, sometimes using lethal violence. The most common crimes committed by offenders with an ASD appear to be sexual offences, arson and criminal damage (Gómez de la Cuesta, 2010; Mouridsen, 2012). Søndenaa et al. (2014) reviewed more than 3000 forensic examination reports from the Norwegian Board of Forensic Medicine and found that 58 per cent of those prisoners who had committed sexual offences had an ASD diagnosis.

Higgs and Carter (2015) have also highlighted an association between ASD and sexual violence. They have suggested that the repetitive narrow interests that are typical of an individual with an ASD could develop in some cases into a risk factor for sexual aggression. This is more likely when their preoccupation is of a sexual nature, and includes the pursuit of a paraphilic interest (see pages 374–7) along with an extensive and addictive use of online pornography (Browning and Caulfield, 2011; Haskins and Silva, 2006; Ray et al., 2004). Attwood (2014) has suggested that in some cases an extensive use of sexually violent pornography by individuals with an ASD may also lead to an inadequate comprehension of the concept of 'consent'. There was significant evidence that Vincent Stanford was an avid and regular user of online sexually violent pornography.

A study by Rogers et al. (2006) concluded that those with an ASD who do use lethal violence and/or commit murder do not necessarily have a more severe version of the disorder. They concluded that 'callous/psychopathic' acts committed by a small number of individuals with an ASD probably reflect what they have described as a 'double hit' in that there is also an additional and significant impairment of empathic response to the distress cues of other people, which is not necessarily a core aspect of ASD itself. This conclusion is consistent with the research of psychiatry professor Michael Fitzgerald, who has identified a subcategory of ASD he has labelled 'criminal autistic psychopathy' (Fitzgerald, 2001, 2010, 2014, 2015). Individuals in this subcategory have an ASD as well as many (and sometimes all) of the key features of an ASPD/psychopathy (e.g. extreme lack of empathy and remorse, limited conscience, using other people for their own ends, and cruelty; see page 140). Younger people aged fifteen or under who fit into this category of criminal autistic psychopathy have some or all the features of both an ASD and a conduct disorder (DSM-5, APA, 2013; see pages 370–1).

Fitzgerald (2015) and Allely et al. (2014, 2017) have concluded from their review of available research that the behaviour of a significant proportion of mass murderers and serial killers is consistent with their fitting into this criminal autistic psychopathy subtype of an ASD. They found numerous examples of mass murderers who had been diagnosed with an ASD or demonstrated significant autistic traits, including:

- Adam Lanza, who in 2012 shot his mother and then 26 children and adults at Sandy Hook Elementary School in Newton, United States, before killing himself
- Anders Breivik, who in 2011 murdered 77 people at a summer camp on the island of Utøya in Norway
- Cho Seung-Hui, who killed 32 people at Virginia Polytechnic Institute in Blacksburg, Virginia, in 2007

- Martin Bryant, who murdered 35 people in 1996 at Port Arthur in Tasmania, Australia.

After Vincent Stanford was charged, forensic psychologist Anna Robilliard reported that he probably had an ASD, and noted that, like others with an ASD diagnosis, he may have lacked the neurological capacity to fully grasp the implications of his criminal activities. His brutal crime places him in the sub-category of criminal autistic psychopathy, while the extreme sexual violence and cruelty he exhibited when he savagely beat, raped and killed Stephanie Scott, confirm that Stanford also had a second disorder, namely a 'sexual sadism disorder'.

Paraphilic disorders

A 'paraphilia' is a strong, recurrent and persistent sexual interest that involves activities other than foreplay and genital stimulation with normal, consenting adult partners. The eight examples of paraphilia described in the DSM-5 (APA, 2013) are:

1. **sexual sadism:** sexual interest in inflicting humiliation, suffering and pain on another
2. **sexual masochism:** sexual interest in being physically harmed by someone else, for example, bondage, whipping
3. **paedophilia:** sexual interest in pre-pubescent children aged ten or less
4. **exhibitionism:** sexual interest in engaging in sexual behaviour or exposing genitals while another is watching
5. **voyeurism:** secretly watching strangers in their normal private activities, especially those that involve undressing
6. **frotteurism:** touching or rubbing against a non-consenting person
7. **transvestism:** sexual interest in cross-dressing

8. **fetishism:** sexual interest in non-genital body parts of a partner or inanimate objects, such as feet, high-heeled shoes, underwear, and items made of rubber, leather or silk.

Several other paraphilias have been described by various clinicians and researchers but are not listed in the DSM-5, such as:

- **zoophilia/bestiality**: sexual interest in non-human animals
- **gerontophilia**: sexual interest in elderly people
- **triolism**: sexual interest in watching a partner engage in sexual behaviour with another.

Most people with these types of atypical sexual interests do not have a mental disorder, but some do. To make a diagnosis of a paraphilic disorder, the DSM-5 (APA, 2013) requires that individuals with one of the atypical sexual interests listed above from the DSM-5 also meet one or both of the following criteria:

1. The individual feels ongoing personal distress about their interest, but not just the type of distress that might result from disapproval by others or society in general.
2. Their sexual desires or behaviours:
   a. involve another person's psychological distress, injury or death.
   b. involve unwilling and non-consenting people or people unable to give legal consent.

Criteria for a sexual sadism disorder

A person can be diagnosed with a sexual sadism disorder if:

- Over a period of six months or longer they have experienced recurrent and intense sexual arousal from the physical or psychological suffering of another person either by their actions or through fantasising, such as watching sadistic pornography.

- The individual has inflicted these urges on a non-consenting other person.

OR

- Their fantasies and urges have resulted in clinically significant distress or impairment in their own social life, work life or other significant contexts.

Vincent Stanford's behaviour confirms that he met the first two criteria for a diagnosis of a sexual sadism disorder. He obtained sexual arousal from both the violent and sadistic pornography that he obsessively watched and from his sexual and sadistic attacks on a non-consenting Stephanie Scott. Murderers with a sexual sadism disorder who commit crimes that involve rape gain their erotic satisfaction mostly from their victim's pain and suffering. They usually mutilate their victim's body and take an item that belongs to them as a trophy (Cantor and Sutton, 2015; Dietz et al., 1990). Stanford burnt Stephanie's body, kept her red bra as a trophy and removed her graduation ring and her engagement ring.

Prevalence of sexual sadism disorders

The general prevalence of sexual sadism disorder is somewhat unclear (Yates et al., 2008) and information is based mostly on research that has focused on individuals in forensic settings. Between 37 per cent and 75 per cent of men who have committed sexually motivated murders have been diagnosed with a sexual sadism disorder (Krueger, 2010).

There is little doubt that Vincent Stanford not only meets the criteria for the criminal autistic psychopathy subtype of an ASD but also the criteria for a sexual sadism disorder – a horrifying combination. His callous, cold-blooded and sadistic actions would have caused Stephanie Scott great fear, pain and suffering. Knowledge of his mutilation of her body added a level of disrespect that would have caused her family, friends and colleagues additional pain and distress.

CHAPTER 13

VINCENT STANFORD

The cast

Vincent Stanford: School cleaner who raped and murdered 26-year-old teacher Stephanie Scott, who was at her school on Easter Sunday
Stephanie Scott: The murder victim, who was due to be married the following week
Aaron Leeson-Woolley: Stephanie's fiancé
Merrilyn and Robert Scott: Stephanie's parents. Robert died in a farm accident in 2016.
Anika Stanford: Vincent Stanford's mother
Marcus Stanford: Stanford's twin brother
Luke Stanford: Stanford's older brother

The motive

Vincent Stanford raped and murdered teacher Stephanie Scott when she went to Leeton High School alone on a Sunday to prepare teaching plans and materials for the substitute teacher who would temporarily replace her while she was away on her honeymoon. He did this simply to satisfy his long standing sexually sadistic fantasies.

Introduction

Like so many of her colleagues, Stephanie Scott was devoted to her high school teaching job. Some people like to assume that teachers work from 9 am to 3 pm and spend endless weeks on holidays between terms. But as anyone close to an educator knows, they are dedicated professionals who work many unpaid hours preparing classes and marking work at home or during those holidays.

Stephanie Scott was no exception. As her 2015 marriage to sweetheart Aaron Leeson-Woolley approached, her mind was still very much on school work. The 11 April nuptials were just days away and there was still plenty to organise, including lesson plans for her temporary replacement. Stephanie worked at Leeton High School in New South Wales, where she had been an enthusiastic and much-loved English and drama teacher for three years. One of five siblings, she had two sisters and two brothers. Their father, Robert, was Deputy Principal at Canowindra High School, also in country New South Wales.

Stephanie's fiancé Aaron Leeson-Woolley had attended her father's school. She met the talented sportsman when Robert accompanied him to various sporting events. Aaron and Stephanie started dating and then became engaged in April 2014. Stephanie's mother, Merrilyn, later described her daughter as a gifted young woman who offered and gave so much to the world. She was 'truly one of the special ones', a person who was kind and touched everyone she met, leaving no person worse off for having experienced her love and goodness.

Despite wedding preparations reaching their final, hectic days, Stephanie was determined to ensure that her school work was up to date and ready for her replacement. When the Easter break began with the final bell on Thursday, 2 April 2015, Stephanie's last work day before her wedding, there was still much to do. Staff held a party for her that day and there was great excitement. The following day was Good Friday. Aaron needed to visit Canowindra for a mutual friend's farewell party, but Stephanie decided to spend the Easter weekend taking care of wedding plans, including a shopping trip to Griffith and collecting travel tickets for their honeymoon. At 12.30 pm, Aaron kissed Stephanie goodbye and told her that he loved her. He was due to return on Easter Sunday. They stayed in touch over the weekend and Aaron made dinner reservations for his return on the Sunday night.

The lead-up to the crime

On the morning of Sunday, 5 April, Stephanie went to school to ensure everything was in place for her absence. Teachers often work during the holidays to clean up their classroom or prepare for an upcoming term. Stephanie wanted to relax while she was on her honeymoon, and preparing lessons for the substitute teacher would help her to do so. Stephanie dropped in on colleague Monique Hardy at about 11 am to collect the school keys. Monique accompanied her to the grounds to show her how to get in. Stephanie parked her car near the school gates, then walked inside alone. She went to the English teachers' staff room, which was locked but not alarmed.

At some stage that day, Aaron texted his fiancée but did not receive a reply. When he got home at around 7.20 pm that night, Stephanie wasn't there. It was completely out of character for her to ignore him, so Aaron became worried and continued to text her without a response. He thought she might have stayed away for the night due to feeling anxious about the wedding preparations and not having him home over the weekend.

Aaron's concern increased when he still couldn't contact Stephanie the following morning. When he reported her missing at Leeton Police Station, inquiries revealed that Stephanie's mobile phone was uncontactable and there had been no activity on her bank accounts since she went shopping on Saturday. Nor had she been active on social media. Naturally, there was a chance Stephanie, 26, had experienced cold feet about the wedding. But she had not raised any concerns with family or friends in person, on the phone or online. Relatives and friends posted appeals on social media, which generated much activity across the country, but there was no response from Stephanie or anyone who had seen her. She had simply disappeared.

What Stephanie's friends and family didn't know was that she was not the only person at the school on Easter Sunday and that the school cleaner, Vincent Stanford, had also been there, even though this wasn't permitted. Stanford lived in Leeton with his mother and older brother Luke, and worked as a casual cleaner at several locations, including schools and other educational facilities. Stanford started working at Leeton High School on 2 March 2015. The five-week temporary position had been due to end on the last day of Term 1, but had been extended. The cleaner had keys to the school, and usually worked from 3.30 am to 8.30 am and then from 3 pm to 6 pm on weekdays.

Stanford, 24, was not meant to attend the school outside those hours, except by arrangement, and was only supposed to be in areas associated with his cleaning duties. But he had somehow obtained alarm access codes, despite the school's policy of not providing them to casual employees. He was regularly seen on campus outside his work hours, when children were on breaks from lessons and in and around the girls' toilets, and he had hung around the school for most of the Easter long weekend. He later said he was bored and 'just wanted to go to work'. The deputy principal saw him at the school on the Friday, when he said he was emptying and hosing out garbage bins. He returned on the Saturday to clean the multipurpose centre and again on Easter Sunday at 7.30 am (*R v Stanford, Vincent* [2016] NSWSC 1434).

The murder and aftermath

That day, Stanford first saw Stephanie when she was in the English teachers' staff room working on her computer. He later said he had no idea that she was there and that he had never met her. After seeing the young teacher, however, Stanford claimed that a feeling came over him that he described as 'Just that I had to kill her. I wasn't angry or anything. Basically emotionless. Just that I had to kill her' (*R v Stanford, Vincent* [2016] NSWSC 1434).

Stephanie sent her last known email at 12.58 pm, confirming payment for one of her wedding expenses. She then went to the administration block, turning off its alarm at 1.31 pm and rearming it at 1.38 pm. As she left the building, Stephanie had to walk along an enclosed corridor towards the locked school gates. She saw Stanford and said, 'I'm going home now. Have a happy Easter.'

After Stephanie stopped to retrieve the keys from her bag to open the gate, Stanford grabbed her from behind with his right arm over her mouth and his left arm around her middle. Walking backwards, he dragged her along a corridor towards a storage room that had been used as a photographic darkroom. Stephanie fought back, scratching her attacker's face and attempting to yell. After he dragged her inside the darkroom, he released her. As he turned to close the door, she tried to run away. But Stanford pushed her, and she fell face down on the floor. He then put his left arm over Stephanie's throat and beat her to the face with his right fist 30 or 40 times. After 45 to 50 seconds, she fell unconscious. Stanford then put on a condom that he had with him and raped her. She was still alive. After removing a 40-centimetre knife from his pocket, Stanford stabbed Stephanie in the neck 'to make sure she was dead'. He left her lying on the floor, went home for lunch and then returned.

After putting yellow masking tape on Stephanie's neck to stop the bleeding, Stanford put plastic into the boot of her car and placed her body on top of it. For the next couple of hours, he used a high-pressure cleaner to clean the murder scene. He then drove Stephanie's car to his house with her body in the boot and walked back to the school to collect his own car, loading blood-soaked wooden MDF panel boards from the storeroom into the back of his ute. Later in the day, someone saw Stanford throw Stephanie's laptop into a canal outside Leeton. That night, he parked her car near a service station and filled a jerry can with petrol. In the early hours of the following morning, Monday, 6 April, he drove the car to the Cocoparra National Park, about 50 kilometres north of Leeton, removed Stephanie's body from the boot and put it on the ground. He removed her clothes and placed them with a sun visor from the car and the plastic from the boot into a backpack. Just after 3 pm, Stanford took six photos of the body before putting branches and petrol on it and setting it alight. Most of the fuel was placed between the upper thighs and lower rib cage.

Stanford left Stephanie's car near a canal just outside Leeton, probably after driving it home. He then removed the jerry can and boot liner and changed his clothes. When he met his mother at a supermarket just after 7.30 am, she later described his behaviour as 'normal'. He told her he had been for his regular walk, gone home and slept for a couple of hours.

After storing Stephanie's belongings in his bedroom wardrobe, Stanford later began disposing of them. He drove around in his ute and dumped items in public bins, including on Leeton's main street. The clothes were not found, but the police recovered the car sun visor and other personal belongings in a Griffith bin. On Tuesday, 7 April, Stanford went to work at the TAFE in Leeton, from about 4.30 am until 8 am. When a colleague asked if he had seen Stephanie at Leeton High School over the weekend, he said he hadn't. When another person said she probably had cold feet about the wedding, Stanford smiled and giggled. Police soon discovered that Stanford's car had been seen at the school over the Easter weekend and questioned him. He told them he had been there cleaning bins but hadn't seen Stephanie, before wishing them good luck with their search.

In the early hours of Wednesday, 8 April, Stanford's older brother, Luke, emerged from his bedroom to see his brother standing near the fireplace burning some of Stephanie's belongings. Stanford then texted his twin brother Marcus to tell him he was going to send him an envelope that he wanted kept safe. He posted Stephanie's engagement ring, a ring her mother gave her as a graduation present and her driver's licence. Marcus sold the rings as requested by his brother for $705. They were later allegedly melted and turned into scrap metal. At about 11 am that day, Stanford went to Leeton Police Station and provided a statement about his movements on Easter Sunday. He said that he had been cleaning all weekend but had not seen anyone at the school other than some 'rollerskaters'. He also claimed to have gone to the Golden Apple Supermarket in Leeton that day, but police later discovered that it was closed at the time Stanford said he had visited it.

Stanford then returned to Cocoparra National Park to see if Stephanie's remains were still there and took more photos of her dead body. Police arrived at his home at 6 pm to ask him to come to the police station for an interview and to seek permission to search the house. Stanford was not home, but his mother gave consent for the search of the home. Police found fresh tyre tracks left by a small car that led from the front of the house into the rear yard and towards a shed. A used condom was on the ground and some yellow tape was found nearby. In Stanford's bedroom, they found a set of keys matching the description of the school keys Stephanie had with her on Easter Sunday. They also found an empty condom wrapper and several condoms still in their wrappers.

The premises were declared a crime scene. When Stanford returned, police found the large MDF boards in the back of his ute and what looked like a blood smear. They seized his car and he agreed to accompany them to the police station. When police took Stanford's camera, the first image they saw was a burnt corpse in bushland. He claimed he had downloaded the photos from a horror movie because he thought they were funny. Police placed him under arrest for murder. Asked why he had numerous fresh scratch marks on his face and arms, Stanford said he had bumped his head and run into a tree branch. He consented to DNA testing.

Stephanie's car was found in Pike Road, Wamoon, about 11 kilometres from Leeton, on Thursday, 9 April. Human blood was found in the boot and on the external bumper bar. Stephanie's remains were discovered on the edge of Cocoparra National Park in the late afternoon of Friday, 10 April. Stanford confessed to her murder on Saturday, 11 April, and was interviewed again on 21 April. During this interview he demonstrated a lack of emotion and did not show 'the slightest hint' of remorse. He later pleaded guilty to Stephanie's murder and to having sexual intercourse with her without her consent in aggravated circumstances.

Items found that linked him to the crime included the used condom, yellow duct tape, personal lubricant, a condom box and a set of handcuffs. The knife used to stab Stephanie was also found nearby, and a red bra that Stanford told police he kept 'maybe because I wanted a souvenir'. When police analysed Stanford's phone and computer, they found he had regularly searched for images of violent rape, violent sex, hardcore pornography and murder. He also searched necrophilia and 'necro-rape'. On 21 February 2015, he had searched 'bride rape', 'bride kidnapping', 'Virgin Bride brutally raped by drunk man/rape videos' and 'Muslim man rapes child bride until she dies'.

It also emerged that Stanford held an account with a security company that supplies handcuffs, batons, knives and the like. On 10 October 2014, he had ordered handcuffs and a half-sword. The day before Stephanie died, he ordered another knife and more handcuffs. Stanford also attempted to buy leg-cuffs, ordered various sex toys online and searched terms including 'widowmaker', 'widow knives', 'sharpest puncture knives', 'sharpest knife tips', 'sharpest knife you can buy', 'best piercing knives' and 'serial killer knives'.

Police also discovered that Stanford had stalked three other girls before killing Stephanie. After moving to Leeton in March 2014, he began covertly photographing, filming and stalking a twelve-year-old local schoolgirl. He took 1805 images of her and photographed other female students and women who passed his house. He also had numerous images of bestiality (people having sex with animals) and pictures of other young girls. Police found an exercise book that referred to the young girl as a slut and detailed his surveillance of her and plans to abduct her. The book contained an image of a female head with a knife striking it, and the car registrations of the girl's father and grandfather. Stanford said he had wanted to abduct the girl but managed to control that urge. He added, however, that if he had given into that urge, he probably would have killed her.

Stanford also used to visit a young woman who worked in a Leeton shop, where he would talk to her and sit outside in his ute. He conducted internet searches of her name, photographed her car and tried to trace her car registration details. He also used to hang around the school and be there when another young woman who often worked back late went to her car. He sometimes said hello and she would say hello back. Police found a photo of this woman on Stanford's phone. His actions were clearly abhorrent and part of a pattern of predatory and antisocial behaviour. Until then, however, he had no criminal history or issues with drugs or alcohol.

The sentencing

At Stanford's sentencing hearing in late 2016, his counsel, Janet Manuell SC, conceded that the offences were serious, but argued they did not warrant a life sentence. Ms Manuell said Stanford's ASD reduced his moral culpability, which, in turn, reduced the need for denunciation and general deterrence. She said Stanford's age (24 at the time of the offences) meant that he could expect to live another 58 years, and he had acknowledged responsibility for his offending conduct, having confessed days after his arrest and later pleading guilty. He was not remorseful, she argued, but that was a function of his autism. Ms Manuell also noted Stanford's lack of prior criminal convictions and noted that he may be amenable to treatment that could possibly reduce the risk of him reoffending (*R v Stanford, Vincent* [2016] NSWSC 1434).

Forensic psychiatrist Professor David Greenberg reported on Stanford's future dangerousness. Stanford refused to speak to Professor Greenberg, but as an acknowledged expert with 30 years' experience in addressing and treating sex offenders and sexually deviant disorders, including sexual sadism disorders, he was well placed to comment. Professor Greenberg found it highly likely that Stanford had an ASD. There were some features of a psychopathic personality, but he could not explore this further. Professor Greenberg felt that Stanford had a likely paraphilic disorder that played a significant role in his underlying motivations. He noted Stanford's repeated denials to police of any sexual element in the murder, only to plead guilty later. The burning of Stephanie's genital area also raised strong suspicion of a sexual element that Stanford was trying to destroy.

Professor Greenberg speculated about whether Stanford had a sexual sadism disorder, noting his sexually deviant interests and violent sexual themes in his internet searches. He also wondered whether Stanford used paraphernalia during the murder, including handcuffs and rolls of tape, which are often associated with sexually sadistic acts. Further, if he was simply intent on rape it would not have been necessary to use such excessive force. The professor also queried whether Stanford had sexually sadistic paedophilic interests given the material concerning the child neighbour, including his admission that if he had abducted her he probably would have killed her. Other questions included whether Stanford had a sexual interest in cross-dressing or fetishism, given that a 'sexy' female costume was found in his wardrobe, and an interest in bestiality, given his internet searches concerning sexual acts with dogs and horses.

Professor Greenberg found that Stanford's current risk of committing a further sexual and violent offence/s would depend upon his response to treatment in the future. 'At this stage, based on the limited information, I am of the view that his risk for sexual and/or violent offence should be regarded as in the "high risk" category range, relative to other sex offenders,' he found. 'Relative to the general male population, his risk of sexual violence must be regarded as in the highest category. However, his response to treatment and management may or may not change this risk assessment in the future. At this point, his prognosis should be regarded as guarded' (*R v Stanford, Vincent* [2016] NSWSC 1434).

In sentencing Stanford on 13 October 2016, Justice Robert Allan Hulme described the case as 'one of great heinousness'. 'The offender had harboured violent thoughts, including killing people, since he was a child,' he said. 'When he saw Ms Scott, his immediate thought was that he had to kill her. He had time to reflect in the hours that he waited for her but persisted with his plan. Nothing she said or did provided him with a rational motive to do what he did. Their only interaction was her wishing him a happy Easter.' Justice R.A. Hulme said Stanford's initial explanations were false and the crime appeared to be premeditated. 'The possibility that Ms Scott was his target from a time well before Easter Sunday is supported by the evidence of his searching on the internet for "bride rape" and the like,' he said. 'It seems apparent that he would not have known that Ms Scott would be at the school on that Easter Sunday. But the matters I have referred to support an inference that he had thought of attacking her before then and when he saw her there that day he saw it as his opportunity and went home to retrieve the various items' (*R v Stanford, Vincent* [2016] NSWSC 1434).

Justice Hulme said Stanford also had a large knife and condom on him on a day he said he was simply there to clean. 'I am satisfied of this beyond reasonable doubt and also that he deliberately left the door to the storage room open in order to facilitate the attack when his opportunity arose,' he said. 'The attack itself involved extreme brutality by a man of substantial size . . . upon a defenceless young woman of modest size who had no means of escape or raising the alarm. The offender's conniving, callous and self-interested conduct continued in the immediate aftermath with his disposal of incriminating items, one of the most despicable acts being his despatch of Ms Scott's engagement and graduation rings and her driver's licence to his brother Marcus in South Australia. Marcus Stanford's conduct in disposing of those items was disgraceful, as I observed in sentencing him. Another despicable act was the offender's return to the Cocoparra National Park and photographing the charred remains. There was also the keeping of Ms Scott's bra as something of a "souvenir"' (*R v Stanford, Vincent* [2016] NSWSC 1434).

Justice Hulme was not convinced that Stanford's moral culpability was reduced by his ASD. 'But even if it was, the extent would be minimal,' he said. 'The calculating manner in which the offender carried out the various activities following the murder (and to some extent before) indicates that he was well capable of making well-considered choices about how to best serve his own interests and to achieve his objectives. There can be no question that the offender is a very disturbed individual. The evidence concerning his searches on the internet in relation to violent rape; his purchases of knives, handcuffs and other devices capable of use in carrying out acts of extreme violence; his surveillance of the child in his neighbourhood and other such things; together with the assessment, albeit guarded, by Professor Greenberg, all indicate to me that the offender will, for a considerable period of time, represent a serious danger to the safety of the community.'

Justice Hulme sentenced Stanford to life without parole. 'I am satisfied that this is a case of murder that clearly falls within the worst category,' he said. 'I am satisfied beyond any doubt that the offender's culpability is so extreme that the community interest in retribution, punishment, community protection and deterrence can be met with only one response. For the aggravated sexual assault, the offender is sentenced to imprisonment for fifteen years. I decline to nominate a proportion of that sentence as a non-parole period as there is no utility in doing so. For the murder, the offender is sentenced to imprisonment for life' (*R v Stanford, Vincent* [2016] NSWSC 1434).

Compounding the Scott family's tragedy, Stephanie's father, Robert, was killed in a farm accident in November 2016, just a month after Vincent Stanford was sentenced. Around that time, reports emerged that Stanford was enjoying life in his isolated jail cell, where he didn't have to talk to anyone – largely because he didn't like talking to people anyway. He had told several others that being around people, especially those who disrupted his routine, stressed him out.

Stanford's twin brother, Marcus, also spent time in jail for his role in Stephanie's murder. In August 2016, Marcus was sentenced to fifteen months' jail after pleading guilty to being an accessory after the fact in disposing of Stephanie's engagement ring and the ring her mother gave her when she graduated. Justice Robert Allan Hulme found Marcus was motivated by 'misguided loyalty to [his] brother'. 'However, given the amount of attention the case had received in the media, I am satisfied he must have known that the two rings had been stolen in the context of the murder of a woman who was much loved by her family, and in her community, and who was looking forward to her impending marriage to the man she loved,' he said. 'The offender must have known that the rings were items of great sentimental value to her fiancé and family. In that context, he simply chose to sell them for a small sum of money in circumstances where they would be unlikely to be returned' (*R v Stanford, Marcus* [2016] NSWSC 1174).

In a report by forensic psychologist Dr Katie Seidler, Vincent Stanford's brother Marcus Stanford described himself as somewhat shy and disengaged socially, due largely to anxiety. He had abused alcohol and cannabis as a teenager, which may have contributed to irresponsible and unproductive behaviour at times. While in the Netherlands, Marcus started studying at a maritime university in Rotterdam but quit after six months due to his lack of interest. When arrested, he was working as a labourer on a South Australian flower farm. He had no previous convictions. 'I am prepared to accept the submission that the offender is unlikely to re-offend and has good prospects of rehabilitation,' Justice R.A. Hulme found. 'This is primarily on the basis that the present offence was committed in a highly specific and unusual context and the offender has not otherwise demonstrated any tendency to criminal offending' (*R v Stanford, Marcus* [2016] NSWSC 1174).

Vincent Stanford's background

Vincent Stanford was born in Franklin, Tasmania, in December 1990. His mother, Anika Stanford, who was referred to in some reports as Anneke Noort, moved him and his twin, Marcus, and their older brother, Luke, to her native Netherlands after her marriage ended when the twins were six. The boys' father lived in Australia and reportedly has not seen Vincent since he was a small child. Anika raised her children in the Netherlands before returning to Australia in 2014 and settling in Leeton. Marcus had returned to South Australia a year or two earlier. Vincent Stanford later described his relationships with immediate family members as 'all right'. But he was not particularly close to Luke.

Stanford's sentencing heard that while he was in the Netherlands, he was involved in a series of troubling events. He attended a specialist behaviour school in 2001 and 2002 because of his unruly and oppositional behaviour, and limited social skills and friendships. In 2003, Stanford was reportedly expelled after an apparently impulsive and serious incident at school. When the principal reprimanded him for being in the schoolyard without authorisation and held onto his coat, the young student apparently grabbed her around the throat with both hands and with such force that she had difficulty breathing. Others at the school later denied this had happened.

That alleged incident apparently followed a fight in which Stanford grabbed another student by the throat. He was reportedly sent to an adolescent psychiatric centre and discharged with a diagnosis of pervasive developmental disorder (i.e. ASD) and oppositional defiant disorder. Stanford then attended a smaller school for students with special needs until he was sixteen. While there, aged fourteen, he had a girlfriend for about six months, but later said that it was 'not something I craved in life'.

In a background article on Stanford, News Corp's Mike Colman described him as 'a cross between Hollywood's Rain Man and the simple-minded giant Lennie from John Steinbeck's book *Of Mice and Men*. A seemingly naive savant with a gift for numbers and love of animals, who had difficulty with changes of routine.' Mike visited the Dutch city of Zoetermeer, where Stanford had lived with Anika, Marcus and Luke. Those Mike spoke to described the family as weird and Vincent Stanford as a reclusive loner who didn't like to talk about his father. But they didn't see him as violent. In fact, he was quiet, polite and helped carry his neighbours' groceries. 'They were always nice and polite, never any problem at all,' said next-door neighbour Marie Louise de Groot. 'They would wave good morning, Vincent would help me carry the groceries, but there was something weird about them, you know? The way they kept to themselves' (Colman, 2015).

In 2003 the family moved to the newer part of the city, less than 60 minutes' drive from Amsterdam. Vincent and Marcus attended Prins Florisschool, a short walk from home. Stanford had behavioural issues, but principal Annette Mulder denied reports that Stanford had been expelled for attacking a teacher. She said Vincent and Marcus graduated when they were twelve, although Vincent did not enjoy his school experience. After leaving high school at seventeen, Stanford worked as a deckhand on a domestic cargo ship and later told friends he quit because the captain was 'too strict'. He then spent his days playing computer games in his room while Anika worked with people who have disabilities. The house was very messy and made worse by the nine cats they kept.

Stanford was close to his mother and would walk to the shops with her, passing the home of contract cleaner Richard Antonisse, who took an interest in him and offered him a job. Anika told Antonisse that her son had autism, but Mike found no evidence that he was medically diagnosed or treated. Antonisse and his wife Mireille taught Stanford some social skills such as eye contact when talking. After six months as a cleaner, Stanford abruptly left Antonisse, saying he intended to enlist in the army, but he was rejected for 'medical reasons'. Meanwhile Marcus attempted to enter the computer games industry and did some unpaid work with a Melbourne-based Dutchman and some Australians to form Bullet Proof Studios, an 'indie' games design company.

When the company failed, Marcus began planning his return to Australia, while Stanford worked with packing and shipping firm Fladderak at Delft, twenty minutes from Zoetermeer. Employed to cut timber to build packing crates, at 1.8 metres and 110 kilograms Stanford earned the nickname King Kong for his unnatural strength. He was also known for his gift for numbers by quickly adding up darts scores in his head. He was dismissed from Fladderak after refusing to work with a group of co-workers he felt were teasing him (Colman, 2015).

Colman added that the murder investigation did paint Stanford as a violent killer, but those who knew him also described a socially awkward young man who had no interest in women but responded to those who taught him social skills. For example, his neighbours who he worked for as a cleaner taught him how to use deodorant. 'When I spoke to people in Holland who knew him, the person they described and the impression I was left with was totally different to what came out in court,' Mike says. 'The cleaner and a man who worked with him, and claimed to be his friend, made a point of saying that he never showed any interest in the opposite sex or even mentioned females.'

When Anika, Vincent, Marcus and Luke moved to Leeton, they were friendly with their neighbours but largely kept to themselves. None of them drank alcohol. After several months, Stanford scored a job as a cleaner. Stanford did not have a girlfriend, and he had no friends or social contacts as he found being with other people stressful and he didn't like it. But he enjoyed dropping in on his neighbours for a cup of tea and some homemade apple tart or scones. After he took the leftovers home to enjoy, Stanford would return the cleaned plate and say thank you. He told people he was relatively comfortable in his cleaning job, as it largely involved early and late hours when few people were around. He was often seen doing chores around the house, but would also spend hours alone on his computer.

The neighbour who shared baked treats with Vincent, Luke and Anika, says Stanford was well mannered, pleasant enough and did not mind small talk. But his eyes were 'as deep as the ocean' and gave very little away. Nor did he have a sense of humour. 'When everybody would make a bit of a joke, he'd just sort of half smile,' the neighbour says. 'He wouldn't get it. He was certainly very much his own person. He had no expression, or very little. You wouldn't know what he was thinking or what he was doing. [But] as far as we were concerned he never did anything in any way to make us suspicious.'

Like many, Stanford's neighbours were shocked when they found out what he had done to Stephanie Scott. While some people knew about him obsessing over several young local girls, others had no idea – including his neighbours. Stanford was always well mannered to those who cooked for him, but had displayed some hints that he was not socially aware. A couple of days before he killed Stephanie, he came over to return a plate and stood right behind one of his neighbours, who was completely startled upon turning around to see him standing so close. 'I didn't know he was there,' the neighbour says. 'I've said, "Vincent, I've told you, don't come up on me like that and frighten me."'

Why did he do it?

How does someone with a relatively ordinary upbringing in a relatively close family develop an uncontrollable urge to kill? It appears that the urge to commit violent acts had been part of Vincent Stanford's psyche for some time before he acted upon it. Before he was sentenced for Stephanie's murder, Stanford told forensic psychologist Anna Robilliard that while he was working as a cleaner in the Netherlands he seriously considered violence against one of his bosses because he thought he was 'disorganised and did not care about the standard of his workers, which really annoyed Mr Stanford, who took pride in his work performance'. 'Mr Stanford said he had absolutely no prior plan to murder the victim Stephanie Scott and he did not know her at all,' Ms Robilliard reported. 'As soon as he saw her at the school where he was working, on the morning he murdered her, Mr Stanford said, "I had to kill her"' (*R v Stanford, Vincent* [2016] NSWSC 1434).

Stanford told the psychologist that he had thought about killing people since he was seven or eight. These thoughts often appeared when people caused him stress, which could build up to an almost intolerable level. The violent thoughts were usually activated when people interrupted his routine, and in the past such thoughts had been triggered by teachers, other students, mental health nurses and even his mother. Stanford said he did not have to be angry to feel violent, and described it as 'just cold-blooded violence'. In Stephanie's case, he was not interrupted by or angry with her. His only explanation was that he had felt a sudden urge to kill her.

Chillingly, Stanford said he had never been bothered by violence; his own or anyone else's. As a child, he used to think it was normal and kept it 'bottled up'. While he now knows that this is not normal, he still has the same thoughts almost weekly, especially when he has to interact with other people. '[H]e said he believes he cannot learn to tolerate people; that "this is just the way I'm arranged – I don't think there is anything I can do to get them [violent thoughts] away",' Ms Robilliard said. 'Asked what he thought about murdering Stephanie Scott, Mr Stanford said he seldom thinks about it at all and "I can hardly remember it . . . it was so long ago". He said he definitely did not enjoy the killing although he acknowledged that killing the victim reduced his tension and the overwhelming urge he had to kill her. He said he did not entertain the urge to kill anyone for a couple of months after that and then the same thoughts returned.

'He repeated that he has violent thoughts and keeps them in check. He also stated that he does not anticipate gaining pleasure from harming others, just relief from his own urge to kill. Asked whether he felt guilty about his crime he said "no, this was something I had to do . . . I couldn't stop myself". Asked about his self-esteem Mr Stanford repeated that "I'm different to other people – I think I've done remarkably well to live with people for 25 years . . . I don't think there are any treatments for my inability to deal with other people" ' (*R v Stanford, Vincent* [2016] NSWSC 1434).

Following psychometric tests and lengthy interviews, Ms Robilliard found Stanford was of 'soundly average' intelligence. A personality disorder test found elevated scores on a number of scales, including the 'sadistic/aggressive' scale said to 'identify people likely predisposed toward aggressive outbursts which might be expressed in a callous manner, with little awareness of the impact of their verbally or physically aggressive actions on others'. A psychopathy test found that Stanford was in the very low range, not consistent with a diagnosis of psychopathy. His scores were mostly in the low or very low range, but he was in the high range for lack of remorse, empathy and non-acceptance of responsibility. Ms Robilliard also identified a degree of depression. Stanford had self-harmed and attempted suicide while in custody, which could have been a reaction to his new situation.

Ms Robilliard believed that Stanford met the criteria for an ASD. She noted that people with such a diagnosis, as opposed to antisocial individuals, 'lack the neurological capacity to grasp the implications and consequences of their criminal activities'. 'Mr Stanford has developed an entrenched self-belief that he is defective,' she said. 'His autistic limitations cause him to fluctuate between despair for himself and unfulfilled expectations of other's [sic] treatment of him which leads to entrenched anger and hatred. He is essentially locked into this internally conflicted state leading to ongoing tension which he described as reaching an intolerable level at times. His strategy for relief appears to be causing harm to himself and others, in this case, the victim. Mr Stanford commented during the interviews that he considered he had done well to control himself as well as he has, "for twenty-five years"' (*R v Stanford, Vincent* [2016] NSWSC 1434). After seeing Stanford, Ms Robilliard noted that he 'described having one feeling, hatred, which could be a consequence of his perception of exclusion and rejection and the source of a generalised social animosity that may have triggered his angry, unpremeditated and overwhelming urge to kill the victim'.

Essentially, Vincent Stanford killed Stephanie Scott because he had a combination of criminal autistic psychopathy and a sexual sadism disorder (see pages 375–7, 415). Stanford had secretly fed his obsession over a long period of time, and came close to attacking other young women before he decided to rape and kill Stephanie Scott. For some reason, on that day, he could no longer resist the urge to act on his sadistic fantasies. It appears that this seemingly quiet young man had several very dark secrets that either did not fully emerge or were not dealt with until it was too late.

CONCLUSION

Vincent Stanford had an unusual combination of psychological disorders that led to the worst possible outcome. As we have stressed, having an ASD does not mean that someone will be violent. But Stanford, who was obsessed with hardcore and violent pornography that he claimed drove him to rape and murder Stephanie Scott, had a combination of ASD and additional 'psychopathic features' plus a sexual sadism disorder. This resulted in him putting his desires ahead of the welfare and life of an innocent woman. Stanford lacked empathy for his victim and was obsessed with sexual violence, which led him to act in such a despicable manner in raping and killing Stephanie.

Most people who have an ASD can learn, understand and abide by society's legal and moral obligations. Most live fulfilling lives and contribute to society through work, family and social activities. Vincent Stanford's ASD did not prevent him from functioning reasonably successfully as a member of his local community, interacting with his neighbours and holding down a job. He was of average intelligence and there is no doubt that he knew right from wrong. But due to the combination of his criminal autistic psychopathy and his sexual sadism he murdered a woman for the sake of the 'thrill' he got from sexually assaulting her and then killing her.

Stanford had also stalked other young women in Leeton, but had not acted on these sexual desires until Stephanie was in the wrong place at the wrong time – alone at school on a Sunday when no one else was there except him. His sexual sadism disorder led to him watching extreme pornography and buying sex-related and mostly violence-oriented paraphernalia that he collected until he decided, for whatever reason, that he wanted to act out his violent sexual fantasies on a real person. The combination of traits and disorders that Stanford displayed is rare, but unfortunately not easy to identify. Few people saw him as potentially violent, and his neighbours found him to be personable if a little strange. They tried to focus on his positive traits and this meant no one realised how potentially dangerous he was until it was too late.

If more details had emerged earlier about his stalking of the other young women, it may have been possible to ban him from accessing the school grounds. But there was no guarantee he would not have found another opportunity to attack someone else somewhere else. The best we can do in these cases is be vigilant, and if someone shows signs of obsessive or stalking behaviour, it should be fully investigated by the relevant authorities.

APPENDIX: WHERE TO GO FOR HELP AND SUPPORT

Ambulance/Fire/Police
Telephone: 000
Website: www.triplezero.gov.au

Suicide Call Back Service
Telephone: 1300 659 467
Website: www.suicidecallbackservice.org.au

Australian Federal Government crisis support page
Website: www.humanservices.gov.au/customer/subjects/crisis-and-special-help

Lifeline
24/7 crisis support and suicide prevention
Telephone: 13 11 14
Website: www.lifeline.org.au

Kids Helpline
Free, confidential 24/7 telephone and online counselling service for those aged 5–25
Telephone: 1800 551 800
Website: kidshelp.com.au

1800 RESPECT
Free, confidential 24/7 national family violence and sexual assault counselling service
Telephone: 1800 737 732
Website: www.1800respect.org.au

Family Relationship Advice Line
Information and advice on family relationship issues and parenting arrangements after separation
Telephone: 1800 050 321
Website: www.familyrelationships.gov.au

MensLine Australia
Telephone and online support, information and referrals regarding domestic violence and relationship and family problems
Telephone: 1300 789 978
Website: www.mensline.org.au

beyondblue
Information and support on anxiety, depression and suicide, and promotes good mental health
Telephone: 1300 224 636
Website: www.beyondblue.org.au

Victorian Centres Against Sexual Assault
Help and counselling for Victorians who have been sexually assaulted

Sexual Assault Crisis Line telephone: 1800 806 292
Website: www.casa.org.au

White Ribbon
Provides domestic violence information and lists national and state-based support organisations
Website: www.whiteribbon.org.au

ReachOut Australia
Relationship and life advice for young people
Website: au.reachout.com

WikiHow: How to deal with emotional abuse
www.wikihow.com/Deal-with-Emotional-Abuse

Wesley Mission
Support for families experiencing domestic violence
Website: www.wesleymission.org.au/news-and-publications/latest-news/wesley-mission-news/support-for-families-experiencing-domestic-violence

Relationships Australia
Support groups and counselling on relationships, and for abusive and abused partners
Telephone: 1300 364 277
Website: www.relationships.org.au

Australian Childhood Foundation
Help for children and young people affected by abuse
Telephone: 1300 381 581
Website: www.childhood.org.au

Blue Knot Foundation (formerly ASCA)
Helps adult survivors, their friends and family and the healthcare professionals who support them.
Telephone: 1300 657 380
Website: www.blueknot.org.au

DVConnect Womensline (Queensland)
Helps women to obtain safe refuge accommodation, confidential counselling and referral to other services, 24/7
Telephone: 1800 811 811
Website: www.dvconnect.org/womensline

DVConnect Mensline (Queensland)
Telephone: 1800 600 636 (9 am to midnight, seven days a week)
Website: www.dvconnect.org/mensline

Translating and Interpreting Service
Access to an interpreter in your own language for the cost of a local call
Telephone: 13 14 50
Website: www.tisnational.gov.au

PANDA
Perinatal Anxiety & Depression Australia
Telephone: 1300 726 306
Website: www.panda.org.au

Parent helplines
NSW: 1300 130 052
Victoria: 13 22 89
Queensland: 1300 301 300
Western Australia: (08) 9368 9368 or 1800 111 546 (country)
South Australia: 1300 364 100

Tasmania: 1300 808 178
ACT: (02) 6287 3833
Northern Territory: 1300 301 300

Spectrum Personality Disorder Service for Victoria
Specialist treatment for people with personality disorders
Telephone: (03) 8833 3050
Website: www.spectrumbpd.com.au

Australian BPD Foundation Limited
Help for people with borderline personality disorder
Telephone: (03) 8803 5588
Website: www.bpdfoundation.org.au

BPD Family
Support for those with a borderline personality disorder and their loved ones
Email: admin@bpdfamily.com
Website: bpdfamily.com

Australian Psychological Society
Find a psychologist: www.psychology.org.au/Find-a-Psychologist

Royal Australian and New Zealand College of Psychiatrists
Find a psychiatrist: www.yourhealthinmind.org/find-a-psychiatrist

GLOSSARY

Adjustment disorder
A short-term condition rarely lasting longer than six months, in which the individual develops distressing emotional or behavioural symptoms within three months of experiencing one or more stressful life events, such as the ending of a significant relationship, developing a serious illness, the failure of a business or losing one's job. Normal bereavement, such as the loss of an elderly parent, is not considered a stressor in this context.

Amygdala
This area of the brain is like a security camera that is responsible for monitoring what you see, touch, smell and hear, so that you can decide what's 'safe' and what's 'dangerous'. If it perceives 'danger', it quickly sends a message to the hippocampus, where stored personal memories provide further information to allow you to decide whether the danger is 'real'. The hippocampus

then connects to the prefrontal cortex in your brain to help you decide what action, if any, needs to be taken.

Antisocial personality disorder (ASPD)

A personality disorder characterised by a pervasive pattern of disregard for and violation of the rights of other people, occurring from the age of fifteen. Some of the typical features of this pattern include deceit, manipulation, impulsivity, irresponsibility, lack of remorse and, in some cases, aggression.

Borderline personality disorder (BPD)

A pervasive pattern of unstable interpersonal relationships, self-image and emotions combined with impulsive behaviours. It begins by early adulthood and presents in a variety of contexts. Its severity is strongly connected to negative experiences in childhood.

Cognitive behaviour therapy

A form of (usually) short-term psychotherapy, developed by Drs Albert Ellis and Aaron Beck, which focuses on supporting a patient to identify and change irrational thinking and expectations, and challenge unhelpful thinking habits.

Comorbidity

The occurrence of one or more disorders either at the same time or, in some cases, with one contributing to the development of the other.

Conduct disorder

An ongoing pattern of antisocial behaviour in a child aged under fifteen that includes behaviours such as lying, theft, truancy, fighting, violence, using alcohol and drugs, and property damage.

Dependent personality disorder (DPD)

A pervasive pattern of behaviour in which an individual is under-confident and perceives that they are unable to function adequately without the help of others. They look for someone to protect, advise and take care of them, fear abandonment and tend to be needy, clingy, submissive and overly compliant in their key personal relationships.

Dissociation

A sense of being outside yourself and watching what you are doing and what is happening to you but in a disconnected way as if you were a stranger looking on. It tends to occur during or after a traumatic experience, and the memory of what actually happened during the trauma may be impaired.

DSM-5: *The Diagnostic and Statistical Manual of Mental Disorders*, 5th edition (APA, 2013)

A classification and diagnostic reference manual outlining a range of mental disorders and the diagnostic criteria for each of them.

Empathy

Empathy is one of the most important building blocks of respect, kindness, compassion, conscience development and moral behaviour. It has four components, each drawing on different skills:

1. **Emotional recognition** is knowing intellectually how someone else is feeling (and perhaps thinking) as a result of seeing their expressions or actions and/or listening to their voice and words.
2. **Emotional resonance** occurs when you actually 'feel' some of the same emotion that you recognise another person is

feeling. For example, when you are listening to someone who is upset as they tell you about something sad that they have recently experienced you might also feel sad and a bit teary.

3. **Empathic concern** occurs when, having recognised and understood how another person is feeling, you react by saying or doing something that might support them or rejoice with them, or help them feel better.
4. **Empathic prediction** occurs when you take the time to think about and anticipate how another person might respond and react to something you are thinking of doing or are planning to do.

Familicide

The killing of one's whole immediate family, i.e. one's partner and most or all of their biological children. **Familicide–suicide** is the killing of one's whole immediate family, followed by the suicide of the parent who killed them.

Filicide

The killing by a parent of one or more of their biological children aged under eighteen.

Filicide–suicide is the killing by a parent of one or more of their biological children under the age of eighteen, followed by the suicide of the parent who killed them.

Grandiosity

An exaggerated belief in one's ability, importance and level of success.

Heritability

The degree to which genetics plays a role in developing a disorder. Heritability is an estimate of how much of the observed differences between people within a specific population (e.g. people in a research study) is due to genetic differences between them. The closer a heritability estimate is to 100 per cent, the more strongly that characteristic or behaviour is influenced by genetic factors. Heritability can range from 0 (no genetic influence) to 1 (100 per cent genetic influence). If a research study of 'singing ability' in 600 adults found that the heritability of 'singing ability' was .45, that would mean that 45 per cent of the differences between those 600 people in terms of their singing ability was most likely due to specific genetic differences between them. Heritability estimates are usually obtained through studies comparing identical twins with non-identical twins.

Histrionic personality disorder (HPD)

This personality disorder is characterised by a persistent and relatively inflexible pattern of behaviour that is excessively emotional and attention-seeking and often overly dramatic.

Infanticide

In the state of Victoria, infanticide is defined as a woman's conduct that causes the death of her child in circumstances that would constitute murder but, at the time, the balance of her mind was disturbed due to not fully recovering from the effect of giving birth to that child in the past two years, or developing a disorder in the child's first two years. While murder in Victoria carries a maximum penalty of life in prison, infanticide carries a maximum five-year sentence.

In New South Wales and Tasmania, infanticide involves a mother deliberately causing the death of her child aged under the age of twelve months, while the mother is suffering from a mental disturbance due to not having fully recovered from the birth. The *NSW Crimes Act* adds 'or by reason of the effect of lactation following the child's birth' and specifies that someone guilty of infanticide faces the same level of punishment as manslaughter, which can be up to 25 years.

Malignant narcissism

A combination of the core features of a narcissistic personality disorder and an antisocial personality disorder.

Mental illness

A clinically significant medical condition that significantly impairs (temporarily or permanently) a person's mental functioning, perceptions and judgement, and strongly indicates that they need to be placed in a context where they can be monitored, given care and/or medical treatment and/or their behaviour can be controlled. It is characterised by the presence of one or more of the following:

- major disturbance in thought, emotions, orientation, mood, perceptions, memory and/or decision-making
- the presence of one or more of the following symptoms: delusions, hallucinations, serious disorder of thought, a severe disorder of mood, and/or sustained or repeated irrational behaviour that indicates the presence of one of the symptoms above
- a lack of accurate awareness of the nature and quality of their actions and a lack of understanding of the wrongness of some of their behaviours.

Mirror neurons

Mirror neurons are specialised brain cells that enable us to feel empathy. When we see another person who is displaying an emotion such as sadness, these brain cells 'fire' in our own brains and we feel some of the same 'sad' feelings ourselves. This explains why we sometimes cry when we are watching an actor express sadness in a movie. People who tend to be very empathic most likely have a more effective mirror neuron system.

Narcissistic personality disorder (NPD)

A personality disorder characterised by an excessive need for admiration, exploiting others, and arrogance.

Paranoid personality disorder (PPD)

A pervasive and ongoing pattern of behaviour characterised by a general mistrust of the intentions of others, suspiciousness and hostility.

Personality disorder

A personality disorder is not a mental illness. It is a pervasive and relatively consistent pattern of behaviour characterised by maladaptive and inflexible thinking, and ineffective management of emotions and behaviour. It is usually accompanied by relatively low levels of resilience under stressful conditions, low levels of empathy towards others and difficulty with adapting to changing circumstances.

Post-traumatic stress disorder (PTSD)

An anxiety disorder that some people develop after witnessing or experiencing a traumatic event that threatened their life or safety (or that of others around them), such as a war, bushfire, car accident, attack or sexual assault. They may become hypervigilant to sights and sounds that recall the trauma, and constantly feel highly anxious.

Prefrontal cortex

This more rational area of your brain interprets and coordinates emotional signals from your **amygdala** and memories from your **hippocampus**, and integrates them to help you reason, solve problems, plan, make decisions and manage your feelings. It also helps you to empathise with the feelings of others.

Psychopath/sociopath

Terms that are sometimes used interchangeably with the term 'antisocial personality disorder', although some have argued that there are significant differences between the three.

Psychotic

When a person is 'psychotic' they are under the influence of a 'psychosis'. A psychosis is a symptom of **mental illness**, and the term indicates that there has been a loss of contact with reality.

Resilience

The capacity to adapt flexibly to the ever-changing challenges of life, cope with inevitable setbacks, losses and disappointments, and 'bounce back' to a state of emotional wellbeing (McGrath and Noble, 2018).

Sexual sadism disorder

A recurrent pattern of behaviour in which an individual achieves sexual arousal and gratification by inflicting fear, pain and suffering on another person (without their consent) through behaviours such as raping, physically beating, stabbing or restraining/imprisoning them. The individual has also usually experienced recurrent and intense sexual arousal through fantasising about doing this or by watching sexually sadistic pornography.

REFERENCES

INTRODUCTION

American Psychiatric Association (2013), DSM-5: *Diagnostic and Statistical Manual of Mental Disorders*, 5th edn, Arlington, VA: American Psychiatric Publishing

American Psychiatric Association (1994), DSM-IV: *Diagnostic and Statistical Manual of Mental Disorders*, 4th edn, Arlington VA: American Psychiatric Publishing

Coid, J., Yang, M., Tyrer, P., Roberts, A. and Ullrich, S. (2006), 'Prevalence and correlates of personality disorder in Great Britain', *British Journal of Psychiatry*, vol. 188, no. 5, pp. 423–31

Millon, T. (2011), *Disorders of Personality: Introducing a DSM/ICD Spectrum from Normal to Abnormal*, 3rd edn, New York: Wiley & Sons

Millon, T., Millon, C.M., Meagher, S. and Grossman, S. (2004), *Personality Disorders in Modern Life*, Hoboken, NJ: Wiley & Sons

Quirk, S.E., Berk, M., Chanen, A.M., Koivumaa-Honkanen, H., Brennan-Olsen, S.L., Pasco, J.A. and Williams, L.J. (2016), 'Population prevalence of personality disorder and associations with physical health comorbidities and health care service utilization: a review', *Personality Disorders: Theory, Research, and Treatment*, vol. 7, no. 2, pp. 136–46

FILICIDE AND FAMILICIDE

Bourget, D. and Bradford, J.M.W. (1990), 'Homicidal parents', *Canadian Journal of Psychiatry*, vol. 35, no. 3, pp. 233–8

Bourget, D. and Gagné, P. (2005), 'Paternal filicide in Québec', *Journal of the American Academy of Psychiatry and the Law*, vol. 33, no. 3, pp. 354–60

Bourget, D. and Gagné, P. (2002), 'Maternal filicide in Québec', *Journal of the American Academy of Psychiatry and the Law*, vol. 30, no. 3, pp. 345–51

Bourget, D., Grace, J. and Whitehurst, L. (2007), 'A review of maternal and paternal filicide', *Journal of the American Academy of Psychiatry and the Law*, vol. 35, no. 1, pp. 74–82

Campion, J.F., Cravens, J.M. and Covan, F. (1988), 'A study of filicidal men', *American Journal of Psychiatry*, vol. 145, no. 9, pp. 1141–4

Flynn, S.M., Shaw, J.J. and Abel, K.M. (2013), 'Filicide: mental illness in those who kill their children', *PLoS ONE*, vol. 8, no. 4, article no. e58981

Fox, J.A. and Levin, J. (2005), *Extreme Killing: Understanding Serial and Mass Murder*, Thousand Oaks, CA: Sage Publications

Friedman, S.H. and Resnick, P.J. (2007), 'Child murder by mothers: patterns and prevention', *World Psychiatry*, vol. 6, no. 3, pp. 137–41

Friedman, S.H., Hrouda, D.R., Holden, C.E., Noffsinger, S.G. and Resnick, P.J. (2005), 'Filicide-suicide: common factors in parents who kill their children and themselves', *Journal of the American Academy of Psychiatry and the Law*, vol. 33, no. 4, pp. 496–504

Johnson, C.H. (2005), *Come with Daddy: Child Murder–Suicide after Family Breakdown*, Perth: University of Western Australia Publishing

Johnson, C. and Sachmann, M. (2014), 'Familicide-suicide: from myth to hypothesis and toward understanding', *Family Court Review*, vol. 52, no. 1, pp. 100–13

Leggett, V. (2000), 'Patricidal familicide', in P. Blackman, V. Leggett, B. Olson and J. Jarvis (eds), *The Varieties of Homicide and Its Research: Proceedings of the 1999 Meeting of the Homicide Research Group*, Washington, DC: Federal Bureau of Investigation, pp. 209–25

Liem, M.C.A. (2010), 'Homicide followed by suicide: an empirical analysis', doctoral dissertation, Utrecht University, Netherlands

Liem, M. and Nieuwbeerta, P. (2010), 'Homicide followed by suicide: a comparison with homicide and suicide', *Suicide and Life-Threatening Behavior*, vol. 40, no. 2, pp. 133–45

Logan, J.E., Walsh, S., Patel, N. and Hall, J.E. (2013), 'Homicide-followed-by-suicide incidents involving child victims', *American Journal of Health Behavior*, vol. 37, no. 4, pp. 531–42

McPhedran, S., Eriksson, L., Mazerolle, P., De Leo, D., Johnson, H. and Wortley, R. (2015), 'Characteristics of homicide-suicide in Australia: a comparison with homicide-only and suicide-only cases', *Journal of Interpersonal Violence*, doi: 10.1177/0886260515619172

Norris, M. (2016), *Look What You Made Me Do: Fathers Who Kill*, Melbourne: Echo Publishing

O'Hagan, K. (2014), *Filicide-Suicide: The Killing of Children in the Context of Separation, Divorce and Custody Disputes*, Basingstoke: Palgrave Macmillan

Panczak, R., Geissbuhler, M., Zwahlen, M., Killias, M., Tal, K. and Egger, M. (2013), 'Homicide–suicides compared to homicides and suicides: systematic review and meta-analysis', *Forensic Science International*, vol. 233, nos 1–3, pp. 28–36

Resnick, P. (2016), 'Filicide in the United States', *Indian Journal of Psychiatry*, vol. 58, suppl. 2, pp. 203–9

Resnick, P.J. (1969), 'Child murder by parents: a psychiatric review of filicide', *American Journal of Psychiatry*, vol. 126, no. 3, pp. 325–34

Roma, P., Spacca, A., Pompili, M., Lester, D., Tatarelli, R., Girardi, P. and Ferracuti, S. (2012), 'The epidemiology of homicide-suicide in Italy: a newspaper study from 1985 to 2008', *Forensic Science International*, vol. 214, nos 1–3, pp. 1–5

Websdale, N. (2010), *Familicidal Hearts: The Emotional Styles of 211 Killers*, Oxford: Oxford University Press

West, S. (2007), 'An overview of filicide', *Psychiatry*, vol. 4, no. 2, pp. 48–57

West, S., Friedman, S.H. and Resnick, P.J. (2009), 'Fathers who kill their children: an analysis of the literature', *Journal of Forensic Sciences*, vol. 54, no. 2, pp. 463–8

Wilson, M. (2009), *A History of British Serial Killing*, London: Sphere

Wilson, M., Daly, M. and Daniele, A. (1995), 'Familicide: the killing of spouse and children, *Aggressive Behavior*, vol. 21, no. 5, pp. 275–91

Yardley, E., Wilson, D. and Lynes, A. (2014), 'A taxonomy of male British family annihilators, 1980–2012', *Howard Journal of Crime and Justice*, vol. 53, no. 2, pp. 117–40

NARCISSISTIC PERSONALITY DISORDER AND MALIGNANT NARCISSISM

(2017) 'Psychiatrists warn about Trump's mental state', letter to the editor from B.X. Lee, *New York Times*, 30 November, www.nytimes.com/2017/11/30/opinion/psychiatrists-trump.html

(2017) 'Transcript of the Yale Duty to Warn Conference', 20 April, Palgrave Macmillan, us.macmillan.com/static/duty-to-warn-conference-transcript.pdf

American Psychiatric Association (2013), *Diagnostic and Statistical Manual of Mental Disorders*, 5th edn, Arlington, VA: American Psychiatric Publishing

Baskin-Sommers, A., Krusemark, E. and Ronningstam, E. (2014), 'Empathy in narcissistic personality disorder: from clinical and empirical perspectives', *Personality Disorders: Theory, Research, and Treatment*, vol. 5, no. 3, pp. 323–33

Blackburn, R., Logan, C., Donnelly, J. and Renwick, S. (2003), 'Personality disorder, psychopathy, and other mental disorders: co-morbidity among patients at English and Scottish high security hospitals', *Journal of Forensic Psychiatry and Psychology*, vol. 14, no. 1, pp. 111–37

Buffardi, L.E. and Campbell, W.K. (2008), 'Narcissism and social networking web sites', *Personality and Social Psychology Bulletin*, vol. 34, no. 10, 1303–14

Burkle, F.M. Jr (2016), 'Antisocial personality disorder and pathological narcissism in prolonged conflicts and wars of the 21st century', *Disaster Medicine and Public Health Preparedness*, vol. 10, no. 1, pp. 118–28

Cheney, K., Arnsdorf, I., Lippman, D., Strauss, D. and Griffiths, B. (2016), 'Donald Trump's week of misrepresentations, exaggerations and half-truths', *Politico Magazine*, 25 September, www.politico.com/magazine/story/2016/09/2016-donald-trump-fact-check-week-214287

Dhawan, N., Kunik, M.E., Oldham, J. and Coverdale, J. (2010), 'Prevalence and treatment of narcissistic personality disorder in the community: a systematic review', *Comprehensive Psychiatry*, vol. 51, no. 4, pp. 333–9

Dodes, L. (2017), 'Sociopathy', in B.X. Lee (ed.), *The Dangerous Case of Donald Trump: 27 Psychiatrists and Mental Health Experts Assess a President*, New York: Thomas Dunne Books, pp. 83–92

Fisher, M. (2016), 'Donald Trump, perhaps unwittingly, exposes paradox of nuclear arms', *New York Times*, 3 August, www.nytimes.com/2016/08/04/world/donald-trump-nuclear-weapons.html

Friedman, H. (2017), 'On seeing what you see and saying what you know: a psychiatrist's responsibility', in Lee (ed.), *The Dangerous Case of Donald Trump*, pp. 160–9

Fromm, Erich (1965), *The Heart of Man: Its Genius for Good and Evil*, London: Routledge & Kegan Paul

Gartner, J.D. (2017), 'Donald Trump is a) bad, b) mad or c) all of the above', in Lee (ed.), *The Dangerous Case of Donald Trump*, pp. 93–109

Gartrell, N. and Mosbacher, D. (2017), 'He's got the world in his hands and his finger on the trigger: the Twenty-fifth Amendment solution', in Lee (ed.), *The Dangerous Case of Donald Trump*, pp. 343–55

Gass, Nick (2016), 'Trump U "really a fraud from beginning to end"', *Politico Magazine*, 25 September, www.politico.com/story/2016/06/eric-schneiderman-trump-university-fraud-223812

Gilligan, J. (2017), 'The issue is dangerousness, not mental illness', in Lee (ed.), *The Dangerous Case of Donald Trump*, pp. 170–80

Glad, B. (2002), 'Why tyrants go too far: malignant narcissism and absolute power', *Political Psychology*, vol. 23, no. 1, pp. 1–37

Goldner-Vukov, M. and Moore, L.J. (2010), 'Malignant narcissism: from fairytales to harsh reality', *Psychiatria Danubina*, vol. 22, no. 3, pp. 392–405

Gunderson, J.G. and Ronningham, E. (2001), 'Differentiating narcissistic and antisocial personality disorders', *Journal of Personality Disorders*, vol. 15, no. 2, pp. 103–9

Holan, A.D. and Qui, L. (2015), '2015 lie of the year: the campaign misstatements of Donald Trump', Politifact, 21 December, www.politifact.com/truth-o-meter/article/2015/dec/21/2015-lie-year-donald-trump-campaign-misstatements

Kernberg, O.F. (1992), *Aggression in Personality Disorders and Perversions*, New Haven, CT: Yale University Press

Kohut, H. (1972), 'Thoughts on narcissism and narcissistic rage', in P. Ornstein (ed.) *The Search for the Self: The Collected Writings of Heinz Kohut*, vol. 2, pp. 615–58, New York: International Universities Press, 1978

Lee, B.X. (2017), *The Dangerous Case of Donald Trump: 27 Psychiatrists and Mental Health Experts Assess a President*, New York: Thomas Dunne Books

Malancharuvil, J.M. (2012), 'Empathy deficit in antisocial personality disorder: a psychodynamic formulation', *American Journal of Psychoanalysis*, vol. 72, no. 3, pp. 242–50

Malkin, C. (2017), 'Pathological narcissism and politics: a lethal mix', in Lee (ed.), *The Dangerous Case of Donald Trump*, pp. 51–68

Media Today (2016), 'Donald Trump: obnoxious boasting compilation', YouTube, 20 May, www.youtube.com/watch?v=20am-Brid9M (An amusing three-minute compilation video of Donald Trump boasting about his abilities)

Millon, T., Millon, C.M., Meagher, S. and Grossman, S. (2004), *Personality Disorders in Modern Life*, Hoboken, NJ: Wiley & Sons

Montefiore, S.S. (2007), *Young Stalin*, London: Weidenfeld & Nicolson

Reisner, S. (2017), 'Stop saying Donald Trump is mentally ill', *Slate*, 15 March, www.slate.com/articles/health_and_science/medical_examiner/2017/03/donald_trump_isn_t_mentally_ill_he_s_evil.html

Ritter, K., Dziobek, I., Preissler, S., Rüter, A., Vater, A., Fydrich, T. and Roepke, S. (2011), 'Lack of empathy in patients with narcissistic personality disorder', *Psychiatry Research*, vol. 187, nos 1–2, pp. 241–7

Sheehy, G., 'Trump's trust deficit', in Lee (ed.), *The Dangerous Case of Donald Trump*, pp. 75–82

Stinson, F.S., Dawson, D.A., Goldstein, R.B., Chou, S.P., Huang, B., Smith, S.M. and Grant, B.F. (2008), 'Prevalence, correlates, disability, and comorbidity of DSM-IV narcissistic personality disorder: results from the Wave 2 National Epidemiologic Survey on Alcohol and Related Conditions', *Journal of Clinical Psychiatry*, vol. 69, no. 7, pp. 1033–45

Tensey, M.J. (2017), 'Part XIII. The dangerous case of Donald Trump: a letter to Congress', *Huffington Post*, 16 November, www.huffingtonpost.com/entry/the-dangerous-case-of-donald-trump-a-letter-to-congress_us_5a061e3be4b0cc46c52e6a5f

Torgersen, S.I., Myers, J., Reichborn-Kjennerud, T., Røysamb, E., Kubarych, T.S. and Kendler, K.S. (2012), 'The heritability of cluster B personality disorders assessed both by personal interview and questionnaire', *Journal of Personality Disorders*, vol. 26, no. 6, pp. 848–66

Twenge, J. and Campbell, K. (2010), *The Narcissism Epidemic: Living in the Age of Entitlement*, New York: Simon & Schuster

Yang, J. and Halliday, J. (2007), *Mao: The Unknown Story*, London: Vintage Books

Zaru, D. (2017), 'It took FOIA for the Park Service to release photos of Obama, Trump inauguration crowd sizes', *CNN Politics*, 7 March, edition.cnn.com/2017/03/07/politics/national-park-service-inauguration-crowd-size-photos

DEPENDENT PERSONALITY DISORDER

Australian Bureau of Statistics (2016), 'Personal Safety', Australia, http://www.abs.gov.au/ausstats/abs@.nsf/mf/4906.0

American Psychiatric Association (2013), *Diagnostic and Statistical Manual of Mental Disorders*, 5th edn, Arlington, VA: American Psychiatric Publishing

Benotsch, E.G., Sawyer, A.N., Martin, A.M, Allen, E.S., Nettles, C.D., Richardson, D. and Rietmeijer, C.A. (2017), 'Dependency traits, relationship power, and health risks in women receiving sexually transmitted infection clinic services', *Behavioral Medicine*, vol. 43, no. 3, pp. 176–83

Bornstein, R.F. (2006), 'The complex relationship between dependency and domestic violence: converging psychological factors and social forces', *American Psychologist*, vol. 61, no. 6, pp. 595–606

Bornstein, R.F. (2005), *The Dependent Patient: A Practitioner's Guide*, Washington, DC: American Psychological Association

Bornstein, R.F., Denckla, C.A. and Chung, W. (2015), 'Dependent and histrionic personality disorder', in P. Blaney, R.F. Krueger and T. Millon, *Oxford Textbook of Psychopathology*, 3rd edn, New York: Oxford University Press, pp. 659–80

Ewing, C. (1997), *Fatal Families: The Dynamics of Intrafamilial Homicide*, Thousand Oaks, CA: Sage Publications

Fazel, S. and Grann, M. (2004), 'Homicide offenders and psychiatric morbidity: a Swedish population study', *American Journal of Psychiatry*, vol. 161, no. 11, pp. 2129–31

Gjerde, L.C., Czajkowski, N., Røysamb, E., Ørstavik, R.E., Knudsen, G.P., Østby, K., Torgersen, S., Myers, J., Kendler, K.S. and Reichborn-Kjennerud, T. (2012), 'The heritability of avoidant and dependent personality disorder assessed by personal interview and questionnaire', *Acta Psychiatrica Scandinavica*, vol. 126, no. 6, pp. 448–57

Grant, B.F., Hasin, D.S., Stinson, F.S., Dawson, D.A., Chou, S.P., Ruan, W.J. and Pickering, R.P. (2004), 'Prevalence, correlates, and disability of personality disorders in the United States: results from the national epidemiologic survey on alcohol and related conditions', *Journal of Clinical Psychiatry*, vol. 65, no. 7, pp. 948–58

Jacobson, N. and Gottman, J. (2007), *When Men Batter Women: New Insights into Ending Abusive Relationships*, New York: Simon & Schuster

Lenzenweger, M.F., Lane, M.C., Loranger, A.W. and Kessler, R.C. (2007), 'DSM-IV personality disorders in the National Comorbidity Survey Replication', *Biological Psychiatry*, vol. 62, no. 6, pp. 553–64

Loas, G., Cormier, J. and Perez-Diaz, F. (2011), 'Dependent personality disorder and physical abuse', *Psychiatry Research*, vol. 185, nos 1–2, pp. 167–70

Millon, T. (2011), *Disorders of Personality: Introducing a DSM/ICD Spectrum from Normal to Abnormal*, 3rd edn, Wiley & Sons

Reichborn-Kjennerud, T., Czajkowski, N., Neale, M.C. and Orstavik, R.E. (2007), 'Genetic and environmental influences on dimensional representations of DSM-IV cluster C personality disorders: a population-based multivariate twin study', *Psychological Medicine*, vol. 37, no. 5, pp. 645–53

Samuel, D.B. and Widiger, T.A. (2010), 'Comparing personality disorder models: cross-method assessment of the FFM and DSM–IV–TR', *Journal of Personality Disorders*, vol. 24, no. 6, pp. 721–45

Seligman, M.E.P. and Maier, S.F. (1967), 'Failure to escape traumatic shock', *Journal of Experimental Psychology*, vol. 74, no. 1, pp. 1–9

Torgerson, S. (2009), 'The nature (and nurture) of personality disorders', *Scandinavian Journal of Psychology*, vol. 50, no. 6, pp. 624–32

Trull, T.J., Jahng, S., Tomko, R.L., Wood, P.K. and Sher, K.J. (2010), 'Revised NESARC personality disorder diagnoses: gender, prevalence, and comorbidity with substance dependence disorders', *Journal of Personality Disorders*, vol. 24, no. 4, pp. 412–26

Walker, L.E. (2016), *The Battered Woman Syndrome*, 4th edn, New York: Springer

Weizmann-Henelius, G., Viemerö, V. and Eronen, M. (2003), 'The violent female perpetrator and her victim', *Forensic Science International*, vol. 133, no. 3, pp. 197–203

HISTRIONIC PERSONALITY DISORDER

Bakkevig, J.F. and Karterud, S. (2010), 'Is the *Diagnostic and Statistical Manual of Mental Disorders*, Fourth Edition, histrionic personality disorder category a valid construct?', *Comparative. Psychiatry*, vol. 51, no. 5, pp. 462–70

Coolidge, F.L., Thede, L.L. and Jang, K.L. (2004), 'Are personality disorders psychological manifestations of executive function deficits? Bivariate heritability evidence from a twin study', *Behavioral Genetics*, vol. 34, no. 1, pp. 75–84

Grant, B.F., Hasin, D.S., Stinson, F.S., Dawson, D.A., Chou, S.P., Ruan, W.J. and Pickering, R.P. (2004), 'Prevalence, correlates, and disability of personality disorders in the United States: results from the national epidemiologic survey on alcohol and related conditions', *Journal of Clinical Psychiatry*, vol. 65, no. 7, pp. 948–58

Torgersen, S., Czajkowski, N., Jacobson, K., Reichborn-Kjennerud, T., Roysamb, E., Neale, M.C. and Kendler, K.S. (2008), 'Dimensional representations of DSM-IV cluster B personality disorders in a population-based sample of Norwegian twins: a multivariate study', *Psychological Medicine*, vol. 38, no. 11, pp. 1617–25

PARANOID PERSONALITY DISORDER

American Psychiatric Association (2013), *Diagnostic and Statistical Manual of Mental Disorders*, 5th edn, Arlington, VA: American Psychiatric Publishing

Arroyo, J. and Ortega, E. (2009), 'Personality disorders amongst inmates as distorting factor in the prison social climate', *Revista Espanola De Sanidad Penitenciaria*, vol. 11, pp. 11–15

Asarnow, R., Nuechterlein, K., Fogelson, D., Subotnik, K., Payne, D., Russell, A., Asaman, J., Kuppinger, H. and Kendler, K.S. (2001), 'Schizophrenia and schizophrenia-spectrum personality disorders in the first-degree relatives of children with schizophrenia: the UCLA Family Study', *Archives of General Psychiatry*, vol. 58, no. 6, pp. 581–8

Ashcroft, K., Kingdon, D.G. and Chadwick, P. (2012), 'Persecutory delusions and childhood emotional abuse in people with a diagnosis of schizophrenia', *Psychosis*, vol. 4, no. 2, pp. 168–71

Baron, M., Gruen, R., Rainer, J.D., Kane, J., Asnis, L. and Lord, S. (1985), 'A family study of schizophrenic and normal control probands: implications for the spectrum concept of schizophrenia', *American Journal of Psychiatry*, vol. 142, no. 4, pp. 447–55

References

Beck, A.T. and Freeman, A. (1990), *Cognitive Therapy of Personality Disorders*, New York: Guilford Press

Benjamin, L.S. (1996), *Interpersonal Diagnosis and Treatment of Personality Disorders*, 3rd edn, New York: Guilford Press

Bentall, R.P., Corcoran, R., Howard, R., Blackwood, N. and Kinderman, P. (2001), 'Persecutory delusions: a review and theoretical integration', *Clinical Psychology Review*, vol. 21, no. 8, pp. 1143–92

Blakemore, S.J., Sarfati, Y., Bazin, N. and Decety, J. (2003), 'The detection of intentional contingencies in simple animations in patients with delusions of persecution', *Psychological Medicine*, vol. 33, no. 8, pp. 1433–41

Fisher, H.L., Appiah-Kusi, E. and Grant, C. (2012), 'Anxiety and negative self schemas mediate the association between childhood maltreatment and paranoia', *Psychiatric Research*, vol. 196, nos 2–3, pp. 323–4

Freeman, D. (2007), 'Suspicious minds: the psychology of persecutory delusions', *Clinical Psychology Review*, vol. 27, no. 4, pp. 425–57

Grant, B.F., Hasin, D.S., Stinson, F.S., Dawson, D.A., Chou, S.P., Ruan, W.J. and Pickering, R.P. (2004), 'Prevalence, correlates, and disability of personality disorders in the United States: results from the national epidemiologic survey on alcohol and related conditions', *Journal of Clinical Psychiatry*, vol. 65, no. 7, pp. 948–58

Hampton, W. and Burnham, V. (2003), *The Two-Edged Sword: A Study of the Paranoid Personality in Action*, Santa Fe, NM: Sunstone Press

Johnson, J.G., Smailes, E.M., Cohen, P., Brown, J. and Bernstein, D.P. (2000), 'Associations between four types of childhood neglect and personality disorder symptoms during adolescence and early adulthood: findings of a community-based longitudinal study', *Journal of Personality Disorders*, vol. 14, no. 2, pp. 171–87

Johnson, J.G., Cohen, P., Kasen, S., Skodol, A.E., Hamagami, F. and Brook, J.S. (2000), 'Age-related change in personality disorder trait levels between early adolescence and adulthood: a community-based longitudinal investigation', *Acta Psychiatrica Scandinavica*, vol. 102, no. 4, pp. 265–75

Johnson, J., Cohen, P., Brown, J., Smailes, E. and Bernstein, D. (1999), 'Childhood maltreatment increases risk for personality disorders during early adulthood', *Archives of General Psychiatry*, vol. 56, no. 7, pp. 600–6

Kendler, K.S., Myers, J., Torgersen, S., Neale, M.C. and Reichborn-Kjennerud, T. (2007), 'The heritability of cluster A personality disorders assessed by both personal interview and questionnaire', *Psychological Medicine*, vol. 37, no. 5, pp. 655–65

Lenzenweger, M.F., Lane, M.C., Loranger, A.W. and Kessler, R.C. (2007), 'DSM-IV personality disorders in the National Comorbidity Survey Replication', *Biological Psychiatry*, vol. 62, no. 6, pp. 553–64

Lobbestael, J., Arntz, A. and Bernstein, D.P. (2010), 'Disentangling the relationship between different types of childhood maltreatment and personality disorders', *Journal of Personality Disorders*, vol. 24, no. 3, pp. 285–95

McGurk, S.R., Mueser, K.T., Mischel, R., Adams, R., Harvey, P.D., McClure, M.M., Look, A.E., Leung, W.W. and Siever, S.J. (2013), 'Vocational functioning in schizotypal and paranoid personality disorders', *Psychiatry Research*, vol. 210, no. 2, pp. 498–504

Miller, M.B., Useda, J.D., Trull, T.J., Burr, R.M. and Minks-Brown, C. (2001), 'Paranoid, schizoid and schizotypal personality disorders', in H.E. Adams and P.B. Sutker (eds),

The Comprehensive Handbook of Psychopathology, 3rd edn, New York: Plenum, pp. 535–59

Millon, T. (2004), *Personality Disorders in Modern Life*, New York: Wiley & Sons

Nicolson, R., Brookner, F.B., Lenane, M., Gochman, P., Ingraham, L.J., Egan, M.F., Kendler, K.S., Pickar, D., Weinberger, D.R. and Rapoport, J.L. (2003), 'Parental schizophrenia spectrum disorders in childhood-onset and adult-onset schizophrenia', *American Journal of Psychiatry*, vol. 160, no. 3, 490–5

Selten, J., Cantor-Graae, E. and Kahn, R. (2007), 'Migration and schizophrenia', *Current Opinion in Psychiatry*, vol. 20, no. 2, pp. 111–15

Stone, M. (2007), 'Violent crimes and their relationship to personality disorders', *Personality and Mental Health*, vol. 1, pp. 138–53

Torgersen, S., Lygren, S., Oien, P.A., Skre, I., Onstad, S., Edvardsen, J., Tambs, K., and Kringlen, E. (2000), 'A twin study of personality disorders', *Comprehensive Psychiatry*, vol. 41, no. 6, pp. 416–25

Yang, M., Ullrich, S., Roberts, A. and Coid, J. (2007), 'Childhood institutional care and personality disorder traits in adulthood: findings from the British National Surveys of Psychiatric Morbidity', *American Journal of Orthopsychiatry*, vol. 77, no. 1, pp. 67–75

ANTISOCIAL PERSONALITY DISORDER

American Psychiatric Association (2013), *Diagnostic and Statistical Manual of Mental Disorders*, 5th edn, Arlington, VA: American Psychiatric Publishing

Baker, E. and Crichton, J. (1995), '*Ex parte* A: psychopathy, treatability and the law', *Journal of Forensic Psychiatry*, vol. 6, no. 1, pp. 101–9

References

Baker, L.A., Bezdjian, S. and Raine, A. (2006), 'Behavioral genetics: The science of antisocial behavior', *Journal of Law and Contemporary Problems*, vol. 69 (Winter), pp. 7–46

Baron-Cohen, S. (2011), *The Science of Evil: On Empathy and the Origins of Cruelty*, New York: Basic Books

Baron-Cohen, S. (2011), *Zero Degrees of Empathy: A New Theory of Human Cruelty and Kindness*, London: Allen Lane

Baskin-Sommers, A.R., Curtin, J.J. and Newman, J.P. (2013), 'Emotion-modulated startle in psychopathy: clarifying familiar effects', *Journal of Abnormal Psychology*, vol. 122, no. 2, pp. 458–68

Blair, R.J. (2007), 'The amygdala and ventromedial prefrontal cortex in morality and psychopathy', *Trends in Cognitive Science*, vol. 11, no. 9, pp. 387–92

Fazel, S., and Danesh, J. (2002), 'Serious mental disorder in 23 000 prisoners: a systematic review of 62 surveys', *Lancet*, vol. 359, no. 9306, pp. 545–50

Gregory, S., Ffytche, D., Simmons, A., Kumari, V., Howard, M., Hodgins, S. and Blackwood, N. (2012), 'The antisocial brain: psychopathy matters', *Archives of General Psychiatry*, vol. 69, no. 9, pp. 962–72

Hare, R.D. (1996), 'Psychopathy: a clinical construct whose time has come', *Criminal Justice and Behavior*, vol. 23, no. 1, pp. 25–54

Hare, R.D. (1978), 'Electrodermal and cardiovascular correlates of psychopathy', in R.D. Hare and D. Schalling (eds), *Psychopathic Behavior: Approaches to research*, Chichester: Wiley & Sons

Hare, R.D., Clark, D., Grann, M. and Thornton, D. (2000), 'Psychopathy and the predictive validity of the PCL-R: an international perspective', *Behavioral Sciences and the Law*, vol. 18, no. 5, pp. 623–45

Harris, G.T. and Rice, M.E. (2006), 'Treatment of psychopathy: a review of empirical findings', in C.J. Patrick (ed.), *Handbook of Psychopathy*, New York: Guilford

Lenzenweger, M.F., Lane, M.C., Loranger, A.W. and Kessler, R.C. (2007), 'DSM-IV personality disorders in the National Comorbidity Survey Replication', *Biological Psychiatry*, vol. 62, no. 6, pp. 553–64

McGrath, H.L. and Edwards, H. (2009), *Difficult Personalities: A Practical Guide to Managing the Hurtful Behaviour of Others*, 2nd edn, Melbourne: Penguin

Marsh, A.A. and Blair, R.J.R. (2008), 'Deficits in facial affect recognition among antisocial populations: a meta-analysis', *Neuroscience and Biobehavioral Reviews*, vol. 32, pp. 454–65

Meffert, H., Gazzola, V., den Boer, J.A., Bartels, A.A. and Keysers, C. (2013), 'Reduced spontaneous but relatively normal deliberate vicarious representations in psychopathy', *Brain*, vol. 136, no. 8, pp. 2250–62

Moeller, F.G., Dougherty, D.M., Swann, A.C., Collins, D., Davis, C.M. and Cherek, D.R. (1996), 'Tryptophan depletion and aggressive responding in healthy males', *Psychopharmacology*, vol. 126, no. 2, pp. 97–103

Ortiz, J. and Raine, A. (2004), 'Heart rate level and antisocial behavior in children and adolescents: a meta-analysis', *Journal of American Academy of Child and Adolescent Psychiatry*, vol. 43, no. 2, pp. 154–62

Raine, A., Fung, A.L.C., Portnoy, J., Choy, O. and Spring, V.L. (2014), 'Low heart rate as a risk factor for child and adolescent proactive aggressive and impulsive psychopathic behavior', *Aggressive Behavior*, vol. 40, no. 4, pp. 290–9

Rotgers, F. and Maniacci, M. (2006), *Antisocial Personality Disorder: A Practitioner's Guide to Comparative Treatments,* New York: Springer

Stout, M. (2006), *The Sociopath Next Door: The Ruthless vs the Rest of Us*, New York: Broadway Books

Thomas, M.E. (2013), *Confessions of a Sociopath: A Life Spent Hiding in Plain Sight*, New York: Crown Publishers

Torgersen, S., Kringlen, E. and Cramer, V. (2001), 'The prevalence of personality disorders in a community sample', *Archives of General Psychiatry*, vol. 58, no. 6, pp. 590–6

Torgersen, S.I., Myers, J., Reichborn-Kjennerud, T., Røysamb, E., Kubarych, T.S. and Kendler, K.S. (2012), 'The heritability of cluster B personality disorders assessed both by personal interview and questionnaire', *Journal of Personality Disorders*, vol. 26, no. 6, pp. 848–66

CRIMINAL AUTISTIC PSYCHOPATHY AND SEXUAL SADISM DISORDER

Allely, C.S., Minnis. H., Thompson, L., Wilson, P. and Gillberg, C. (2014), 'Neurodevelopmental and psychosocial risk factors in serial killers and mass murderers', *Aggression and Violent Behavior*, vol. 19, no. 3, pp. 288–301

Allely, C.S., Wilson, P., Minnis, H., Thompson, L., Yaksic, E. and Gillberg, C. (2017), 'Violence is rare in autism: when it does occur, is it sometimes extreme?', *Journal of Psychology*, vol. 151, no. 1, pp. 49–68

American Psychiatric Association (2013), *Diagnostic and Statistical Manual of Mental Disorders*, 5th edn, Arlington, VA: American Psychiatric Publishing

American Psychiatric Association (1994), *Diagnostic and Statistical Manual of Mental Disorders*, 4th edn, Arlington, VA: American Psychiatric Publishing

Attwood, T., Henault, I. and Dubin, N. (2014), *The Autism Spectrum, Sexuality, and The Law*, London: Jessica Kingsley Publishers

References

Baxter, A.J., Brugha, T.S., Erskine, H.E., Scheurer, R.W., Vos, T. and Scott, J.G. (2015), 'The epidemiology and global burden of autism spectrum disorders', *Psychological Medicine*, vol. 45, no. 3, pp. 601–13

Bjørkly, S. (2009), 'Risk and dynamics of violence in Asperger's syndrome: A systematic review of the literature', *Aggression & Violent Behaviour*, vol. 14, no. 5, pp. 306–12

Browning, A. and Caulfield, L. (2011), 'The prevalence and treatment of people with Asperger's syndrome in the criminal justice system', *Criminology and Criminal Justice*, vol. 11, no. 2, pp. 165–80

Cantor, J.M. and Sutton, K.S. (2015), 'Paraphilia, gender dysphoria, and hypersexuality', in P.H. Blaney and T. Millon (eds), *Oxford Textbook of Psychopathology*, 3rd edn, New York: Oxford University Press, pp. 589–614

Centers for Disease Control and Prevention, US (2015), 'CDC estimates 1 in 68 school-aged children have autism; no change from previous estimate', press release, CDC, 31 March, www.cdc.gov/media/releases/2016/p0331-children-autism.html

Dietz, P.E., Hazelwood, R.R. and Warren, J. (1990), 'The sexually sadistic criminal and his offenses', *Bulletin of the American Academy of Psychiatry and the Law*, vol. 18, no. 2, pp. 163–78

Fitzgerald, M. (2015), 'Autism and school shooting', in M. Fitzgerald (ed.), *Autism Spectrum Disorder – Recent Advances*, London: InTech Publishing

Fitzgerald, M. (2014), 'Criminal autistic psychopathy', in M. Fitzgerald (ed.), *Psychopathy: Risk Factors, Behavioral Symptoms and Treatment Options*, New York: Nova Science, pp. 105–50

Fitzgerald, M. (2010), *Young, Violent and Dangerous to Know*, New York: Nova

Fitzgerald, M. (2001), 'Autistic psychopathy', *Journal of the American Academy of Child and Adolescent Psychiatry*, vol. 40, no. 8, p. 870

Freckelton, I. (2013), 'Autism spectrum disorder: forensic issues and challenges for mental health professionals and courts', *Journal of Applied Research in Intellectual Disabilities*, vol. 26, no. 5, pp. 420–34

Ghaziuddin, M. (2013), 'Violent behavior in autism spectrum disorder: is it a fact, or fiction?' *Current Psychiatry*, vol. 12, no. 10, pp. 23–32

Ghaziuddin, M., Tsai, L. and Ghaziuddin, N. (1992), 'Comorbidity of autistic disorder in children and adolescents', *European Child and Adolescent Psychiatry*, vol. 1, no. 4, pp. 209–13

Gómez de la Cuesta, G. (2010), 'A selective review of offending behavior in individuals with autism spectrum disorders', *Journal of Learning Disabilities and Offending Behavior*, vol. 1, no. 2, pp. 47–58

Hart-Kerkhoffs, L.A., Jansen, L.M., Doreleijers, T.A., Vermeiren, R. and Minderaa, R.B. (2009), 'Autism spectrum disorder symptoms in juvenile suspects of sex offenses', *Journal of Clinical Psychiatry,* vol. 70, no. 2, pp. 266–72

Haskins, B.G. and Silva, J.A. (2006), 'Asperger's disorder and criminal behavior: forensic-psychiatric considerations', *Journal of American Academy of Psychiatry and Law*, vol. 34, no. 3, pp. 374–84

Higgs, T. and Carter, A.J. (2015), 'Autism spectrum disorder and sexual offending: responsivity in forensic interventions', *Aggression and Violent Behavior*, vol. 22, May–June, pp. 112–19

Im, D. (2016), 'Template to perpetrate: an update on violence in autism spectrum disorder', *Harvard Review of Psychiatry*, vol. 24, no. 1, pp. 14–35

Joshi, G., Petty, C., Wozniak, J., Henin, A., Fried, R., Galdo, M., Kotarski, M., Walls, S.U. and Biederman, J. (2010), 'The heavy burden of psychiatric comorbidity in youth with autism spectrum disorders: a large comparative study of a psychiatrically referred population', *Journal of Autism and Developmental Disorders*, vol. 40, pp. 1361–70

King, C. and Murphy, G.H. (2014), 'A systematic review of people with autism spectrum disorder and the criminal justice system', *Journal of Autism and Developmental Disorders*, vol. 44, no. 11, pp. 2717–33

Kroncke, A.P., Willard, M. and Huckabee, H. (2016), 'Forensic assessment for autism spectrum disorder', in A.P. Kroncke, M. Willard and H. Huckabee, *Assessment of Autism Spectrum Disorder: Critical Issues in Clinical, Forensic and School Settings*, Basel: Springer, pp. 345–73

Krueger, R.B. (2010), 'The DSM diagnostic criteria for sexual sadism', *Archives of Sexual Behavior*, vol. 39, no. 2, pp. 325–45

Lerner, M.D., Omar, S.H., Eli, C., Northrup, L.L. and Bursztajn, H.J. (2012), 'Emerging perspectives on adolescents and young adults with high-functioning autism spectrum disorders, violence, and criminal law', *Journal of the American Academy of Psychiatry and the Law Online*, vol. 40, no. 2, pp. 177–90

Mouridsen, S.E. (2012), 'Current status of research on autism spectrum disorders and offending', *Research in Autism Spectrum Disorders*, vol. 6, no. 1, pp. 79–86

Murrie, D.C., Warren, J.I., Kristiansson, M. and Dietz, P.E. (2002), 'Asperger's syndrome in forensic settings', *International Journal of Forensic Mental Health*, vol. 1, no. 1, pp. 59–70

Ray, F., Marks, C. and Bray-Garretson, H. (2004), 'Challenges to treating adolescents with Asperger's syndrome who are sexually abusive', *Sexual Addiction and Compulsivity*, vol. 11, no. 4, pp. 265–85

Robison, J.E. (2016), *Switched On: A Memoir of Brain Change and Emotional Awakening*, New York: Speigel & Grau

Robison, J.E. (2007), *Look Me in the Eye: My Life with Asperger's*, New York: Three Rivers Press

Rogers, J., Viding, E., Blair, R.J., Frith, U. and Happe, F. (2006), 'Autism spectrum disorder and psychopathy: shared cognitive underpinnings or double hit?' *Psychological Medicine*, vol. 36, no. 12, pp. 1789–98

Simonoff, E., Pickles, A., Charman, T., Chandler, S., Loucas, T. and Baird, G. (2008), 'Psychiatric disorders in children with autism spectrum disorders: prevalence, comorbidity, and associated factors in a population-derived sample', *Journal of the American Academy of Child and Adolescent Psychiatry*, vol. 47, no. 8, pp. 921–9

Søndenaa, E., Rasmussen, K., Helverschou, S.B., Steindal, K., Nilson, B. and Nøttestad, J.A. (2014), 'Violence and sexual offending behavior in people with autism spectrum disorder who have undergone a psychiatric forensic examination', *Psychological Reports: Disability and Trauma*, vol. 115, no. 1, pp. 32–43

Tick, B., Bolton, P., Happe, F., Rutter, M. and Rijsdijk, F. (2016), 'Heritability of autism spectrum disorders: a meta-analysis of twin studies', *Journal of Child Psychology and Psychiatry*, vol. 57, no. 5, pp. 585–95

Woodbury-Smith, M.R., Clare, I.C.H., Holland, A.J. and Kearns, A. (2006), 'High functioning autistic spectrum disorders, offending and other law-breaking: findings from a community sample', *Journal of Forensic Psychiatry and Psychology*, vol. 17, no. 1, pp. 108–20

Yates, P.M., Hucker, S.J. and Kingston, D.A. (2008), 'Sexual sadism: psychopathology and theory', in D.R. Laws and W.T. O'Donohue (eds), *Sexual Deviance: Theory, Assessment, and Treatment*, New York: Guilford, pp. 213–30

GLOSSARY

McGrath, H. and Noble, T. (2017), *Bounce Back! A Positive Education Approach to Wellbeing, Resilience and Social–Emotional Learning*, 3rd edn, Melbourne: Pearson Education

COURT AND MEDIA REFERENCES

PART I FILICIDE AND FAMILICIDE

Chapter 1 Geoff Hunt

Geoffrey Francis Hunt, Kim Jeannine Hunt, Fletcher Austin Hunt, Mia Isobel Hunt and Phoebe Amelia Hunt: Findings, 9 October 2015, NSW State Coroner Magistrate Michael Barnes sitting in Wagga Wagga. File nos. 2014/267678, 2014/266683, 2014/266621, 2014/266598, 2014/26634

Interview with Councillor Rodger Schirmer, 2017

Chapter 2 Arthur Freeman

Anderson, Paul. *Arthur Freeman made chilling threat two months before murdering Darcey*, www.news.com.au 29.3.2011, https://goo.gl/Svmxxn

R v Freeman [2011] VSC 139 (Coghlan J)

Freeman v The Queen [2011] VSCA 214 (27 July 2011). Maxwell, P. Appealed from *R v Freeman* [2011] VSC 139 (Coghlan J)

Freeman v The Queen [2011] VSCA 349 (9 November 2011) (Warren CJ, Nettle JA, Beach AJA)

Chapter 3 Akon Guode

R v Guode [2017] VSC 285 (Lasry J)

Family destruction: Damien Little and Darren Milne

Darren Milne, Susana Estevez Castillo and Liam Milne: Findings, 6 May 2016, Coroner David Day sitting in Wyong. File numbers 2015/00031540, 2015/00031518, 2015/00031516

PART II NARCISSISTIC PERSONALITY DISORDER AND MALIGNANT NARCISSISM

Chapter 4 Man Haron Monis

State Coroner of NSW, *Inquest into the Deaths Arising from the Lindt Café Siege: Findings and Recommendations*, 2017

The Martin Place Siege Joint Commonwealth – New South Wales Review, January 2015

Several interviews with specialist criminal trial lawyer Manny Conditsis, 2017

Chapter 5 Megan Haines

'Roy Morgan Image of Professions Survey 2017', Roy Morgan, finding no. 7244, 7 June 2017, www.roymorgan.com/findings/7244-roy-morgan-image-of-professions-may-2017-201706051543

R v Haines (No. 3) [2016] NSWSC 1812

Sunday Night, Channel 7, 20 November 2016, reporter Peta-Jane Madam

Chapter 6 Robert Xie

R v Xie [2017] NSWSC 63

Sunday Night, Channel 7, 26 February 2017, reporter Melissa Doyle

PART III DEPENDENT PERSONALITY DISORDER

Chapter 7 Michael O'Neill

DPP v O'Neill [2015] VSC 25 (Hollingworth J)

Supreme Court of Victoria, Court of Appeal, *Director of Public Prosecutions Appellant v Michael O'Neill Respondent*, [2015] VSCA 325. Appealed from *DPP v O'Neill* [2015] VSC 25

R v Verdins [2007] 16 VR 269

Chapter 8 Chamari Liyanage

Liyanage v The State of Western Australia (2017) WASCA 112

Chapter 9 Anthony Sherna

DPP v Sherna [2009] VSC 526 (Beach J)

Chapter 10 Cia Xia Liao

R v Liao [2015] VSC 730 (Lasry J)

PART IV PARANOID PERSONALITY DISORDER

Chapter 11 Ian Jamieson

DPP v Jamieson (Ruling) [2016] VSC 406 (Hollingworth J)

DPP v Jamieson [2016] VSC 407 (Hollingworth J)

PART V ANTISOCIAL PERSONALITY DISORDER

Chapter 12 Michael Cardamone

R v Cardamone [2017] VSC 493 (Lasry J)

Whorouly Newsletter, October 2014

PART VI CRIMINAL AUTISTIC PSYCHOPATHY AND SEXUAL SADISM DISORDER

Chapter 13 Vincent Stanford

R v Stanford, Vincent [2016] NSWSC 1434

R v Stanford, Marcus [2016] NSWSC 1174

Colman, M. (2015), 'Stephanie Scott: murder suspect Vincent Stanford "a reclusive loner"', News Corp Australia Network, 17 April, www.news.com.au/national/stephanie-scott-murder-suspect-vincent-stanford-a-reclusive-loner/news-story/62462ccd14fcb0807c84572ff1624bc5

Several interviews with anonymous neighbour of Vincent Stanford, 2017

FURTHER READING

Narcissistic personality disorder

Dawson, T. (2015), *Narcissistic Personality Disorder: Narcissistic Men and Women How to Spot Them, Check Them and then Avoid Them*, CreateSpace Independent Publishing Platform

Ellington, A. (2016), *Encountering a Narcissistic Sociopath*, Litchfield, IL: Revival Waves of Glory Books & Publishing

Lechan, C. and Goodman, B.L. (2012), *The Everything Guide to Narcissistic Personality Disorder: Professional, Reassuring Advice for Coping with the Disorder – at Work, at Home, and in Your Family*, Avon, MA: Adams Media

McNally, R. (2017), *Narcissism: How to Beat the Narcissist! Understanding Narcissism and Narcissistic Personality Disorder*, CreateSpace Independent Publishing Platform

Ronningstam, E.F. (2005), *Identifying and Understanding the Narcissistic Personality*, New York: Oxford University Press

Antisocial personality disorder

Babiak, P. and Hare, R.D. (2006), *Snakes in Suits: When Psychopaths Go to Work*, New York: HarperCollins

Dutton, K. (2013), *The Wisdom of Psychopaths: What Saints, Spies and Serial Killers Can Tell us about Success*, New York: Scientific American/Farrar, Straus and Giroux

Hare, R.D. (1999), *Without Conscience: The Disturbing World of the Psychopaths Among Us*, New York: Guildford Press

McGrath, H.L. and Edwards, H. (2009), *Difficult Personalities: A Practical Guide to Managing the Hurtful Behaviour of Others*, 2nd edn, Melbourne: Penguin

Stout, M. (2006), *The Sociopath Next Door: The Ruthless Versus the Rest of Us*, New York: Broadway Books

Thomas, M.E. (2013), *Confessions of a Sociopath: A Life Spent Hiding in Plain Sight*, New York: Crown Publishers

Domestic violence

Norris, M. (2016), *Look What You Made Me Do: Fathers Who Kill*, Melbourne: Echo Publishing

Bancroft, L. (2003), *Why Does He Do That? Inside the Minds of Angry and Controlling Men*, New York: Berkley Books

Bancroft, L., Silverman, J.G. and Ritchie, D. (2012), *The Batterer as Parent: Addressing the Impact of Domestic Violence on Family Dynamics*, Thousand Oaks, CA: Sage

O'Brien, C. (2016), *Blame Changer: Understanding Domestic Violence*, Melbourne: threekookaburras

Dependent personality disorder

Frank, J. (2016), *Dependent Personality Disorder: Cognitive Behavioral Therapy Self Help Guide*, Warsaw: Cleal Publishing

Histrionic personality disorder

Geoffreys, C. (2015), *Histrionic Personality Disorder: The Ultimate Guide to Symptoms, Treatment and Prevention*, CreateSpace Independent Publishing Platform

Autism

Robison, J.E. (2007), *Look Me in the Eye: My Life with Asperger's*, New York: Three Rivers Press

Robison, J.E. (2016), *Switched On: A Memoir of Brain Change and Emotional Awakening*, New York: Speigel & Grau

PERMISSIONS

Court material that appears in this book is reproduced with the following permission:

Supreme Court of Victoria

Material from Supreme Court of Victoria and Supreme Court of Victoria Court of Appeal cases *DPP v Sherna* [2009] VSC 526 (Beach J), *R v Liao*, [2015] VSC 730 (Lasry J), *R v Freeman* [2011] VSC 139 (Coghlan J), *Freeman v The Queen* [2011] VSCA 214 (Maxwell J), *R v Freeman* [2011] VSC 139, *Freeman v The Queen* [2011] VSCA 349 (Warren CJ, Nettle JA, Beach AJA), *R v Guode* [2017] VSC 285 (Lasry J), *DPP v O'Neill* [2015] VSC 25 (Hollingworth J), *DPP v Jamieson* (Ruling) [2016] VSC 406 (Hollingworth J), *DPP v Jamieson* [2016] VSC 407 (Hollingworth J), and *R v Cardamone* [2017] VSC 493 (Lasry J), is reproduced with permission from the Council of Law Reporting in Victoria.

Supreme Court of Western Australia

Material from *Liyanage v The State of Western Australia* (2017) WASCA 112 is reproduced with the permission of the Supreme Court of Western Australia.

Supreme Court of New South Wales

Material from *R v Stanford, Vincent* [2016] NSWSC 1434, *R v Stanford, Marcus* [2016] NSWSC 1174, *R v Haines* (No. 3) [2016] NSWSC 1812 and *R v Xie* [2017] NSWSC 63 © State of New South Wales, through the Department of Justice.

NSW Coroner's Court

The following reports/findings are reproduced with the permission of the NSW Coroner's Court.

Geoffrey Francis Hunt, Kim Jeannine Hunt, Fletcher Austin Hunt, Mia Isobel Hunt and Phoebe Amelia Hunt: Findings, 9 October 2015, NSW State Coroner Magistrate Michael Barnes sitting in Wagga Wagga. File nos. 2014/267678, 2014/266683, 2014/266621, 2014/266598, 2014/26634

Darren Milne, Susana Estevez Castillo and Liam Milne: Findings, 6 May 2016, Coroner David Day sitting in Wyong. File numbers 2015/00031540, 2015/00031518, 2015/00031516

State Coroner of New South Wales, *Inquest into the Deaths Arising from the Lindt Café Siege; Findings and Recommendations*, 2017

Australian Government Department of Prime Minister and Cabinet, New South Wales Government Department of Premier and Cabinet

The Martin Place Siege Joint Commonwealth – New South Wales Review, January 2015. Licensed from the Commonwealth of Australia under a Creative Commons Attribution 3.0 Australia

Licence. The Commonwealth of Australia does not necessarily endorse the content of this publication.

Names

The names of children have only been used in this book where they are deceased or their names have been widely reported in the media and referred to publicly by their next of kin. Several sources requested that they remain anonymous, and we have respected this.

Accuracy

The authors have made every effort to ensure that the material used in this book is accurate and up to date. Any errors or omissions are unintentional, and we invite readers to contact Pan Macmillan if anything needs correcting for future editions.

ACKNOWLEDGEMENTS

Many people helped to make this book possible, and we thank them all. In many cases the subject matter was distressing, but a number of people either directly or indirectly involved with the cases covered helped us with our research and with insightful comments about the perpetrators.

Special thanks to our publisher, Pan Macmillan, particularly our talented copy editor, Nicola Young, who did a wonderful job; our supportive editor, Alex Lloyd, who expertly guided and supported us through the process; and non-fiction publisher Ingrid Ohlsson, who has showed faith in this project from the start. We would also like to thank the authors' families and friends for their support and special thanks to, in no particular order, Manny Conditsis, Cr Rodger Schirmer, Mike Colman, Kris Paltoglou, Tracy Stockdale, Erika Stockdale, Georgie Loudon, Lynette Mordue, Channel 7, the NSW Coroner's Court, and the Supreme Courts of Victoria, New South Wales and Western Australia.

Heartfelt thanks also to the many people who provided information anonymously, whom we cannot thank by name. We appreciate your vital support.

MORE BESTSELLING NON-FICTION BY CHERYL CRITCHLEY AND DR HELEN McGRATH

WHY DID THEY DO IT?

The cases that stunned Australia – and left us all with one question: why did they do it?

Gerard Baden-Clay was described as charming and successful, with a picture-perfect life, until he murdered his wife, Allison. John Myles Sharpe killed his pregnant wife and their young daughter with a spear gun. Simon Gittany flung his fiancée off the balcony of his upmarket inner-city apartment, having proposed lovingly to her, in public, just two months before. These and other crimes, committed by people described as average, ordinary, normal . . .

In *Why Did They Do It?*, respected journalist Cheryl Critchley teams with esteemed psychologist Dr Helen McGrath to dissect the cases and identify the personality disorders of each of the killers. Using psychological analysis, combined with scientific evidence, they identify the reasoning and motives of the men and women whose brutal crimes shocked the nation.